Producing Dreams,
Consuming Youth

Producing Dreams, Consuming Youth

Mexican Americans and Mass Media

VICKI MAYER

RUTGERS UNIVERSITY PRESS

New Brunswick, New Jersey, and London

Library of Congress Cataloging-in-Publication Data

Mayer, Vicki, 1971–
    Producing dreams, consuming youth : Mexican Americans and mass media / Vicki
Mayer.
        p.   cm.
    Includes bibliographical references and index.
    ISBN 0–8135–3326–0 (cloth : alk. paper) — ISBN 0–8135–3327–9 (pbk. : alk.
paper)
    1. Mexican Americans and mass media. I. Title.

    P94.5.M47M38 2003
    320.23'089'6872073—dc21

                                                                        2003014203

British Cataloging-in-Publication information is available from the British Library.

The publication program of Rutgers University Press is supported by the Board of
Governors of Rutgers, The State University of New Jersey.

Manufactured in the United States of America

To Raúl

Contents

Acknowledgments

THIS BOOK HAS transformed through many permutations over the past five years thanks to the help of many people along the way. My dissertation adviser and friend, Ellen Seiter, looked at first drafts and taught me more than anyone else about being an academic and a scholar. Other mentors in graduate school, John Caldwell, Dan Schiller, and Dee Dee Halleck, were supreme teachers and role models for a politically engaged research agenda. George Lipsitz has continued to guide me long after I left San Diego.

I also cannot forget the crucial inputs of my friends and colleagues in San Antonio and Davis: Debbie Nathan, Clemencia Rodríguez, Robert Huesca, Estela Reyes López, Pablo Vila, Kent Wilkinson, Beatriz Pesquera, Sergio de la Mora, Kent Ono, Carolyn de la Peña, Roger Rouse, and Raúl Aranovich. Their comments have left imprints on this manuscript, though I have often been a stubborn listener to their advice. I can never repay Ann Hepperman and Samantha Arnold for their time and dedicated research assistance over the years.

I have interacted with amazing people during this project. The generosity of professionals at Studio M, Tejas Records, and KTFM opened doors for me in Tejano. Each interviewee provided invaluable insights into their fields and professions. Manny Castillo and San Anto Cultural Arts deserve the highest praise for their patience, support, and warmth. Although I have tried to let these participants' voices speak through my words, any errors in their interpretation are my own.

Introduction

WHEN I THINK OF the representation of Mexican Americans in mass media, two images come to mind. Both are covers from national newsmagazines. Both show Mexican Americans in the personages of young people, who often-embody visions of the future.[1] Yet the future projected in each one is so strikingly different that it is unclear if either image is accurate, fair, or representative.

First, the 12 July 1999 cover of *Newsweek* announces "Latin U.S.A." across the magazine's center in roughly the same lettering as a "Made in the U.S.A." label. Indeed, the three people behind the title look much like a fashion advertisement; two men stand three-quarters turned to the camera while a woman between them stands face forward, her shoulders rolled back. Each one is an emerging star in their cultural field: Oscar de la Hoya is a boxer, Shakira is a pop singer, and Junot Díaz is a writer. Each one also represents a different Latino identity: Mexican American, Colombian American, and Dominican American respectively. Although de la Hoya figures most prominently in the photo—perhaps to signify his fame or a synecdoche of the largest Latino population in the United States—in all other respects, the members of the triad share the same representational strategy. They are strong, hip, and confident. Each one stares at the reader with serious but also alluring, flawless faces. The subtitle asserts "Young Hispanics Are Changing America," but a red, white, and blue color scheme also belies how "American" these figures are. Set against a bright blue and white sky background, these beautiful, affluent people may be ethnic, but they are as American as the flag.

Compare this to the 11 June 2001 cover of *Time Magazine*. Titled "Welcome to Amexica," the cover pictures a brown-skinned girl and boy staring into a telephoto lens, slightly distorting the image we see by bringing them in close range. The mood of the photo is upbeat; the children wear happy pinks, purples, and blues. They seem playful rather than serious, or worse, menacing. Unlike covers *Time* dedicates to a single person, such as their annual *Man of the Year* edition, the boy and girl crowd the photo's frame. Even the block letters "Amexica" overlap, pushed together by the gaping mouth of the female child. Her mouth, a set of crooked teeth and gums placed at the center of the photo, threatens to swallow the reader. Her garish clothing, a purple tank top, a floppy silk flower, oversized sunglasses, and a pink parasol, further emulates the carnivalesque. She is a clown toying with the idea of overturning the status quo by accentuating her difference. In contrast, the boy in the background looks uncomfortable. He sits passively in an infant's stroller, the mirror opposite of the girl. Both children wear sunglasses, obscuring their eyes and rendering their personal identities anonymous, while their racial identities are clearly marked as brown, Mexican, others. The subtitle tells the reader: "The Border Is Vanishing before Our Eyes, Creating a New World For All of Us." The idea of a new world hearkens to the rhetorics of primitive discovery, as in Columbus, except it is not clear what remains of the old world. The border between us and them is simply vanishing.

Recognized or anonymous, trendsetters or strange, socially included or excluded: these are the binaries reserved for the representation of Mexican Americans in mainstream mass media. The socially included are brokers of popular culture in the United States. They push cultural boundaries, but only within the established paradigms of literature, music, and sports. They set trends so that other Americans can consume their products. The socially excluded sit passively and consume whatever comes their way. They are premodern and thus threaten to destabilize modern American society. As the titles infer in both cases, Mexican Americans are not exactly "Americans." They are either "changing America," connoting a comfortable alteration, as in a change of clothing, or they are affecting an entirely "new world," as in an alien invasion. The covers of *Time* and *Newsweek* mediate what it is to be an "American" and on what terms. By representing Mexican Americans as a market or a threat, mass media has generally obviated other potential images of Mexican Americans, especially as political participants.

This book looks at the ways mass media portray Mexican Americans from the unique perspectives of the Mexican Americans who produce and consume these images everyday. To do so assumes both the important role that mass media images play in constructing the identities of Mexican Americans in the United States and, conversely, the active roles that Mexican Americans play in making, using, and contesting those images. Mexican Americans' personal investments in media industries stretch beyond reductive analyses of good or bad images to encompass the ways that diverse people look to radio, television, and film to mediate the complexities of ethnicity, gender, and class in the United States today. By looking at some of the paradoxes that Mexican Americans face in representing their own cultures, this book offers some answers as to why certain images of Mexican Americans are more visible than others, who gains and loses from their presence, and what alternatives there might be for the future.

Mexican Americans consume mass media images, texts, and music as much as other Americans do, though not in the same way. Historically, Mexican Americans have protested images such as the *Time* cover as negative, arguing that they reinforce prejudice and stereotypes in society as a whole. From film boycotts in the 1910s, to letter writing campaigns to the FCC in the 1960s, to a "brownout" directed at television networks in the 1990s, Mexican Americans have targeted media representations as central pillars of racism in the United States.[2] With a camera in hand, many Mexican Americans then followed in the footsteps of New Latin American filmmakers by creating their own images to counter mainstream cultural representations and preserve working-class cultures of "the people."[3] In their wake, Mexican American producers strategically celebrated diverse Mexican American identities, breaking essentialist notions of gender, race, class, and sexuality.[4] This kind of resistance to mass media has survived in the alternative media production culture of community-based arts organizations throughout the United States. My own observations and participation with one such group allowed me to see both the rich heritage of Mexican American cultural arts production and the difficulty of sustaining alternatives to mass media production and consumption. For many Mexican Americans who have contested degrading media images, change could only be effected from *inside* the media industries that produced them. The *Newsweek* cover, in many ways, represents the fruits of their labor.

Mexican Americans have been involved in mass media production since the early twentieth century, when pioneers like Pedro González broadcast local Spanish-language music to field-workers in Los Angeles County.[5] Long before Shakira and de la Hoya, middle-class Mexican Americans and U.S. production companies, interested in quick profits from "race records," marketed working-class Mexican *corridos* throughout the 1920s.[6] According to George Sánchez, the development of an original Mexican American identity was intimately related to the expansion of mass culture industries for Mexican Americans.[7] Recording, broadcasting, and popular music invited Mexican Americans into imagined communities while encouraging producers and consumers to develop their own memberships in these communities.[8] With each generation, media production was an increasingly popular avenue for Mexican Americans to earn both class mobility and status by promoting the popular cultures of its audiences. The Chicano movements of the 1960s and 1970s drew special attention to the political importance of Mexican Americans' participation in mass media industries, eventually helping more Mexican Americans become part of the industries that they had protested earlier.[9] More than two decades later, some Mexican American media producers who remembered this era framed their entrance into mass media industries as the last stage in a civil rights movement to gain public recognition for all Mexican Americans. Recognition, however, depended on their ability to sell Mexican Americans as a profitable market.

As illustrated by the *Newsweek* cover, Mexican American media producers have gained more visibility, but only within capitalist imperatives that have assigned their products exchange value. In an economy oversaturated with mass media products, Mexican Americans could offer the labor and resources that could sell culturally unique products. Characterized by outsourcing and nonunion labor, mobile capital and digital technologies, the post-Fordist shift in production since the mid–1970s has incorporated Mexican American media producers who pursued niche markets and narrowcast (as opposed to broadcast) audiences.[10] In other words, some Mexican Americans have capitalized upon a new economy where multiculturalism sells. The process has been turbulent; Spanish-language media producers still receive comparatively little financial backing, few distribution outlets, and less market value than their English-language counterparts. In addition, Mexican Americans' coalitions within mass media industries have been historically fragile, subject to the ebbs and flows of capital both in the United States and Mexico. Perhaps the Tejano music industry has best illustrated these fragile coalitions in recent times. After the niche market for Tejano went bust in the mid–1990s, workers in the business restructured their practices to compete with Latin, pop, Mexican regional, and country industries. The new economy has globalized the potential for Mexican American media while subjecting its producers to new challenges as businesses downsize or vertically integrate under multinational corporations.

This, however, is only half of the story. With the exception of the success of some cultural brokers and media industry executives, most Mexican Americans do not create the media images they consume. The empowerment of certain Mexican Americans in the new economy has not been shared by the majority of Mexican Americans, whose place at the lowest rungs of the labor market form what social scientists call an "underclass."[11] The same state that used neoliberal policies to accommodate post-Fordist changes in media production also dismantled the social programs that would ensure that more Mexican Americans could receive the education, training, and services needed to enter mass media industries. It is particularly ironic that young Mexican Americans, who have been the most vulnerable to neoliberal reforms, are the most visible in Mexican American media. Statistics show 40 percent of Latino adolescents lived in poverty during the late 1990s.[12] Yet young Mexican Americans at this time often appeared in media images of private family life, where their public identities could only be defined through individual consumption and family values. Despite the loss of consumer power relative to other citizens in the United States, mass media increasingly portray Mexican American youths as good consumers in mediated worlds. As Christy Haubegger, founder of *Latina* magazine, has explained to corporate America, "Remember, we may only be 11 percent of the country, but we buy 16 percent of the lipliner."[13]

Lacking the power to represent themselves in most spheres of their lives, Mexican American children and teenagers look to media they do not produce for "communities of resemblance" with other Americans.[14] Film, radio, and televisual forms mediate cultural identities to Mexican Americans, which they can then accept and contest through rituals of consumption, conversation, and collection. They address and reflect private pleasures and public identities, stabilizing and destabilizing boundaries between local communities and national political/economic formations, such as working-class viewers, female fans, or Mexican American citizens. In my experiences working with Mexican American adolescents, mass media helped youths stake out identities as not only members of their communities but also as *certain kinds of members*, reaffirming two decades of media audience studies that show people interpret media to express their nationality, gender, sexuality, ethnicity, race, and age.[15] Lacking access to alternative sources of information, mass media consumption has been a formative experience, helping young Mexican Americans imagine themselves in relation to other cultures. Like a past generation that, in George Lipsitz's words, constructed Mexican American identities through "David Bowie, Bryan Ferry, the Ramones and the Sex Pistols *as well as* Lydia Mendoza, Los Lobos, and Poncho Sanchez," the Mexican American teens in the late 1990s claimed multiple identities as part of the Mexican American experience.[16] They watched *Jerry Springer, Oprah,* and *Cristina.* They followed local news and international serials. They listened to at least five different radio stations in English and Spanish. These texts were not limited to one language, culture, or market; though it was through them that young Mexican Americans without a political voice accessed their memories of a collective past and developed hopes for a brighter future.

This book attempts to listen to those voices, as well as the voices of those who try to channel young Mexican Americans' voices toward economic, social, and cultural goals. For all that young people have spoken through their mass media consumption, they have spoken to populations that often either disregarded their tastes for reality programs and pop music as "low-class" or

used these tastes as evidence of their future buying potential. Passive or active, like the images in *Newsweek* and *Time*, Mexican American youths were
caught in a field of cultural hierarchies that they could bend, through creative appropriations and reversals, but not break. Even as producers of their
own media texts, young people returned to a conundrum in which their cultural identities could not be separated from the forces that degrade or commodify them. Given the limited choices in the neoliberal state, young media
producers saw themselves as equal consumers more than as equal citizens.

In the Shadow of the Alamo: Mexican American Producers and Consumers

This book focuses on the city of San Antonio, Texas, as a conceptual space
and a physical place for investigating Mexican American cultures and media.
In San Antonio, one sees how abstract ideas of identity collide with political
economy in the production of culture. At the time I conducted the research
for this book, nearly 530,000 Mexican Americans (U.S. citizens of Mexican
heritage) lived in San Antonio, or 45 percent of the city's total population.[17]
Statistically, this meant that San Antonio had the greatest proportion of Mexican Americans in any city with over one million residents in 1990. Located
between the Mexican borderlands and the capital-rich metropolises of Dallas, Houston, and Austin, San Antonio has tried to use its cultural difference
to its advantage in the new economy. It was a prominent cultural tourism des-
tination, second only to Santa Fe in the southwestern United States. Meanwhile, the city also became an artery for international trade promoted by the
passage of the North American Free Trade Agreement in 1994. At a time when
the country had adopted a laissez-faire political economy, San Antonio stood
in for the nation as a purveyor of multicultural goods and services. Here, Mexican Americans actually experienced the effects of the dismantling of the welfare state, an information-based service economy, and a globalized media
environment. As in the past, different Mexican Americans experienced these
changes quite differently.

Cultural production has always reflected the multiplicity of Mexican
Americans' identities in San Antonio. Churches, plazas, cantinas, and movie
houses were central cultural cores of Mexican American, working-class life
in the first half of the twentieth century.[18] These sites were largely denigrated
by the elite class of Mexican Americans who flooded the city during the Mexican Revolution and promoted their supremacy as "whites" over lower-class
Mexican "mestizos" or "greasers."[19] From about 1920 to 1940, Richard García
writes that this group used "culture as a vehicle through which to gain and

maintain political and philosophical hegemony."[20] Upper-class women frequently coordinated public symphonies, Shakespearean plays, and poetry readings to display their cultural capital to non-Mexican elites and improve the lives of the working masses of Mexican Americans by "educating" them to appreciate refined culture.[21] Meanwhile, the Mexican American middle class emerged from the working class, often by becoming merchants of their own culture. Cultural tourism boomed in the 1930s, when middle-class Mexican Americans began marketing rodeos and homemade hot springs to railway tourists looking for entertainment and salubrious leisure. Later, they transformed the working-class morality play, *Los Pastores*, into a tourist attraction that stirred cultural pride for those who could afford tickets to the mission performances.[22] The middle class also initiated small-scale newspapers, radio stations, and record production labels. They used these media both to transmit popular cultural forms, such as local stories (*dichos*) and songs (*corridos*), and to commercialize emerging cultural forms, such as *conjunto* music.

When I arrived to San Antonio in the summer of 1997, the number of media industries operating in the city had increased, though the number of Mexican Americans producing media was restricted to a small set of consumers. San Antonio was the center for the production of Tejano music nationally and a strong competitor in Spanish-language advertising. Several radio and television affiliates directly targeted the Mexican American population and a few publications distributed only to areas most frequented by Mexican American patrons. Film production was growing due to the establishment of a large studio and production facilities. Professionals in these industries possessed different backgrounds and training, though they were all part of the city's middle-class population—a class that was shrinking from the late 1970s to the mid–1990s.[23] In contrast to the producers, over 70 percent of Mexican American households earned less than $25,000 per year, with more than half of those earning less than $15,000.[24] As Mexican American media professionals publicized the growing Latino consumer market, San Antonio itself was the second poorest city in the country.

Questions of cultural identity complicate this scenario further. I remember brushing up on my Spanish before coming to San Antonio thinking I would need it on a regular basis. In 1994, 55 percent of Mexican Americans in San Antonio reported that they did not speak Spanish, and only 7 percent said they were monolingual Spanish speakers.[25] I used Spanish more to watch television programs and listen to Tejano music than to talk to anyone about these media. I also recall someone asking me why I was writing about "Mexican Americans" and not "Chicanos" on a trip to California from Texas. I first reacted by saying that no one ever called themselves a "Chicano," though it prompted me to think why one constructed identity was better than another. Census figures in 1990 reveal that San Antonio Americans of Mexican descent worked within the range of options to construct themselves both ethnically and racially. Although all were limited to a box marked "Hispanic" in the survey, only 65 percent considered themselves racially white. A remaining 34 percent of Hispanics asserted that they belonged in the "other" racial category—suggesting that they did not feel White, Black, Asian, or American Indian. While it would be inaccurate to extrapolate the social histories of Mexican Americans in San Antonio, Texas, based on a few statistics, the numbers do suggest a wide range of cultural identities that Mexican Americans occupied and self-reported.

My own location in this matrix of ethnic and class identities set me apart from both Mexican American media producers and consumers. As an Anglo American, I was in the statistical minority, but the most powerful segment of the city's population. During my four years in San Antonio, I moved between class identities much easier than most of my research participants, from a graduate student without a car or steady income to a lecturer at the city's elite private university and finally an assistant professor. My educational status and background in media production opened doors to communities of media producers and consumers that I probably could not have entered otherwise. I was never an organic member of communities I studied, but over time, these field sites were part of my consciousness as a resident of San Antonio. I began advocating for community media through the city's cable advisory board, in academic grant proposals for the cultural arts organization, and through outreach efforts from the universities where I taught. I wrote for the local alternative newspaper and became an ardent fan of Tejano music and its venues. The balance between detachment and attachment to the field at least blurred some of the issues around my privilege and power as the ethnographer, though as I wrote about people who did not write this book, I was aware that these boundaries remained.

I began my work as an observer-participant with a nonprofit cultural arts center located in the city's West Side, a working-class and working-poor area populated almost entirely by Mexican Americans. I volunteered there to help children and teenagers learn to make videos about the topic of their choice, many of which directly quoted or reinterpreted their favorite films, television programs, and songs. For more than two years, I did my research by helping where I could: teaching kids how to edit, driving them home at night, videotaping a mural blessing, or gluing sashes at a fundraising event. It was a time in my graduate studies when I could work within the community I was studying and come home each night to write field notes about media talk, making media, and social relationships around media. The young people in this site were both producers and consumers, using the tools and knowledge of mass media to construct images of themselves and their communities.

As my study extended to Mexican American media professionals, the field site, its ethnographic subjects, and my position as the researcher changed. Using snowball techniques, I began interviewing Mexican American professionals around their work schedules and conveniences, a process recently dubbed "appointment ethnography."[26] Whereas the traditional ethnography at the cultural arts center required time to get to know a few people, this ethnographic project demanded patience both because of the interviewees' status as professionals in their respective field and my comparative status as a student or a newly titled member of the academy. As I worked through the networks of acquaintances, the field expanded to Mexican Americans with different roles in all types of media industries. Despite these unique locations, the participants cited similar economic challenges as Mexican American media workers. They were the ones who most clearly related Mexican American citizenship to consumer power. In the final phase of the ethnography, I followed the production process for Tejano music in 2001 to show how Mexican American media workers have created an entire industry in which cultural consumption is an expression of cultural power.

These two communities, and the methods I have used to understand them, guide the organization of this book. The first half of the book focuses particularly on how Mexican Americans produce media, given their own cultural perspectives and what their industries will allow. Chapter 1 begins with a history of Mexican Americans' involvement in mass media industries in San Antonio, both as producers and as a target audience. Here I present a framework for thinking about the multicultural and multinational structuring of San Antonio's mass media industries in a changing political economy. This framework provides the background for thinking about Mexican American producers as a community that struggles to represent its cultural identities within the limits of the marketplace. Chapter 2 presents this community, its members, and the experiences they have as workers in mass media industries. Within the framework of a neoliberal state, members of this community best articulate the political importance of media production and consumption as practices for integrating Mexican Americans into the nation through cultural representation. These representations, and the cultural negotiations involved in producing them, are the subjects of my investigation in chapter 3 of the Tejano music industry and my analysis in chapter 4 of two films about Mexican American youths.

The second half of this book centers on a group of Mexican American young people who consume mass media and integrate its texts into their daily lives. Chapter 5 introduces these youths through the community of participants at San Anto Cultural Arts, a nonprofit organization dedicated to giving local residents access to arts resources, including video. Questions of access, identities, and communities persist through a discussion of the young volunteers' media consumption in chapter 6 and video productions in chapter 7. Here, the multiplicity of Mexican Americans' media tastes and practices were part and parcel of the ways they presented themselves to their peers, parents, and authorities. Together, the chapters in the second half of the book illustrate the ways media both enables and limits young people as they define themselves as ethnic, gendered, and cultural members of their city and nation.

The overriding message in this book is that if we want to understand Mexican Americans' relationships with mass media, then we have to understand the ways that heterogeneous communities of Mexican Americans confront the cultural norms in mass-mediated representations that are pillars of belonging in the United States. Film, television, video, and radio mediate different cultural experiences of the nation. By comparing working-class Mexican American young people and middle-class Mexican American adults, voices emerge that speak of the differences felt by Americans of Mexican heritage, an articulation of the hierarchies and exclusions within the United States itself. San Antonio, Texas, is perhaps the ideal place to study Mexican American communities because it is so unlike every other American city. It does, however, provide one scenario of what Mexican American communities could be in the future. The 2000 Census indicates that the United States looks more similar to San Antonio than different. The U.S. Mexican American population has increased by 53 percent since 1990.[27] By 2005, Census officials project Mexican Americans, together with other Latino groups, will be the most populous minority in America.[28] If the research from this book is any indication, then the representations of this group, including who produces, who consumes, and who is impacted by them, will be of the utmost importance to understanding the diversity and contradictions of Mexican American identity in the United States.

Producing Dreams,
Consuming Youth

Chapter 1

Mexican American
Mass Media in San Antonio

To UNDERSTAND HOW Mexican Americans produce and consume mass media, these processes must first be contextualized in a history that shows how their productive labor and consumer pleasures *could be* expressed within political and economic limits. For cultural historians, the uneven development of mass media industries, regulatory controls, and consumer markets are not just a forgotten background to a present story; they are the conditions that structured the current discourses of Mexican American inclusion in a mass media economy.[1] In San Antonio, Mexican Americans were always at the forefront nationally in producing mass media and targeting a Mexican American audience. San Antonio was one of the first cities in the United States with a Spanish-language newspaper, and the city later fostered the first Spanish-language radio station and Spanish-language television station. While they are impressive entries into largely Anglo American dominated environments, Mexican American mass media are also testaments to the changing political-economic discourses toward mass media and ethnicity in the twentieth century.

What are Mexican American mass media? Practically speaking, the term *Mexican American* refers to anyone from or with descendants in Mexico. At the same time, it would be difficult to say that any mass media industry can be limited to members of one ethnic or racial group. Mass media industries' dependence on investors and clients, as well as networks of producers, distributors, and exhibitors imbricate each industry in networks of other industries.

I

Many authors define Mexican American—along with Hispanic, Mexican American, or Chicano—mass media as print, broadcast, or film texts that are produced by members of those specific identity groups.[2] For my purposes, Mexican American mass media are print or visual texts that are produced principally by Mexican Americans or for Mexican American target audiences. This definition recognizes that Latin Americans, Anglo Americans, and Mexican Americans often work together in the production and distribution of media texts that may specifically target Mexican Americans, as well as other populations. Another option, defining Mexican American media as texts and images that mediate Mexican American culture, is inadequate because it is often impossible to identify who is Mexican American and what cultural attributes he or she should have.[3] In short, the definition of Mexican American mass media in this chapter casts a broad net around several types of mass media producers and target audiences who may have different class and ethnic backgrounds but prominently include Mexican Americans.

With a broad cultural definition of Mexican American mass media, the development of these industries occurred within the political and economic constraints imposed both in the United States and in Mexico. The articulation of a corporate liberalist discourse in the United States by the turn of the twentieth century naturalized the assumption that media industries must maximize individual liberties while constraining industries to maintain social stability. Although politicians and industry professionals negotiated different ways of maintaining corporate liberalism over history, Mexican American media remained within the limits of the discourse. At the same time, Mexico provided much of the labor, capital, and raw resources that Mexican American mass media industries needed to tap into their target market. Over the past century, Mexico was in dialogue with corporate liberalism in two ways. First, foreign companies, particularly from the United States, looked to Mexico as a place to sell media, from Hollywood films in the 1920s to global pop music in the 1980s, hence making superprofits above what could be sold domestically. Second, Mexican professionals wanting to create or sell mass media in the United States adopted corporate liberalism as the "American business model." In San Antonio, the Mexican application of corporate liberalism sometimes led to uneasy relationships between Mexican Americans and Mexican management, unveiling racial dynamics behind the discourse. This history thus reflects back to our initial question about what Mexican American mass media are. For if we bring issues of identity to the forefront of political-economic research into media industries, we see the complex ways that race, class, and nationality have been interwoven in the expansion of media by, about, and for Mexican Americans.[4]

Constructions of Mexican American Media

Beginning in the early twentieth century, the history of Mexican American media production in San Antonio itself involved multiple allegiances between media producers within and across media. The structural organization of these media reflects, first, the political and economic constraints on certain kinds of industrial developments and, second, the ways producers define Mexican Americans as particular types of audiences/consumers, for these homologies are uneven. Further, the structural organization of these industries reveals to what degree Mexican Americans shaped these definitions themselves or in conjunction with Anglo American or Mexican-national producers. Roughly, there are four constructions that describe the relationship between Mexican American media producers and their imagined audiences: segmentation, massification, panethnicization, and fragmentation. The term *construction* here seems useful in describing the continuity and flexibility in these relationships over time. For although these constructions arose historically, marking the industrial development of media technologies, the expansion and conglomeration of companies, and the formation of new markets, these constructions carry on today, often in new material forms. The term *construction* recognizes the changing definitions of Mexican American media as coterminous but not dependent on any one technology or market factor, a point elaborated upon at the end of the chapter.

SEGMENTATION

By the beginning of the century, San Antonio was home to a multiethnic population of Mexicans, Germans, Irish, Chinese, and African Americans, as well as Jews and Scots-Irish descended southerners. Although Mexican Americans certainly took part in the city's internal economy, buying and selling products, they were not yet part of a media market. As América Rodríguez states, "Hispanic consumers had always been there in the marketplace, but they hadn't been 'discovered,' named, and conquered—as an audience."[5] Then, the Mexican Revolution brought thousands of Mexican immigrants and exiles to San Antonio. Among them, wealthy and schooled members of Mexico's oligarchic families fled across the border to avoid persecution by the punitive revolutionaries. These immigrants were the new labor and market for a Mexican American mass media product.

The first construction for Mexican American producers and audiences was a segmented market of elites living in San Antonio. Started in 1913 by Antonio Lozano (a wealthy Mexican immigrant himself), *La Prensa* hired exiled Mexican journalists to produce a professional newspaper for the Mexican

Revolution's well-heeled exiles. Lozano's target audience was small when compared to working-class and poor Mexican migrants, but it was economically and culturally important to San Antonio. "A good number of them were members of the middle class, the enlightened and educated and monied class."[6] Serving a niche market, La Prensa's labor and audience were unstable. Many people came to San Antonio precisely because it was the closest major city to their Mexican homes, where they often planned to return after the war. Lozano could not count on them for the paper's long-term sustainability, despite the fact that more of them eventually stayed than returned after the war.[7] Furthermore, anti-immigrant sentiments among Anglos peaked from 1915 to 1930, threatening all Mexican Americans with deportation.[8] The Texas Rangers, a rural police force supported by the U.S. Cavalry, terrorized Mexican Americans throughout south Texas in service of an elite Anglo American landholding class.[9] Given this social threat, many Mexican elites operated economically, politically, and culturally within an Anglo-dominated social order while considering their return to a potentially hostile homeland.

The dual marginality Mexicans felt in the United States became the strategic basis for La Prensa's commodification of a segmented Mexican American readership. On one hand, La Prensa covered the Mexican Revolution and daily life in Mexico. For example, the paper's literary page specifically targeted elite readers with reprinted essays by esteemed scholars and intellectuals from Spain and Latin America.[10] On the other hand, La Prensa covered issues that reflected the political needs of middle-class Mexican immigrants in the United States. As such, La Prensa printed war coverage and Latin American essays alongside reports on Mexican American rights, education, and community struggles. This balance between Mexican and United States–based contents for a limited audience proved particularly resilient in San Antonio until the paper's closure in 1963 (it would be revived later). The social mobility of certain segments of San Antonio's Mexican population sustained La Prensa's readership, and the specificity of the content eliminated Anglo American competition for a similar print audience.

MASSIFICATION

Meanwhile, the expansion of radio broadcasting in the 1920s and 1930s, followed by television in the 1950s, provided the conditions for the second construction of Mexican American media in San Antonio. These were the early days of broadcast network advertising systems. Federal broadcasting regulations stressed two agendas for commercial stations.[11] First, they were to serve local communities primarily. Second, they were to operate in the public interest. The stations complied with these mandates in a contradictory way; they had to expand entertainment programming to raise advertising capital to buy larger transmitters that would reach greater numbers of the community.[12] New stations nationally lacked capital to make many original programs. As a result, they often became "mere outlets for network programming" in the 1930s to survive the tides of capitalist competition.[13] In San Antonio, however, broadcast programming took an alternative route.

Spanish-language radio created a hybrid system, combining standard network programming with alternative programs directed specifically at Mexican Americans. Anglo-owned radio stations had difficulty selling advertising for the early-morning or late-night time slots in the programming schedule. Mexican and Mexican American radio brokers capitalized on these empty segments by buying them, arranging their own programs, selling advertisements, and pocketing the profit. Felix Gutiérrez and Jorge Schement report that the first broker began broadcasting in San Antonio on KONO-AM in 1928.[14] Broadcasting in Spanish, the radio brokers targeted a mass Mexican American audience, using Mexican radio genres, such as the *radionovela,* and American radio genres, such as the quiz show.[15] Local announcements also revealed the important events in working-class life.[16] As the programs gained popularity, the radio formats became shorter and faster paced to match the tone and cadence of advertising breaks.[17] The individual personalities of the brokers, though, were the most distinctive qualities of the radio programs, providing direct contact with advertisers and a point-to-mass contact with listeners.[18] While many of the successful brokers became radio station employees, at least one broker, Raúl Cortez, bankrolled enough capital to start his own full-time Spanish-language radio station, KCOR 1350-AM.[19] KCOR and its sister television station, KCOR 41-TV, represent industrial strategies to construct Mexican Americans as part of a mass San Antonio audience. Launched respectively in 1946 and 1955, they were the first full-time Spanish-language broadcasting media industries in the United States.

Radio and television broadcasting at this time functioned largely through Mexican American labor, Mexican-national talent, and Anglo American sponsorship. Mexican American brokers and owners imported popular Mexican actors to create loyal listener bases that they could sell to advertisers. Famous personalities, such as Lalo Astol, became influential entrepreneurs on their own, moving between radio and television programs and charging extra for song dedications and personal commercial endorsements in the 1940s and 1950s.[20] In television, San Antonio's KERN-TV, an Anglo-owned station, featured "Buscando Estrellas," a traveling variety show that rotated production locations every thirteen weeks to new cities in south Texas.[21] Mexican actor José Pérez (Pepe) del Río hosted the program from 1951 to 1956 under the sponsorship of Pioneer Mills, a German American–owned flour company in San Antonio. In 1956, Pepe del Río moved to KCOR-TV to host "Cine en Español," based on old movies from Mexico, Argentina, and Spain. This was, coincidentally, the "Golden Age of Mexican Cinema," a time period marked by Mexico's heavy exportation to the United States and throughout Latin America.[22] Cortez also promoted a chain of local Anglo-owned movie theaters that showed only Mexican films.[23] These arrangements illustrate the ways Mexican Americans, Anglo Americans, and Mexican nationals collaborated in order to mobilize a mass Mexican American audience for sale to advertisers.

These arrangements also reveal the structural barriers to Mexican American media at this time. Although more than half of the talent on KCOR-TV was Mexican, latent racism guided hiring practices. At least one listener survey in San Antonio concurred: "The complaint is that the American version of Spanish is either too *pocho* (i.e., too intermixed with English words or constructions) or too 'peasanty' (i.e., agricultural terms are used in discussing non-agricultural subjects)."[24] By denigrating Mexican American Spanish as nonstandard and unprofessional, the survey implied that the Mexican Americans speaking this language were also not worthy of respect. This latent racism also permeated advertising mentalities, conjuring images of old, rural farmers who did not fit a strong consumer profile. At one time, Cortez encouraged his listeners to send box tops to a potential advertiser to prove the consumer strength of Mexican Americans.[25] Under these conditions, many Mexican American workers remained with English-language music radio stations because they "were cautious in either acknowledging their heritage or . . . for fear of blatant discriminatory policies" against them.[26] Even Cortez, who fought to promote Mexican American audiences, sold KCOR-AM and KCOR-TV to an Anglo owner, McHenry Tichenor, when limited advertising revenues could not offset the costs of importing Mexican talent for programs.

Meanwhile, the creation of Mexican American radio and television broadcasts facilitated the media's easy collaboration with San Antonio's music recording industry. Small record labels existed throughout the city well before broadcasting began. Throughout the 1920s, middle-class Mexican Americans and national Anglo American production companies interested in quick profits from "race records" marketed Mexican *corridos* to working-class Mexican Americans and migrant labor.[27] While the Great Depression froze national production for a mass market, radio and television programs continued to give Mexican and Mexican American musicians access to a mass audience in San Antonio. In the 1940s, radio stations promoted *conjunto* (later called Tejano) music, a regional music genre produced by and for working-class Mexican Americans.[28] Abandoned by national record production companies, local companies again flourished, such as Real and Discos Ideal.[29] These companies capitalized on a new market of Mexican Americans who found work in war industries and thus had more disposable income for music.[30]

When KCOR-TV began broadcasting in the 1950s, Tejano music provided an easy programming format, particularly since the radio and television stations shared a production studio. For example, *conjunto* musician Flaco Jimenez became a superstar in part due to the symbiosis created by mass media promotions. *Texas Monthly* reporter Chester Rosson writes: "[Jimenez's band] Los Caminantes already had a regular program over radio KCOR in San Antonio and played at clubs throughout the area.... In May 1956 Los Caminantes first recorded on the local Rio label and gained a Thursday evening slot on San Antonio's Channel 41, KCOR-TV. Within two years they were San Antonio's favorite Tex-Mex band."[31] At this time, television ownership and viewing was still a privileged activity; only middle-class Mexican Americans could afford the forty to seventy dollars needed to buy a UHF converter to watch Spanish-language television.[32] The joint broadcasts thus combined middle-class and working-class Mexican American audiences for locally recorded music. Together, broadcast industries and record labels used Mexican American labor, Anglo American capital, and Mexican cultural producers to construct a Mexican American mass audience for media.

PANETHNICIZATION "lumping"

Panethnic media rose in the United States amidst the increasing conglomeration of mass media industries and commodification of mass audiences globally. By the 1960s, large broadcast, film, and print companies dominated mass media systems of production and distribution in the United States. The Federal Communication Commission (FCC) assisted corporations' growing economies of scale and vertical integration through rulings that asserted the indivisibility of regulated competition and the public interest—rulings that served the interests of the dominant corporations.[33] In turn, these corporations had invested heavily in Latin American mass media industries, from professional training schools and management to technological resources and organizational structuring. These investments resulted in Latin American media corporations that functioned often within state-protected regulations but according to an American business model. In Mexico, Don Emilio Azcárraga Vidaurreta created the Televisa broadcasting empire by managing these tensions. As the sole Mexican agent for RCA Victor Records in the 1930s, Azcárraga Vidaurreta invested in Los Angeles Spanish-language broadcasting, fostering synergy between RCA records, radio station playlists, and concerts to be performed in his own theaters.[34] In addition, he maintained close ties to the Partido Revolucionario Institucional (PRI), the country's ruling party from 1929 until 2000, allowing Televisa's hegemony over private broadcasting to go virtually unchallenged.[35] From this foundation, Azcárraga Vidaurreta inaugurated the panethnic construction of Mexican American media when he purchased KCOR-TV in 1961.

Panethnic media differed from massified media in scale, both in terms of financial investment and distribution networks. The strong financial presence of multinational investors—initially Mexican nationals but later other Latin Americans—signified a departure from media industries started and financed by Mexican American individual entrepreneurs. The interest of Latin American companies brought many of San Antonio's Mexican American media into international arenas for distribution and investment as profitable pieces of an extended network that relied on content from other parts of the globe.[36] Further, whereas massified media targeted a local Mexican American audience, panethnic media further homogenized the imagined audience into Spanish-speaking consumers without regard for their national origin or immigration history.[37] Panethnic media professionals presumed they could exploit a cultural-linguistic market shared by Latin Americans on the basis of language and history, and they looked for silver-bullet approaches to content, in which one media product could be shipped all over the world with little to no changes.[38] Mexican Americans in San Antonio thus became part of a complex web of multiethnic Latinos and multinational players in a globalizing media market.

Expanding into television, Azcárraga hoped to use San Antonio's KCOR, now renamed KWEX-TV Channel 41, to create a unified mass media market for all Spanish speakers on both sides of the U.S.-Mexican border.[39] He created both the Spanish International Communications Corporation (SICC) and the Spanish International Network (SIN) to expand his reach legally as a Mexican citizen. SICC was a station group for which SIN managed programming and sales. From 1962 to 1972, SICC purchased or merged with five other television stations: KMEX in Los Angeles (1962); WXTV in New York (1968); WLTV in Miami (1971); and Fresno/Hanford (1972).[40] In addition, SIN's owners, the Azcárraga family, expanded their Mexico City–based programming network, Televisa, to cover 63 percent of all television stations outside of the capital.[41] Although Azcárraga used minority investors with U.S. citizenship to legalize purchases for SICC's development, the Mexican family bankrolled the company through its close association with SIN, which provided content from Mexico.

San Antonio was crucial to the cultivation of the panethnic Mexican American market in two important ways throughout the 1970s. San Antonio was one of SIN's two hub cities for the distribution of Mexican programming in the United States. As the nearest cities to Mexico City, the San Antonio and Los Angeles affiliates received programming via terrestrial microwave, which they then distributed through a "bicycle network" to the other stations.[42] This was an expensive proposition. In the beginning, KWEX kept a running tab of its imports with Televisa and billed at approximately forty dollars per hour of programming. Posting net losses until 1967, KWEX managed to stay afloat through capital loans, program subsidies and maintaining limited personnel.[43] Then, in 1976, Televisa began paying KWEX for carrying the network's live programming from Mexico, increasing local revenues significantly.[44] Ultimately, the relationship between KWEX, SIN, and Televisa resulted in each institution's profiting from the panethnic construction of producers and audiences.

In addition, San Antonio's advertising agencies and other media outlets strove to use the idea of the panethnic consumer to open national markets for Mexican Americans and Latinos in general. In 1979, SIN commissioned Yankelovich, Skelly and White to do the first market research on Latinos in the United States.[45] One year later, Lionel Sosa, a Mexican American from San Antonio, opened Sosa and Associates to service clients willing to invest in the newly quantified Hispanic market.[46] Using SIN's research numbers, Sosa and Associates combined the Mexican American consumer into a panethnic package with other Spanish-speaking peoples, because "U.S. advertising agencies and their corporate clients had to be convinced on two points: (1) that U.S. Mexican Americans were a desirable consumer group for their products, and (2) that Spanish-language television was the best way to convince U.S. Mexican Americans to buy these products."[47] In other words, San Antonio's advertising industry grew largely in the 1980s as an extension of panethnic television broadcasting. Sosa and Associates became Sosa, Bromley, Aguilar, Noble and Associates during that time and spurred several other Mexican Americans to open Mexican American advertising agencies in the city, including Hispano Marketing; Montemayor y Asociados; Bromley, Aguilar and Associates; Cartel Creativo; García LKS; and Creative Civilization. In the 1990s, these advertising agencies billed millions of dollars for panethnic advertising campaigns for Procter and Gamble, Coca Cola, Sprint PCS, Levi's, AT&T, Gillette, Texaco, Labatt U.S.A., Anheuser-Busch, Dr. Pepper, Ralston-Purina, JCPenney, Continental Airlines, American Airlines, Nationwide Insurance, and the U.S. Department of Health and Human Services.[48] These accounts made the panethnic construction of Mexican American media one of the most lucrative avenues for San Antonians to profit nationally.

While expanding into new territories for Mexican Americans in media, panethnic mass media, nevertheless, produced its own tensions between Mexican nationals, Mexican Americans, and the state. Azcárraga Vidaurreta, and later his son, Emilio Azcárraga Milmo, used U.S. citizens as fronts for SIN and its affiliate stations to avoid abutting Section 310b of the Communication Act, which requires national citizens to own at least 80 percent of stock in television stations. When a Latino media interest group brought charges against SIN's station group, SICC, in 1980, the FCC investigated the legitimacy of the network and its holdings.[49] Six years later, the FCC decided not to renew the licenses of some of SIN's affiliates in breach of the foreign ownership law. Hallmark Cards/First Capital bought those stations and others and formed the Univision Network, based on SIN and its holdings. Televisa responded by refocusing on panethnic content for Univision, such as a national news program, until it could buy back some ownership shares in 1992, when Hallmark sold the network to Jerrold Perenchio. Although Mexican nationals never stopped influencing Univision's operations and programming, they did so within more restricted boundaries and with more inclusion of Mexican American professionals.

The survival and subsequent explosion of panethnic mass media reconfigured San Antonio Mexican American media consumers in terms of other national media markets. Whereas Mexican American mass media professionals struggled to even catch the attention of media advertisers in the 1950s, advertisers sought panethnic media outlets in the 1980s as easy entries into growing Spanish-speaking markets. Private marketing firms by that time had begun to measure San Antonio's Mexican American population, their media consumption, and buying power using standard audience research methods. In 1998 San Antonio ranked seventh nationally as a Hispanic demographic area, with a buying power of over $9.5 billion.[50] Placed behind Los Angeles, New York, Miami, Houston, Chicago, and San Francisco, San Antonio media producers had to sell their largely Mexican American consumer figures against more diverse Latino populations. Meanwhile, San Antonio media that claimed the largest shares of the local consumer market, such as KWEX-TV, garnered the highest advertising rates and profits.[51] Both of these trends in the panethnic construction of Mexican American media fortified local media that could capture a Mexican American market locally while devaluing their inability to capture a wider panethnic market nationally. In this sense, the panethnic construction defined San Antonio Mexican American consumers both inside and outside of the local region, exerting pressure on media in other constructions to count all Latino consumers for revenue.

FRAGMENTATION

By the mid–1990s, panethnic definitions of Mexican American media had extended globally, making them the most widespread in their history, but in San Antonio, Mexican American media also fragmented into new local ways. This fourth, fragmented construction of Mexican American mass media signified the simultaneous expansion and concentration of industrial producers, their contents, and their target audiences. In one sense, mass media industries began targeting niche segments of Mexican American consumers with more diverse contents, using new technologies and marketing strategies. In another sense, Mexican American mass media became more integrated into larger media conglomerates. These trends both conformed to a sea change in North American regulations over mass media industries, which favored the commodification of new media contents and their audiences while also favoring the concentration of capital in the hands of fewer corporations based in the United States. For Mexican Americans in San Antonio, the changes had ambiguous effects. More media meant more job opportunities for many Mexican Americans in all creative and managerial fields, just as the concentration of ownership tended to push Mexican Americans out of the upper echelons of managerial hierarchy. Caught in between cooperation and competition with both Anglo Americans and Mexican nationals, Mexican Americans bridged the global, national, and local in fragmented ways.

In the 1990s, the sheer numerical growth of San Antonio media outlets that claimed to hire Mexican Americans reflected the fragmented construction of Mexican American media. In 1981 San Antonio had approximately twenty-five radio stations, five television stations, two daily newspapers, and four regional newspapers; of these, five radio stations and KWEX-TV were Spanish-language media outlets.[52] By the end of the century, these numbers had nearly doubled, with forty-two radio stations (eight Spanish language), thirteen television stations, three community access channels, two daily newspapers, and at least nine weeklies. These numbers do not even take into account the thousands of Web-based media outlets that were available through free Internet terminals in San Antonio Libraries. Unlike in previous decades, Mexican Americans worked across media industries, regardless of language or culture. To some degree, affirmative action practices in media industries and pressure from Latino advocacy groups eased Mexican Americans' entry into more of these workplaces, setting employment goals in some locations as high as 50 percent.[53] It is also true, though, that "race, gender, and ethnicity have now joined socio-economic status as potentially marketable boundaries of difference," making Mexican American workers more desirable to attract a Mexican American niche market.[54]

Fragmented media producers pursued specialized local Mexican American markets while making inroads into panethnic, multiethnic, or multiclass markets. Joseph Turow calls this tendency "hypersegmentation," in which media workers, assisted by new technologies, can tailor content as precisely as possible to the consumer habits and tastes of individuals.[55] The rebirth of *La Prensa* in 1989 and the creation of new print media in the 1990s signified this type of tailoring. Originally published as a Mexican American elite paper for other Mexican American elites, *La Prensa* diversified its production, staff, and target audience in the 1990s. Distributed in area businesses and home-delivered on the city's south side, *La Prensa* became a bilingual newspaper with "a Hispanic perspective."[56] Marketing materials for the paper aimed for a linguistically diverse San Antonio readership, while niche marketing to middle-class Hispanic consumers, such as Spanish teachers and "Hispanic business people [who want] to polish their knowledge of the Spanish language."[57] Other publications followed suit. Avista published *Vajito*, a bimonthly magazine for lowrider fans, and *The Juice* for "urban hip hop and Mexican American hip hop communities."[58] Prime Time Inc. offered ten different weekly newspapers specializing in multiethnic middle-class neighborhoods and military bases.[59] *Que Onda*, a bilingual Houston publication, began a San Antonio edition in 1997 for middle-class Tejano fans.[60] Finally, Alternative Media Inc. purchased San Antonio's largest weekly newspaper, *The Current*, as part of a national strategy to corner left-leaning Hispanic, African American, and gay markets.[61] Like the new *La Prensa*, local publishers created new print media that carved out niche readers from lucrative segments of the Mexican American populace.

As Mexican American niche media diversified their target audiences, though, media ownership became more concentrated between companies operated outside of San Antonio. Changes in media regulations circumscribed this economic trend by supporting the vertical integration of some of the United States' largest media industries while also limiting the role of Mexican national producers and Mexican American advocacy groups. The legal resolution that led to the creation of Univision ironically also accompanied a wave of deregulatory acts aimed at liberalizing media markets for companies based in the United States. Decreasing limits to media ownership, vertical integration, and synergies across media and nonmedia industries encouraged corporate media giants to partner or buy out panethnic Spanish-language corporations to consolidate their market shares.[62] At the same time, deregulation still favored mass media companies owned by U.S. citizens. Tariffs on mass media products and limits on foreign ownership of broadcast industries remained even after the North American Free Trade Agreement (NAFTA) would reportedly open trade borders.[63] Some Mexican American advocacy groups, such as the National Council of La Raza, have supported restrictions, anticipating that the measures would encourage Mexican American ownership and management in those industries.[64] Yet this did not happen; instead, the tariffs reflect the ways Mexican Americans relied on cooperation with Anglo Americans to capitalize upon fragmented Mexican American media markets.

The ethnic and national implications of concentration have been apparent in San Antonio's media market since the 1950s, when a successful Anglo newspaper owner, McHenry Tichenor, bought out KCOR-AM along with several other Spanish-language stations in Texas.[65] Although at that time he could not alone own the Mexican American radio market in San Antonio under federal regulations, he eventually integrated into one of the largest radio conglomerates in the world, thus capturing the city's Mexican American market. In the 1970s, Tichenor sold KCOR and KQXT, an adult contemporary station in San Antonio, to Heftel, a much larger panethnic Mexican American broadcasting company.[66] When the 1996 Telecommunications Act deregulated ownership rules, Heftel's majority owner, San Antonio's Clear Channel Communications, became one of the largest radio station owners in the world, buying mainstream radio stations throughout the United States. Merging again with Tichenor in 1997 and Jacor in 1998, the company signed a $23.5 billion deal with AMFM, which brought the company's holdings to 830 stations.[67] In San Antonio, Clear Channel and Heftel (renamed the Hispanic Broadcasting Company) owned four of the five top-rated Spanish-language radio stations as well as five English-language radio stations.[68] Clear Channel's concentration of Spanish-language stations was consistent with their expansion nationally in other "ethnic formats," such as African American hip-hop, rap, and R&B.[69] Only Cox Radio, which owned five FM and two AM stations, challenged Clear Channel's economy of scale in San Antonio.[70] Clear Channel and Cox, both Anglo-owned corporations, together dominated the top seventeen of the top twenty-two radio stations in the San Antonio market.[71] As a result, San Antonio had eight Spanish-language radio stations that employed and targeted Mexican Americans in 2000 but only one station with a Mexican American owner.

Ownership concentration in the market also required large, fluid sources of capital in order to afford losing millions on media outlets before ever turning a profit. For example, the most likely new television network to emerge in the early twenty-first century, Sí TV, needed heavy local investment combined with national partnerships and international support vehicles. Unlike segmented media, which catered to local communities through small production and distribution chains, Sí TV needed to reach the wealthiest segments of a national, panethnic Mexican American market. To do so meant securing the financial support of both local entrepreneurs from around the country and multinational corporations. A majority investor, Bruce Barshop posted the start-up funds for Sí TV to then secure a deal with Galavision, a counterprogramming vehicle for Univision that also supported Televisa with content. Barshop was a San Antonio venture capitalist who managed one of the city's largest real estate companies.[72] In 1993, Barshop expanded into the entertainment industry with a string of comedy clubs extending throughout Texas, and then entered television with the initiation of the Mexican American Laugh Festival, an annual Showtime exclusive. These networks eased Sí TV's entrance into television in a way that other fledgling networks could not afford. With Galavision's support, Sí TV expected to produce "a dozen Mexican American–themed, character-driven shows to premiere each season just so that one or two might make it past the first season and have a chance to be nourished into a hit show."[73] By 2000, its most successful program, *The Brothers Garcia*, moved to the Nickelodeon network, where a Mexican American–themed, English-dominant program targeted an enviable youth market, one that has both a multicultural sensibility and a middle-class access to cable television.[74] This example raises the complicated issues of culture given economic trends toward ownership consolidation, global expansion, and technological barriers to entry.

The tendency toward fragmented media in some ways limited what kinds of Mexican American culture could be marketed to which consumers, since media outlets only targeted certain kinds of consumers and since market entry became more expensive over the long term. This was especially true in Spanish-language media, where American-based advertisers were loath to invest in the new market. The histories of Univision and Telemundo demonstrated that corporations should be ready to absorb millions in debt in order to post a profit.[75] These hefty losses discouraged new Mexican American–owned operations from entering a market that nearly guaranteed they would lose money in the short term. The major multinational corporations that did enter the market often operated "two-tier marketing plans" to reach rich and poor consumers with separate types of cultural messages.[76] These plans sought to divide Mexican Americans into socially exclusive groups with their own media, producers, and visions of cultural differences. Importantly, the media targeted at the upper tier of rich consumers received the most financial resources in the form of advertising and investor backing—meaning that Mexican American media producers' survival depended upon choosing the medium and messages that could either cooperate or coexist within the confines of national or international corporate objectives. In the future, the growth of the economy for fragmented media will be intimately related not only to the growth of Mexican American media as a viable market locally but also to the national trends that regulate the cost of market entry in the postdigital age.[77]

Corporate Liberalism and Capitalism

Although Mexican American mass media has passed through several types of economic organization, contents, and audiences, elements of all four mass media constructions can still be found in San Antonio today, though the survival of many seem precarious. Homemade broadsheets and pamphlets distributed among the city's Mexican American immigrants hearken to a segmented construction without having the elite base that really bifurcated the owners and audiences from the rest of the Mexican American population. Like other massified media, KEDA-AM, known as "Radio Jalapeño," began in 1966 through the entrepreneurial efforts of Manuel Davila, whose family still owns and operates all aspects of the station. Despite family members' pride in their ability to self-sufficiently serve a multigenerational, mass Mexican American audience with Mexican-regional and Texas-based music, the station has had difficulties competing against panethnic media in recent years.[78] Even the success of fragmented mass media industries has been hard to gauge. Panethnic media occupy a lion's share of San Antonio's Mexican American media, dominating broadcast, recording, and print industries as well as the flow of content internationally. Fragmented media often rely heavily on panethnic media for global content, and massified media have difficulties competing for advertising investment without global distribution chains. Whether this reliance on panethnic media's access to global money and markets eventually shuts down a construction of Mexican American media in San Antonio is yet to be seen. However, it is reasonable to assume that media that can successfully target the most profitable segments of Mexican American audiences will be able to resist the pulls of panethnic media over many industries.

Mexican Americans in San Antonio have been forerunners in producing mass media content for Mexican Americans, though they have not been the sole creators, distributors, or audiences for these products. Together with Mexican nationals and Anglo Americans, Mexican Americans labored within the same capitalist structures and corporate liberal discourse to reproduce capital and invest its surplus into new consumer markets. At the same time, the construction of Mexican American mass media has changed over time to reflect the economic conditions for an ethnic media in the United States. The table here illustrates the similarities and differences across Mexican American media constructions with regard to economic structuring in this discourse:

Table 1.1
Historical Constructions of Mexican American Media in San Antonio,
Texas

	Segmented	Massified	Panethnic	Fragmented
Ownership	Individual	Individual	Corporate	Corporate
Investment	Local/regional	Local/regional	Global	Global
Target Market	Niche	Mass	Mass	Niche

These economic trends underscore the changing meaning of Mexican American media not only over time but also with the entry of new owners and investors whose use of new media technologies imagined new kinds of audiences. For Mexican Americans entering mass media, it has been important to know the contours of the economic landscape. Similarly, Mexican American media consumers have had to be aware of economic change. Mexican American target audiences segregated, aggregated, and reconfigured with each subsequent construction of mass media. This meant variances in the availability of certain kinds of media, for producers often have ignored consumers outside of their desired demographic.[79]

Though everyone involved in Mexican American mass media at a certain time worked in the same economy, Mexican Americans labored under unique conditions. Sometimes ignored and other times enlisted as "experts," Mexican Americans have had to face the racist ironies embedded in corporate liberalist discourse. For although the discourse deems all market players as equals, Mexican Americans experienced varying degrees of difference in relation to Mexican nationals and Anglo Americans. Mexican American mass media passed through several racial crises in the past century when Mexican American workers either faced exclusion or Mexican-national investors, for their workplaces became the targets of legal discipline.[80] Here the law and its regulatory functions were hardly neutral. The complex ethnic and national relations involved in the formation of Mexican American media underscore the class inequalities between capital-rich Anglo Americans and working-poor Mexican Americans, the national inequalities between United States citizens and Mexican citizens, as well as the cultural biases favoring Mexican-national traditional talent over Mexican American new talent. While national and cultural biases dissipated somewhat in the panethnic period and during the Chicano movements in the 1970s, class inequalities are still evident today.

Currently, the United States and Mexico support the hegemony of a corporate class of media elites. Over time, this class has incorporated Mexican nationals and Mexican Americans, but social class hierarchies have remained stable. Fewer Mexican Americans still occupy ownership positions in Mexican American mass media industries, and more Mexican Americans are target audience members than creative personnel. Thus, more Mexican Americans may be part of or feel the effects of Mexican American mass media, but this is not the same as holding power in the states that manage these industries. Nicos Poulantzas writes that the capitalist state "has always functioned in a specific relation with the hegemonic class or a specific faction of this [power] bloc, and it has always been at the service of this specific class or faction."[81] For top Mexican American professionals in mass media industries, the servicing of hegemony has been most apparent even when their powerful voices cannot be heard in mainstream corporate circles.

Chapter 2

Mexican Americans
Making Media, Making Citizens

W<small>HEN</small> S<small>AN</small> A<small>NTONIAN</small> A<small>DOLFO</small> A<small>GUILAR</small> became president of the Association of Hispanic Advertising Agencies (AHAA) in 1999, he brought the organization's annual conference to his hometown. There, in a hotel ballroom, he gave an optimistic but cautious welcome speech to AHAA members. Praising the trade magazine *Advertising Age* for creating a Hispanic advertising awards contest, Aguilar presented the organization with three challenges for the future of the Hispanic advertising industry. First, Hispanic advertisers still needed to educate corporations about the importance and changing nature of Hispanic consumers. Further, they needed to stress the importance of their ability to sell to that market. Finally, Hispanic advertisers must begin to reach out to their ethnic communities, both socially and politically. "We can no longer ignore the importance that Hispanics attach to being in their communities," Aguilar said. By using rhetoric of political empowerment, these three goals expressed a connection between Mexican American media production and citizenship, not just for Aguilar but for an entire community of Mexican American advertisers. This chapter explores how San Antonio's Mexican American professional media producers have reinterpreted economic production through the lens of a political struggle for media rights and economic justice, thereby transforming themselves into empowered citizens.

It cannot be underestimated how conscious Mexican American media producers were in San Antonio that they did more than make television advertisements, magazine supplements, and radio spots. Mexican American media production in the city has a long history with political movements organized to build and publicize linkages between Mexican American citizenship and mass media. Mexican American mass media have existed in San Antonio since the beginning of the twentieth century, but the existence of these industries has not necessarily reflected Mexican Americans' economic or political power. For the most part, Mexican Americans remained segregated on the city's west and south sides, where political activism addressed the inequalities of both ethnicity and class.[1] Nationally, political activism among Mexican Americans came to a head during the civil rights movement in the late 1960s and 1970s. Using a discourse of a civil rights crisis that encompassed all aspects of minorities' lives in the United States, many activists protested against mass media as sites where stereotypical images of Mexican Americans perpetuated racism and marginalization in the wider society.[2] San Antonio was one of the hotbeds of boycotts (brownouts), letter-writing campaigns, and media advocacy groups such as the Involvement of Mexican Americans in Gainful Endeavors (IMAGE) and the Federation for the Advancement of Mexican Americans (FAMA). Tied directly to other political organizations through overlapping memberships, IMAGE and FAMA integrated mass media production and representation into a direct-action politics for social change. One of those with multiple allegiances, Albert Peña advocated holding a public Yellow Pages bonfire if the city's telephone company continued a stereotypical advertising campaign.[3] As the first Mexican American County Commissioner in Bexar County and one of the original founders of Mexican American Unity Council and the Mexican American Legal Defense and Educational Fund, Peña's visibility brought the connection between mass media representation and political representation into the public sphere.

Yet by the mid–1970s, many Mexican Americans from mass media activist groups had become what Chon Noriega calls "realistic radicals," in that they became part of the system that they were trying to change.[4] By raising consciousness around unjust media representations, hiring disparities, and prejudices within media markets, San Antonio opened a space to enter some of the very institutions they had criticized. Allegiances fragmented between Mexican Americans who entered mass media institutions, joined their professional organizations, and adopted their rhetoric, and Mexican Americans who continued to press for structural changes in mass media institutions from the outside.[5] For those who entered mass media industries, they became part of the history of Mexican American mass media as described earlier. This chapter, however, tells another side to the story—that is, how Mexican American media producers saw themselves in relation to that history.

In the late 1990s, Mexican Americans working in mass media cited multiple definitions of their cultural and occupational communities. Using a snowball approach to meet people in San Antonio's mass media industries, I selected a small sample of fifteen Mexican Americans and five Anglo Americans to interview further about their history, goals, and experiences in mass media industries. Each of my subjects worked in diverse areas of Mexican American mass media in San Antonio, from advertising to newspapers, and played diverse roles in those industries, from casting to video postproduction. Despite the variations among interviewees, they often traced shared narratives of Mexican American identity and common struggles to produce media for Mexican Americans. In their own words, Mexican American media producers often saw themselves as actors in the final stage of a civil rights movement: one that recognizes them as a cultural market. The following interviews with media producers explain how they define their own cultural and economic identities in mass media industries.

Talking With Mexican American Media Producers

Interviews with media professionals were resources for understanding the contexts for production and how individuals conceive of their own agency in these contexts. As such, the interviews were narratives, constructed by the interviewer and interviewee in an artificial situation. I reached most of the interviewees through my personal contacts in San Antonio. Having studied Mexican American audiences in San Antonio, I told my contacts that I wanted to know more about the people who produce media for them. Within these parameters, the narratives of being a Mexican American, knowing about Mexican Americans, and producing media for Mexican Americans diverged into various topics, often within the same interview. Interviews generated "a stream of narrative, involving an intricate braiding of stories. Interviewees, in telling stories about themselves, in relation to others, reconstitute[d] themselves." Responding to me then as an Anglo, female graduate student, the media professionals offered me diverse self-narratives. Some were sympathetic to my project and some were suspicious with the knowledge that I came from outside of the cultures they inhabited. These utterances were "double-voiced" because they respond to me and to the interview topic as well as the people and topics of interviews in the past.[8] This is to say that the dialogues between my interview subjects and me were structured by our social and institutional positions.

The producers' narratives about Mexican American media production were at once very personal and social. Sitting in a formal interview setting, the producers pieced together fragments of their own past with the knowledge that they were not the only ones to suffer discrimination both in private and public settings. Then they referred me to other producers they knew who had had similar experiences. This kind of study illuminated how the producers themselves imagined themselves as a community within other communities, namely a nation of mainstream media workers and a San Antonio Mexican American populace. Like all communities, Mexican American media producers were never a unified mass; their differences produced their own tensions both within the group in terms of gender, region, and generation and outside the group in terms of what Mexican American media should be. These tensions are particularly interesting in demonstrating not only the diversity of peoples within an imagined community but also the limits imposed on their membership.

WHO ARE MEXICAN AMERICAN MEDIA PRODUCERS?
HISTORY AND MEMORY

When interviewees spoke about themselves, the social history of Mexican Americans in south Texas filtered through their own stories, shaping their assessments of their pasts, the present, and predictions for the future. This shared history—for instance, of the Chicano movement—and its associated discourses of complicity and resistance, provided Mexican Americans with a surplus of meanings, symbols, and signs that overdetermined how they interpreted their own experiences. For example, shared discourses shaped individuals' stories about their own experience into public understandings of class mobility, racial stigmatization, or family values.[9] Indeed, all of these public discourses appeared in interviewees' descriptions of their own lives and work.

All of the interviewees demonstrated a conscious attention to the role ethnicity and cultural identity played in their profession. In general, the Mexican American producers divided by age into two groups: those who were forerunners in their respective media fields and their subsequent employees. The forerunners shared similar narrative themes in their interviews, including histories of discrimination, assimilation, and activism. The later generation shared common stories of Mexican American pluralism and diversity. Together, their narratives composed a complex picture of what it meant to be a Mexican American media producer in San Antonio in the 1990s. On one hand, their common concerns stemmed from the history of Mexican American media in San Antonio, which increasingly valued Mexican American media professionals through the 1980s and 1990s with the expansion of panethnic and fragmented mass media. On the other hand, though, the interviewees spoke about this history individually as people from different places, as men and women, and as working-class and middle-class subjects. The personalization of these experiences produced a constant tension between what the interviewees wanted to say about themselves and what could not be articulated about the industry as a whole.

FORERUNNERS AND THE OLD SAN ANTONIO

I knew when I was talking with the first generation of mass media professionals that I was not the only one to ask them about their history and trade. As top national executives or business leaders in the community, they were often hailed to give lectures for conferences, schools, or city gatherings in which they had to present themselves to the public. These forerunners, seven in this sample, spoke easily about their histories, emphasizing the divide between Anglo-dominated and minoritized Mexican American communities in San Antonio and in mass media industries at large. They also articulated the importance of their role in bridging the gap between Mexican American and Anglo American consumer markets. By developing more professional strategies, making more positive representations, or opening more access to media texts, this group of professionals mostly framed their aims as citizenship issues and thus themselves as fighters in a quest to gain more rights for Mexican American consumer-citizens. Meeting with these individuals, I knew that they possibly had the most power to influence Mexican American mass media from within the power elite. Their rhetoric about consumer and citizenship empowerment thus could not be easily dismissed, for it was spoken with the power of their industries behind it.

Almost without exception, the forerunners in the mass media industries cited humble beginnings. Ruben Ramos, a longtime Tejano musician and record label owner, told me over lunch how he got involved with the music:

> I was born in Sugarland in 1940. I was a son of migrant workers of
> cotton fields. I was raised in the cotton fields, but always with a lot of
> music around. Not that we had radios. We didn't even own a radio,
> but the truck man, "el truckero," used to have all the doors open and
> the radio on. Of course my mom was a guitar player. She and the
> neighbors used to have social parties back then. My brother was a
> fiddle player; so the music is in my blood. My grandfather was kind of
> a musician, but all his sons were musicians, ten of them; basically,
> they were the city slickers, because we were from the country and my
> sister got a taste of the band on stage; so she didn't want to go back to
> Sugarland and pick up cotton.

Ramos's story about south Texas grounds him in the region—an important qualification for Tejano music—but, more important, it grounds him in the nation. Ramos's humility, work ethic, and strong sense of family are all defining characteristics of the American success story. His eventual rise through the ranks of the industry, from a cotton-picking musician to an independent recording studio and label owner, follows a familiar plot in the lives of Mexican American media professionals who overcame adversities.

Discrimination and exclusion were among the principal adversities that the older generation faced. Themes of racial prejudice recurred in each interview, establishing the narrators' connection to other Mexican Americans regardless of other differences. *La Prensa* publisher Tino Durán, *Vajito* publisher George Velasquez, Telemundo station manager Arthur Emerson, and advertising agency owner Aguilar all spoke of having been segregated from public spaces, of hearing disparaging slurs, and of suffering overt physical repression when growing up in San Antonio. Lionel Sosa, in his autobiographical account of Hispanic advertising, also experienced racial segregation, having grown up in the predominantly Mexican American and economically disfranchised west side of the city.[10] Durán remembered an incident when his family went to a restaurant just outside San Antonio:

> My stepfather got up. He was short; he wasn't very big and he says, "I was in the Army and served the United States Army. I'm an American citizen." And the guy from around the little window where he was looking out, I guess he was a cook. He came out—well the knife looked about that big, might have been that big [*demonstrates with hands*]—but I saw a big knife and he had a big belly and he had a sweaty shirt and he came out and says, "Mexican, get the hell out." My stepfather started to take off his coat. My Mom and I dragged him out of there and he started crying in the car. My Mama started crying and I started crying. I really didn't know what I was crying about, but I know something had happened.

In Durán's narrative, American citizenship and Mexican slurs stood as polar ends of his childhood experience. During this pre–civil rights era, legal, political, and economic obstacles in the United States made the racial formation of Mexican Americanness visible and denigrated in all social interactions.[11] The older generation vividly remembered this era and used memories to construct a narrative of their second-class citizenship.

Mass media became one place to fight discrimination against Mexican Americans. If the aims of Chicano mass media groups in San Antonio were largely reformist in nature, then the generation of Mexican Americans who came into mass media industries during this time learned quickly how to work within the mainstream. Few of the forerunners were part of the Chicano movement. Even Velasquez, who acted and traveled with the Teatro Campesino in the Southwest, said the political experience taught him good business acumen:

> We did a lot of Campesino scripts; then we published our own. . . .
> We were concentrating on the local empowerment and voter
> registration to form a third party. So we did all of that. . . . It was all
> no government support or funding. . . . We didn't want to be shackled
> by any of the restrictions—like you can't do this you can't do that;
> you can't say this, you can't say that—you know they have got you by
> the balls. That was our thing to be totally independent; so we could
> say what we want and say it how we wanted to say it. The theater was
> kind of run like a band, we started with—I put a $100 in an account
> and we lasted 15 years until 1980/81. We sponsored two national
> theater festivals and we raised it all ourselves.

Velasquez's experiences as an activist provided him with the foundation for starting an independent magazine about lowriders. He honed his writing skills through theater scripts and newspaper articles. Through organizing finances, he learned how to create a business that was not dependent on Anglo-dominated institutions for support. Finally, he wanted to produce a product for an audience that he felt he identified with but that was ignored. Although he struggled as a Chicano activist for political independence, Velasquez worked in media industries to achieve financial independence for his magazine.

While Velasquez and others strove for independence, few could attain it. Their work demanded that they integrate into industrial chains of command, ones that at the time were dominated by Anglo Americans. The need to fit into the system created an identity crisis for some of the professionals, because they felt they had to reject different parts of their identity depending on their location. In the workplace, they became Anglicized. Emerson said that people learned to Anglicize the pronunciations of their names, saying, for example, "Sal-AY-zar instead of Sal-a-zar." When Aguilar entered the world of advertising, he said he "did not fit what ad agency types were like back in that particular era." He explained:

> I just didn't have the right type of social experience to be able to fit
> into what to me seemed like an impossible industry to penetrate. I
> remember even as an intern going to make a call with . . . an account
> person at an agency. I walked in with them, very kind of sheepishly
> behind them and they were hugging each other and kissing each other
> and saying how great it was to see them. I said to myself, wow, I could
> never do that—that's not me, it seemed like too much of a
> "schmoozed" type of a job and it just wasn't part of my personality. So,
> it felt a little bit distant and odd to me.

At home, interviewees said they felt out of place as well. Aguilar remembered feeling like a loner as a Mexican American trying to enter advertising, a world associated with an Anglo American identity. Born and raised on San Antonio's south side, Aguilar went to the University of Texas at Austin in the early 1970s to study advertising and marketing: "I would go to the Chicano parties, you know, and all of my Chicano friends were studying Chicano Studies. And, they were in sociology and psychology and all these wonderful things and here I was kind of like lone *bandido* in advertising and marketing." As with other interviewees of his generation, cultural marginalization was part of a common past that had to be overcome along with poverty, discrimination, and exclusion from their industries.

The people I talked with were the survivors of these overwhelming odds. To succeed, they embraced the professional standards and goals of their areas—even if these goals eliminated other Mexican Americans from the industry. One of the first graphics professionals for Tejano music, Ruben Cubillos, for example, started designing albums, posters, and other merchandizing products because he felt the industry was not being taken seriously enough: "To me, my whole heart told me that these [album covers] were ransom notes—that people weren't even doing images. They were just slapping on photos and slapping on type. Who cares what it was? It was Little Joe; it was Ram Herrera. It was whatever. Who cares? There was no theme, there was nothing, there was no campaign. Nobody had put it in perspective. I was like, 'One day I'm going to do this.'" Cubillos moved from being a Tejano musician and fan, to becoming a graphic artist, and finally to directing an advertising agency, A Big Chihuahua, which represented Jack Daniels in the 2000 Tejano Music Awards. To be the best in the industry, though, meant taking no prisoners, Latino or otherwise. Over the years, Durán said he had to drive Mexican American–owned publications out of business if they could not compete. "There's room for you and only you, nobody else. . . . It's not a greedy statement, but you have quality and the other people don't. If they can't play the same game you play, they shouldn't play the game," he said. In fact, Cubillos, Durán, and other forerunners' pride and prowess in their professional lives as Mexican Americans was more important to them than opening the industry to all Mexican Americans.

The Mexican American forerunners adopted the same attitudes as other executives who believed in a liberal world of economic winners and losers without regard to race or ethnicity. A high school video production teacher, George Ozuna, said he learned this corporate mentality when he once worked for a local television affiliate. When his Mexican American supervisor took credit for a popular public service announcement for the Bilingual/Bicultural

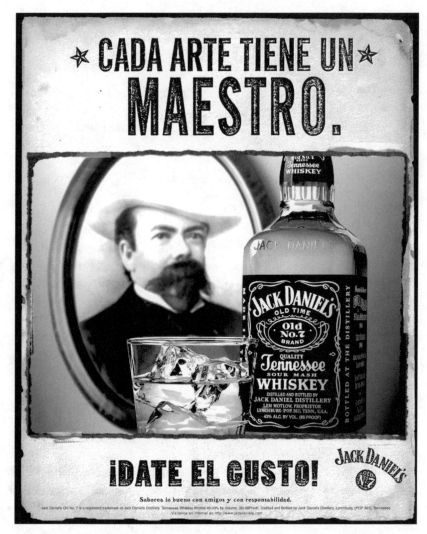

FIGURE 1. "Every Art Has Its Master." An advertisement relates Jack Daniels's story to Hispanic consumers in a culturally relevant way. *Photo reprinted with permission of Ruben Cubillos, A Big Chihuahua.*

Coalition for Mass Media, he reflected, "What it taught me was that if you do something, take responsibility for it and take credit for it. And at the same time, be wary. In this world, there are people who care and there are also predators and you've got to kind of watch yourself." Ozuna left commercial production, but those who stayed embraced its individualistic and market-driven ideology.

In an open market, by this logic, race and ethnicity had little bearing on the principles of creating, buying, or selling, whether it was a car or a mass media text. After telling me about initially feeling uncomfortable in the dual worlds of Chicanos and Anglos, Aguilar said he felt ultimately at home in advertising. "Fortunately this business is really grounded on more fundamental types of marketing and advertising principles," he said. In other words, Aguilar and other interviewees envisioned mass media as a space where they could potentially gain respect as Mexican Americans and achieve success in the industry, even if others could not. Durán concluded his story about the racist restaurant cook saying that he bought the building after he became a business owner. Owning *La Prensa* enabled him to own other properties, even the ones that seemed off-limits to him when he did not have money. Once at the top, Mexican Americans could use their capital to fight against the individual injustices they had felt in the past. Over the years I lived in San Antonio, members within this power elite invested dollars back into the communities that they themselves came from. Almost always the gesture accompanied a speech, retelling the story of discrimination, hard work, and success that had led to their empowerment, and, they hoped, others' as well.

The older generation of interviewees developed personal success stories in which they became symbolic protagonists for a larger Mexican American community. In their accounts, they paralleled the historical discrimination of Mexican Americans with their own struggle to work within Anglo-dominated mass media industries. By succeeding in the mass media, then, the older generation saw itself as contributing something positive to all Mexican Americans. Emphasizing their humble beginnings and obstacles to overcome, they chose events as plot points, revealing a gripping drama between protagonists and antagonists. Indeed, these stories are part of human nature.[12] What is intriguing, though, is how the interviewees chose the public discourses of Mexican American oppression to motivate their own action in the field. On the one hand, the stories were inspirational. They demonstrated an American Dream narrative that paid attention to the inequities that Mexican Americans faced in the pre–civil rights period. On the other hand, the stories glossed over the narratives of the Mexican Americans who could not overcome such odds and who may have been actually eliminated from mass media industries by their Mexican American peers and competitors. Michael Leiman writes that minorities historically became part of the professional-managerial class at the expense of the rest of the community, because corporate capitalism relies on a racialized underclass to provide cheap labor.[13] Among the people I interviewed, all of the members of this elite group were male—reinforcing a masculinist perspective of the hero whose success can rescue the rest of the community. When women were present, they were simply reinforcements to the protagonists, helping their husbands and providing what advertising magnate Lionel Sosa called "the backbone for our culture."[14] This narrative changed as Mexican American women became active themselves in mass media industries, a trend present among a later generation of Mexican American media producers.

YOUNG TURKS AND THE NEW SAN ANTONIO

Too young to have experienced Jim Crow or remember the civil rights movement, a newer generation of Mexican American media producers became the employees of the industries that the older generation helped create. In this group of fifteen media workers—including editorial cartoonist Leo Garza, advertising/film director Mike Cevallos, advertising creative director Luis Garcia, voice actress/advertising producer Laura Barbarena, and newspaper/e-zine editor James Garcia—nearly none of them owned the means for producing their own media texts. Many of them occupied two roles, if not two separate jobs, within mass media industries. Although some had advanced further than others during the time they spent in broadcasting, publishing, and advertising, all of them negotiated their labor with the Anglo American, Mexican American, and Mexican-national executives in their industries. Unlike these executives, however, the newer generation of media workers had different narratives of how their identity contributed to their quests for professional achievements and economic power.

To begin, the composition of the newer generation of media workers was both more numerous and more diverse in terms of gender, socioeconomic class, and geographic background. They were quick to point out their differences from other Mexican Americans in terms of language, cultural practices, and political stances. In general, I had an easier time talking with people in this group. After all, we were all about the same age and class status when we sat down to talk. Yet, the talks themselves focused on dissimilarities, on how little they, as Mexican Americans, shared across classes, regions, and generations. Some of these comments seemed to deconstruct stereotypes that they felt others, including myself, might have. Some of them told me about their middle-class backgrounds, growing up in all-Anglo neighborhoods. Others said they barely spoke Spanish, especially after leaving home for college. One interviewee, Luis Garcia, attended English-language schools in Mexico before moving to Austin for college. Like him, many of the newer generation said they did not grow up in San Antonio; they hailed from various parts of Texas, exhibiting greater geographic mobility in their adolescent and adult trajectories. Cevallos grew up in San Antonio and moved to north Texas for college.

Barbarena grew up in Austin before moving to San Antonio for work. James Garcia lived in various parts of the country because his father enlisted in the military. Garza started his career in Laredo and later moved to a town north of San Antonio to raise his own family. Diverse geographic backgrounds disrupted a common narrative thread in the interviews about growing up as a Mexican American in a Mexican American community. The interviewees were not necessarily male, poor, or Catholic. As Barbarena related self-consciously, "I'm Mexican, but I'm not dark-skinned. I wasn't raised Catholic. I was raised Baptist. I'm a recovering Baptist; you can put that."

The interviewees' reluctance to generalize their personal narrative to all Mexican Americans could be interpreted as both a sensitive way of not universalizing their experience to others and a distancing strategy in a society that valued individual success. Unlike the older generation, the newer generation did not have to reconcile some Chicano activists' calls for a unified struggle with the corporate imperative for competition. As such, many of them did not claim common cause with Mexican American activists who led public media protests, proposed letter-writing campaigns, and strategized media brownouts. Garza, who defined himself as part of the "generation that came between sixties activism and now," said he did not relate to the Brown Berets as an older generation might have, especially because in his hometown of Laredo "the politicians in office were Hispanic" already. Instead, many of them adopted the reformist language of the older generation of media workers as the most effective way to change media industries and their representations. For example, Cevallos said he did not relate to "militant Latinos" who have criticized the absence of Latinos in the media without ever having worked in the industry. "I tend to approach that battle in a different manner," he said, adding, "You know, we're going to do our own film, our own way. And if we're going to have to spend our own money, well then we'll do it, but we'll have total control for that. And that's our angle on trying to make a difference." This statement echoed Velasquez's words about the Teatro Campesino in emphasizing the importance of independence and control, yet in a completely commercial media context. Two decades after Chicano activists advocated reform from within media industries, many younger producers did not identify with media resistance movements conducted outside these industries.

Mexican American media producers often said they learned about their ethnic identity through *consuming* Spanish-language media. Whereas the older generation described a split between Mexican American and Anglo American worlds in producing mass media, their heirs described feeling more part of a Mexican American community when they consumed mass media. This was particularly true with music. Almost none of the interviewees claimed to like Tejano or Spanish-language music until they were older, when their re-introduction to the music symbolized an almost spiritual reconnection with their Mexican American identity. Music producer Michael Morales was a pop singer before he and his brother produced Tejano music. Although they enjoyed producing pop, he felt like Tejano spoke to their roots. He explained, "We were raised like middle class white kids, so it's been kind of a rebirth for us to get, to be immersed, back into the music, get us back to kind of our, our Latin culture that had been all but nonexistent in our lives to that point." In a similar way, Barbarena described herself as a "Born Again Chicana." She reminisced how she once hated her parents' Tejano music and Spanish-language television programs. She went to college and studied an exclusively English-language curriculum to pursue a theater career. She said it did not occur to her to enter into Spanish-language media market until she began consuming Spanish-language cultural products in the mid–1990s. Only then, she said, did she value her father's Mexican and her mother's Mexican American heritage: "And now my fiancé is a mariachi and I produce in Spanish." In both Barbarena's and Morales's stories, mass media consumption stimulated their desire to produce media for Mexican Americans.

Longtime media workers coined the word *retro-assimilation* to describe the newer generation's zeal for learning Spanish or consuming more Spanish-language media. Emerson and Durán said retro-assimilation occurred when economic conditions made Spanish a sought-after job skill and Mexican American culture a salable commodity. Durán explained

> Because of NAFTA, because there is a lot of Anglos that are taking
> Spanish—I just came from Incarnate Word High School. My
> daughter is in the honor roll. She's a senior, and I saw that about nine
> of ten little girls and some Anglo did very high on the Spanish
> Achievement Scholastic Award, a scholastic test. And I'm saying,
> "Why?" Because Mama and Dad are saying, "I want you to speak
> Spanish. I want you to be proficient in Spanish because you live in
> San Antonio, and that language is spoken here very much so."

According to Durán, the new generation saw their Spanish as marketable to media industries in the same way that his generation saw Spanish-language products as marketable to Mexican American consumers. Despite their diversity, the new generation retro-assimilated a Mexican American identity that the previous generation of Mexican American media workers had helped commodify.

When the newer generation began producing Mexican American mass media, they found more opportunities to use their cultural knowledge than their predecessors had found. Whereas the older generation had to struggle to be hired into large media corporations, some of those corporations now recruited Mexican American workers who could sell to panethnic Latino markets. Luis Garcia, who attended the University of Texas after growing up in Mexico, stated his bilingual/bicultural background made him more marketable to advertising agencies. He attributed his value to a bi-directional shift in the way Mexican Americans and mass media executives saw each other:

> Hispanics now are sort of coming to terms with who they are and are comfortable expressing their "Latinness," you know, the idea that it's cool to be different. Ethnic diversity is valued. It's an interesting thing now in this country. [It used to be that] unless you're a blue-eyed, blonde American you're not going to succeed in this country. That's not true anymore. Ethnic diversity is valued. In my case it was a great asset growing up and graduating and being able to land a great job with a great company. [I was] working on the Coca Cola business almost right out of college, which would have taken me five or six years if I would've gone the English route in an agency training program. I would have been buried through the ranks . . . before I got to work on a client like Coca Cola with direct contact with them. I literally had it immediately because there were very few people doing this thing called "Hispanic marketing."

Garcia said that the fact that Sosa and Coca Cola valued his cultural identity and bilingual skills reinforced his ability to express his cultural differences in the industry. In contrast to members of the older generation who Anglicized their names and otherwise tried to fit into the Anglo business culture, the newer generation could emphasize their differences because they represented a potential market segment.

Retro-assimilation, combined with the cultures of Mexican American media professionals, created favorable conditions for the new generation to enter mass media industries to expand the market for Mexican American consumers like themselves. They became socialized into the business culture created by the older generation, one that valued cultural identity as a way of tapping into consumer markets. At the same time, the newer generation's self-branded diversity pressured those industries to diversify the types of Mexican Americans included in market segments. This move among media workers fit the overall market trend in the early 1990s toward fragmented Mexican American mass media, in which the recognition of Mexican Americans' cultural differences helped split them into more profitable niche markets. In purely economic terms, fragmented media industries extracted more value from the middle-class workers who could use their diverse experiences to creatively target likeminded consumers.[15] In human terms, however, the newer group of media workers balanced their integration into a Mexican American corporate structure while preserving their own identities as particular types of Mexican Americans. For these workers, the ability to sell one's identity often signaled success in their personal narratives because it meant they were doing a good job while being themselves.

Cevallos's experience was indicative of the balance some of his peers maintained between corporate integration and cultural individuation. At first, he felt he was different from the Latino professionals at Sosa and Associates, many of whom were more experienced and knew better Spanish. He said, "As a Mexican American, I'm going to be thirty, and I was raised speaking English. So it was also kind of scary being among people and professionals that this is their forte: speaking Spanish and talking to the Hispanic market. So that was a little intimidating at first until I became more familiar, or more comfortable with messing up. . . . But I'm a Latino and I'm proud of that too. And they see that and they know. It's just like this common thread that we have."

In his narrative, the socialization process occurred quickly. Soon he began to direct commercials for the agency. It was after Cevallos said he felt accepted and accepted others in the Latino business that he began to use his own cultural background in his work. He realized his individual differences were valuable in targeting other Mexican Americans like him: "[My coworkers] will come and ask me about a particular angle that, you know, 'Well, growing up did you watch *The Dukes of Hazzard?*' Yeah, I watched that,' I said. 'But my mom also watched novelas.' So I have a different perspective than they have and it helps their insight—how to reach English-dominant Hispanics." Cevallos's ability to represent a generational, language, and age demographic as someone who grew up watching a 1980s television program added value to his stock in the company. With pride, he concluded the story by saying that the camaraderie he felt between himself and other Latinos at work made him feel like part of a community, not despite but because of their differences.

Thinking of Mexican American media professionals as a community is useful for understanding how each generation of media professionals narrated their cultural identities in ways that were similar to and different from other Mexican Americans. In the organizational structures of their industries, the professionals networked with each other and combined their individual skills to produce profitable media. As the industries grew during the 1980s and 1990s, so, too, did these networks, creating eventually a Mexican American media business culture for workers in San Antonio. In many ways, this business culture was no different from that in Anglo-dominated media industries, in that each new generation of workers had to adopt the old business culture before changing it. The socialization of media workers depends on the development of a community of likeminded industry workers who comply with the company rules and infrastructure.[16] However, Mexican American media business culture was significantly different since it depended on the constant identification and reidentification of workers as Mexican Americans. The workers I interviewed remembered how becoming part of mass media industries involved a process of identity transformation, of becoming less or more Mexican American. Unlike in Anglo professional communities, Mexican Americans networked outside their immediate industries to find support in these transformations. For the interviewees, Hispanic advertising, publishing, and commercial associations evoked fond memories, because they saw them as places for building community within the business norms and professional bureaucracies of their fields.

But the interviewees' memories were also untrustworthy, causing them to create narratives that expressed some feelings while hiding others. Whereas race, ethnicity, and gender emerged as important themes in the interviews, class often was less audible. Within two generations of media professionals, race replaced class as the axis of difference between Mexican American media professionals and their work in comparison with the mainstream. Meanwhile, talk about racial differences increased as the newer generation of media professionals elaborated on the diversity among Mexican Americans. This schism in the producers' discourses reflected both a political shift in the language of race and an economic shift in the value of Mexican American media professionals. For an earlier group of professionals, the civil rights movement of the 1960s slowly disaggregated race from class, placing race at the center of the language of social inequality.[17] At the same time, panethnic (and later fragmented) mass media industries increasingly valued the Mexican American professional as someone who could commodify Mexican American cultures. Thus, while a newer generation of Mexican American media professionals who grew up after the civil rights movement may have been more diverse in sociological terms, their differences also became increasingly desirable in a fragmented Mexican American media market. For many, the only way to articulate how they could be both Mexican Americans and media professionals was by seeing themselves as experts in marketing pluralism.

The self-narratives of the Mexican American media producers, how they came into the industry and their experiences, were symbolically significant in the ways that producers related their own stories to identity politics in a capitalist market. For many, media production was a new terrain for Mexican Americans to shed a discriminatory past, erase social stigmas around Mexican American identity, and ultimately merge into a pluralistic business class. Narratives about ethnic identity not only resolved the class tensions in each of the producers' lives as they became more upwardly mobile but also justified the importance of racial equity within capitalism.[18] Producers often formulated these desires for racial equity as "rights," hence legitimating the market as a place to empower a certain kind of Mexican American citizen.

Present Successes and Challenges

Echoing Aguilar's speech in the beginning of the chapter, Mexican American media producers spoke of achieving goals as both mass media professionals and as representatives of an imagined Mexican American community. The interviewees wanted to achieve parity with Anglo American media producers in terms of economic value and hiring as well as access to resources and research. For many, equity was a citizenship issue. During the 1960s and 1970s, legal attempts by some Chicano organizations to secure equal employment in media industries failed institutionally but spotlighted the identity politics of mass media. They argued that equal hiring and treatment of Mexican Americans in all aspects of media production would counter the negative effects on Mexican American citizens of underrepresentation and stereotyping. Thus while reaffirming the economic and juridical framework for mass media industries, activists succeeded in promoting Mexican American mass media hiring as a political issue in the public interest.[19] Over time, these groups divided between activists and professionals, with the latter group advocating less radical changes from within the system.[20] Two decades later, Mexican American media workers in San Antonio continued to frame their work and routines in terms of a political struggle, but this time only in the parameters of what was professional and good for market growth. This was particularly evident in the Tejano music industry, in which many workers adopted general market standards of professionalism to expand the economy for Mexican Americans who were both consumers and citizens.

THE RIGHT PERSON FOR THE JOB

Sitting in a modernistic glass-walled office in a warehouse-turned-art-gallery in San Antonio, Aguilar's presence demanded respect from his fellow advertising colleagues. Yet in our talk, he compared his present success to days when he felt like the token minority in the agency. Anheuser-Busch had declared the 1980s the "Decade of the Hispanic" in terms of Hispanics' consumer value, but American corporations had little notion yet of how to create and cater to the market.[21] Using an ironic tone, Aguilar said he began working first for Coca Cola, where the company had "discovered this new thing called Hispanic Marketing." He continued, "So, they had a very interesting strategy. They said, we're gonna hire a Mexican, a Puerto Rican, and a Cuban because they perceived that to be the most dominant groups. So, guess what? I got to be the Mexican!" Aguilar's tone mocked the idea that the inclusion of one Mexican American into a media industry was more than a token gesture, especially because the group had so little resources to work with.

More important than hiring was the need for resources in order to compete on level fields with Anglo Americans. This meant equal access to investment capital and creative labor, as well as distribution or exhibition networks. In Aguilar's early experience, he felt the group operated at a disadvantage, having a smaller budget and fewer people to work with. Without these resources, Mexican Americans felt they could not produce media of the same quality as Anglo American media:

> In the early days, you know we were expected oftentimes to just literally translate the general market ad campaign and maybe even do a little voice over on a general market ad. And here you had these, these ah . . . blonde, blue-eyed actors in these commercials trying to lip-sync them with Spanish language. I mean it was horrible. It was very, very bad. And, then it kind of evolved to the point where we got to produce our own creative work using Hispanic talent and Hispanic casting. The problem at that point was that we had such small budgets that were dedicated to [us] that we couldn't go out and produce these mega-grandiose, high-production-value-type of commercials. So even though they were what I would call "Hispanic-specific creative" ads, the production values were not where they needed to be because the budgets were so small [approximately one-tenth of the general advertising budget].

Aguilar pointed to several financial and creative obstructions preventing his creation of a Mexican American media market. For example, comparatively low advertising rates, unsophisticated research methods, and ignorance of potential niche markets were structural barriers to Spanish-language media production.[22] The history of Mexican American media reveals the difficulties of allowing Mexican Americans to excel professionally as experts in an unrecognized market.

Even independent workers faced institutional racism in finding funding and resources. In Velasquez's case, distributors and investors misrecognized the Mexican American market for his magazine *Vajito* due to persistent stereotypes about working-class Mexican Americans and lowrider culture. Grocery stores sometimes refused to carry the magazine because distributors thought "it was gang related": "It was a lot of bull, because it was just cars. . . . They wouldn't, you know, where you put a *Time* magazine out, they wouldn't carry

Figure 2. Tejano star Elida featured in *Vajito* in 1997. *Reprinted with permission of George Velasquez.*

it. . . . There were no Hispanic magazines distributed." To get the magazine into stores, Velasquez said he had to network personally with individual distributors, but he said the relationship continued to be tenuous. When the magazine sold out, the distributors claimed they would not carry the bimonthly magazine unless it was published monthly. Velasquez said this obstruction was harder to surmount, eventually causing the magazine to fold. Publishing monthly would have required more capital, and the Velasquez family was unable to secure a bank loan for the expansion. Such structural forms of racism have made it difficult for Mexican American media producers to compete against other Americans who have easier access to capital and corporate media distribution connections. All the interviewees said that these problems continue, though their scope has changed.

It was not until the late 1990s that San Antonio media industries began touting the diversity of their staffs. In-house diversity, they argued, prevented the underrepresentation of Mexican Americans in media out of the workplace. In journalism and publishing, local newspapers such as the *Current* hired Mexican American writers to represent, in James Garcia's words, "what this community looks like." In 1999 *San Antonio Express-News* editor Robert Rivard said that 30 percent of the newspaper's staff was Hispanic and that he aimed to have 10 percent more by the end of the next year.[23] These commitments were in line with the American Society of Newspaper Editors' goal to make newsrooms a mirror of U.S. ethnic and racial demographics by the end of the century. In other words, diversity in hiring codified a set of assumptions that Mexican Americans would represent Mexican Americans in the community. Mexican Americans were not necessarily tokenized in this new scenario but were pigeonholed into positions that management felt represented Mexican Americans. This was a catch–22 for interviewees who questioned the rules under which Mexican Americans had been included. Durán had the most direct critique:

> I don't like what corporate America does. . . . They get a Mexican American, or a Latin American or a Latino in the position that deals only with the special Hispanic segment, okay? . . . When I call Budweiser, I deal with Alicia Zepeda. When I call Sears Roebuck, I call Gilbert Davilla, national. When I call Phillip Morris, I speak to Frances Gomez. . . . Are we discriminating? Are we isolating a Hispanic into a crystal ball and that's his bailiwick? He can't leave there because he speaks Spanish. Although he's bilingual in both languages, English and Spanish, there's been a restriction. I want an ad from Car Max, "Call the Bravo Group." "Oh, who do I speak to?" "Ugh, Roger Dominguez." "Why?" "Because Roger Dominguez handles the Hispanic segment." I mean, they know what they're doing, but the fact remains: why not general market?

By pigeonholing media professionals, Durán addressed the continuity of limited options Mexican Americans have in media industries. According to the interviewees, these labels devalue Mexican Americans' expertise as media professionals and, in some cases, justify lower pay scales and less career advancement for the privilege of working for the company.[24] In advertising, Aguilar said that hiring "a couple of Latinos down the hallway" makes it hard for independently owned agencies to compete and also perpetuates a stereotype that all Latino advertising is essentially the same. These forces pull Mexican American media workers in diverging ways, pushing them to defend their expertise over the Mexican American market while asserting their professionalism in the general market. The interviewees wanted to be good media producers, not good "ethnic-media" producers: an important distinction for creating a pluralistic workplace that is also fair.

Perhaps the biggest gap in representation was the dearth of female Mexican American media professionals as compared to men. The corporate hiring or contracting of Mexican American mass media workers revealed the same gender inequalities present in the general labor market.[25] Linda Alacazar, who cast talent for Latino productions nationally, commented, "It's still a male dominated industry." Attributing the lack to the near invisibility of Latina writers for mass media, Alacazar said acting opportunities for Mexican American women were hard to find. "There's one female role and there's thousands of women going for that role," she explained. In advertising, Cevallos confirmed the scarcity of Mexican American females in directorial positions and shooting crews. Although more women were creative and art directors, the majority of female duties in media production concerned detail-oriented tasks, such as budgets or organizing. Gender divisions in Mexican American media production not only reproduced gender inequities in Anglo American industries, they also pigeonholed Mexican American women in precisely the way Mexican American men have been trying to avoid.

Mexican American media producers were caught in difficult binds between wanting to blend into mass media industries as equals while maintaining their cultural differences as Mexican American media professionals.[26] They wanted to be the experts for producing Mexican American media while gaining equal recognition and treatment as media professionals in other fields. In this respect, generational differences did not matter. Over time, though, what some media producers saw as the improvement of industrial conditions and the challenges ahead were framed as a citizenship struggle: one in which media professionals needed to fight for their rights, but within the industrial framework. On the horizon, producers had faith that nondiscriminatory industry activities would result in parity between Mexican American markets and Anglo American ones, thus achieving the hiring and representational goals of reform-minded activists from the previous generation. In Tejano, generations of producers pulled together in envisioning this struggle.

BRINGING THE PAST INTO THE PRESENT
IN TEjANO MUSIC PRODUCTION

The word *Tejano* in Tejano music already belies the cultural tensions inherent to the political economy of the musical genre. The word itself, a misappropriation of the Spanish feminine modifier *tejana*, references a Texas-born Mexican American music worker. Referencing a person much as a commodity, the production of Tejano music had highly personal meanings to the twenty-five Tejano producers I interviewed. As radio programming manager J. D. Gonzales explained, "We have our own music, our own food, we had everything, but we're sort of an individual culture without a name. So whenever you put a name on the music [Tejano] . . . all of a sudden you have an identity, and that's very important to any culture." Perhaps for this reason, workers' personal histories in the industry incorporated a history of Tejano music—one that rarely matched the official histories of the genre.[27] Like other producers, the Tejano interviewees saw themselves involved in a continuing struggle to achieve cultural visibility and respect for a larger Mexican American community through a commercial industry. They took pride in times when a Tejano musician gained recognition through national media, such as when Sunny and the Sunliners appeared on Dick Clark's *American Bandstand* in 1963.[28] Since then, few Tejano musicians have gained such notoriety, but the ones that achieved gold record status or won an industry award became icons in the eyes of their peers. The Tejano workers measured success by their profits because they further signified public recognition for their cultural labor.[29]

Cultural recognition, for them, entailed a professionalism that did not debase Mexican American culture or the Mexican American consumer. Musicians spoke of being pigeonholed into Spanish-language recordings and performances. As one producer said, "When you're Mexican American and you play great music . . . or the executives get excited about what you do, many times I've heard [them say] things like . . . 'You've really got something, can you play accordion?'" To add insult to injury, interviewees criticized the disregard for professionalism in producing for a Spanish-speaking audience. Songwriters slammed writers using ungrammatical or incoherent lyrics in songs. Workers in radio and production houses targeted mispronunciations, especially by outsiders who insisted on Anglicizing words.[30] These criticisms often compared the treatment of Mexican American culture with other ethnic groups they felt received more respect. Even within Latin music organizational networks, Tejano has had little visibility. The Latin Grammys has never featured a Tejano award recipient outside of the limited category entitled "Best Tejano Album." In a democracy, they reasoned, all ethnic groups should receive equal treatment in public culture.[31]

Issues of respect inevitably intertwined with economic rights. In their narratives about the genre, Tejano producers placed themselves in relation to the objective inequalities between the genre as a whole and other musical genres. In the slumping music economy of the late 1980s, executives of multinational record labels enthused over the prospects that Tejano would become part of a global market for Latin music.[32] This recognition, however, did not respect Mexican Americans' equal rights as music industry laborers. Even at the market's height in the early 1990s, Tejano workers, from songwriters and record producers to graphic artists and roadies, could only expect to earn one-tenth the wages that a general market worker would at the same level.[33] This translated in practical terms into less technology, fewer creative personnel, and less exposure in the business. The major recording labels Sony and EMI exacerbated economic disparities for Tejano musicians by refusing to include them in the American Federation of Musicians' Phonograph Record Labor Agreement since 1996.[34] Arguing that Tejano was a "Latin division," the lack of a binding contract depressed wages and erased potential benefits. The American Society of Composers, Authors and Publishers (ASCAP) only recognized the importance of Tejano songwriters by appointing the association's first and only representative to the south Texas region in 2001. At the time, the ASCAP representative Velia Zamora said, many Tejano songwriters "still don't know their [intellectual property] rights and are not getting their fair share [of royalties]."

To fight for their rights, Tejano workers spoke of an array of tactics for evoking incremental changes from within the music industry. For some, the expansion of new independent sources for production, labeling, and marketing was a positive safeguard against prejudices toward other musical genres in the mainstream. An independent record label, for example, could preserve a local culture by catering to a smaller Mexican American niche market. For others, the only way to resist industrial inequities was through the largest corporate channels of power. Producers looked for new national investors for Tejano divisions in recording. Distributors sought megastores for sales, such as Wal-Mart and Target. Record label executives wanted large corporations to dedicate music clubs and radio stations to promote Tejano music. Tejano music club owners sought backing from Budweiser or other large beverage companies. All of these activities had profitable aims to be sure, but they were also limited forms of resistance, given the economic structures and professional values that they had already embraced. When framed in the discourse of "rights," economic expansion became a natural progression from the political achievements that social movements began decades earlier, and media professionals became the champions of this struggle.

Mexican American Media Producers and the New Language of Citizenship

On the penultimate day of the AHAA conference that I attended, about forty conference attendees went to the west side of San Antonio to see the official unveiling of a mural commissioned by *People en Español*. The association chartered a trolley to bring the well-heeled Latinos from advertising, publishing, and the press to a block party held in the middle of the street. The mural, which was painted by youth volunteers with San Anto Cultural Arts, featured multicultural children holding hands around a globe. Called "Mano a Mano," the mural's central theme was social harmony. Yet despite the speeches praising the mural's message, the young Mexican Americans who painted the mural remained separated from the media professionals. They stayed around their friends and family while the press took photos of some of the executives. Less than one hour later, the visitors left. The neighborhood residents stayed until long after the barbecue was served.

Implicit in the talk of opening access to resources, hiring diversity, and increasing market size for Mexican American media was a circuit of power between Mexican American producers, consumers, and citizens. Mexican American media producers saw themselves as *serving* Mexican Americans as consumers *and* citizens, thereby reaffirming that they, too, were good citizens. Production and citizenship were not at odds in my interviews with them; their economic capital opened the door to create corporate partnerships with Mexican American communities in ways that many social services ignored in the 1990s. Reduced to shoestring budgets, public departments managed under neoliberal policies welcomed private initiatives to cover the expanding needs of the underserved citizenry. In San Antonio, both Anglo American and Mexican American officials and politicians sought investment in social services and, in particular, the arts, where the city's quest for a profitable cultural tourism industry superceded the seeming frivolity of murals and other public art projects.[35] Mexican American media professionals thus had golden opportunities to become cultural citizens by becoming patrons of the cultural goods and services that the city would no longer finance.

As responsible citizens, Mexican American media workers mediated between corporations, Mexican American communities, and the state with pride. Directed mainly at poor and young Mexican Americans, local media industries' good works included literacy campaigns, back-to-school fairs, hospital fund drives, after-school projects, and an annual art show to "recognize up-and-coming Hispanic artists and give them a move in the right direction."[36] Publicizing what they felt were the needs of disadvantaged Mexican Americans,

Mexican American media executives asserted their own authority in satisfying those needs and campaigned for the resources to dedicate to those solutions. Aguilar said, "I carry my Latino badge with me everywhere I go. I walk the halls of Corporate America . . . to convince these companies to give something back to the community." Under his guidance, AHAA launched its first Latino Voters Registration Campaign to double the number of Latino voters registered in the United States. In the same year, San Antonio's Univision affiliate and the Mexican American Legal Defense Fund (MALDEF) teamed up for a national Census 2000 campaign aimed at Mexican Americans.[37] These massive endeavors signified the harmonious potential for media production and the production of citizens moving in the right direction.

In the process, producers' citizen activities also rallied consent to the neoliberal policies of the state and the corporate institutions that underwrote them. Corporate sponsorship and the marketable branding of charity went together as producers had to justify their community involvement in terms of profit. One professional said he realized that outreach could be altruistic and profitable when working on an advertising campaign for Crest:

> [Crest] had such a poor share in the Hispanic market that it was
> driving down their overall market share. Conversely, Colgate had
> such a strong share in the Hispanic market because they had strong
> Latin American equities [in the toothpaste market] and because they
> were doing free things in the neighborhood and doing free dental
> check-ups in the Hispanic community. They had forged a relationship
> with the community in such a way that they were really killing, you
> know, helping erode the overall Crest brand share.

Corporations' charitable endeavors doubly celebrated consumerism as the solution to social ills, both through the free goods, like toothbrushes, and the brands that they promoted, like Crest.[38] In the long run, Mexican American media producers' benevolent investments in Mexican American communities made good business sense because they connected the producers more to communities they identified with and sold products to. I use the term *identification* loosely because the communities that producers identified with and donated their help to were rarely the places they resided. As corporate partnerships expanded nationally and globally, these community ties were even more tenuous, based sometimes only on a common language or national origin.[39] With each generation, consumption was the only common bond that held the majority of Mexican American media producers to the Mexican American communities they identified with.

Identification as citizens was always muddled by the contested politics of ethnicity and class in San Antonio and the United States at large. Mexican

American media workers assimilated into their fields of production in return for higher social and class status from the majority of working-class and working-poor Mexican Americans. They lived through the contradictions involved in fighting ethnic inequalities in the media industries where they worked while becoming more wedded to the institutions that perpetuated class inequalities.[40] At the top of their fields, Mexican Americans had become cultural citizens, empowered to speak on the behalf of Mexican American communities and their needs through charitable and profitable works. Nevertheless, their empowerment came at the expense of others who were then faced with the choices of consenting to participate in public projects that they themselves did not develop or control. Mexican American media producers may have lacked material or cultural resources in relation to Anglo American workers in general market industries, but, in return, they gained the symbolic capital to construct Mexican Americans as citizens and consumers across cultural and political spheres of life.[41]

The construction of Mexican Americans as consumers and citizens was very important to the producers, because they never lost sight that they were consumers and citizens too. After all, the producers themselves talked about "knowing themselves" through the music they had listened to, the television they had watched, and the books they had read. It is this kind of symbolic "self-determination" that producers felt every citizen pursued.[42] This belief reaffirmed not only the political significance of Mexican American media production in helping to create citizens but also the importance of amplifying the consumer choices aimed at a Mexican American market.[43] Yet the process of producing media that maximizes Mexican American choices was complicated, both by diverging ideas of who Mexican American consumers were and what would be profitable among them. Given the struggle to break into the mainstream and create organizational networks for Mexican American media, Mexican American media producers were in constant negotiation of what Mexican American media should be, both in form and content and for whom.

Chapter 3

Tensions in the Tejano Industry

THE WORD *TEJANO* emerged from within the Mexican American musical community to describe a new style of music and its presumed Mexican American listeners.[1] Yet the word *Tejano* also signified a new kind of competition over a mass Mexican American audience as consumers and commodities. Record labels introduced Mexican American consumers to a new commodity, the Tejano recording, when large corporations began purchasing smaller independent record labels in the 1980s.[2] By the late 1990s, three global companies invested in Tejano: EMI-Latin, Sony Discos, and, to a lesser extent, BMG.[3] Their new products found a distribution outlet through Spanish-language radio stations eager to sell a Mexican American audience to advertisers. According to locals, one of the first of these stations, KXTN, dubbed the word *Tejano* as a misappropriation of the Spanish modifier *tejana* in order to compete with KEDA 1540-AM, which had been known as "La Tejanita" since the Polcas family bought the station in 1972.[4] In this sense, the very word *Tejano* emerged from both longstanding musical traditions and the commodification of Mexican American audiences.[5] This chapter investigates the interlacing of cultural identity and economic forces in the production of Tejano music.

Nineteen ninety-four was perhaps the peak year for Mexican American producers in the Tejano music industry. Locally and regionally, Tejano had emerged as a profitable genre with global potential. Tejano clubs and radio stations had mushroomed across San Antonio. KXTN Tejano 107.5-FM received the highest advertising rates of any station in the city, English or Spanish.[6] This station joined others in the region that played an all-Tejano format.[7] Almost every weekend featured free concerts and paid events in San Antonio, Dallas, Houston, Austin, and Corpus Christi. Nearly 61,000 people gathered for Tejano night at the Houston Livestock Show and Rodeo, perhaps the largest crowd in Tejano's history.[8] The headliners for these large performances, Selena, La Mafia, and Emilio, performed as far away as New York and maintained fans as distant as Europe and East Asia.[9] Their success rested on the frenzied activities of major recording labels, which had bought some of the major independent labels in the late 1980s and had infused the entire industry with new financial capital, professional management, and networking opportunities around the world. Their sales hit 400,000 copies, a record for an industry that barely sold 50,000 in 1991.[10] A columnist commenting on the 1996 Tejano Music Awards Show wrote: "Tejano music is now a red-hot international business that is growing at a dizzying pace. The small local record producers—for decades the only ones who even noticed Tejano artists—are now dodging takeover bids from the majors while they hustle to compete with international record giants that can drop as much money into a promotion party as the little guys once dropped into producing and promoting an entire series of albums."[11] By all accounts, what was happening in Tejano music in 1994 reflected the aspirations of an entire community of Mexican American media producers who sought cultural recognition via economic success. Everything seemed like a win-win situation.

Then, suddenly, Tejano changed in the latter half of the decade, from a sizzling new genre to a music industry "limping along."[12] While other forms of Mexican American mass media expanded, massified, and diversified during the late 1990s, the Tejano industry contracted. Sales flattened; development downsized. Artists were let go, and new contracts were hard to come by. Large recording labels looked to stretch their dollars further, often outsourcing their products to the lowest bidders, or keeping profitable processes such as song copyrighting in-house. Although every major music distribution outlet in the city, from mom-and-pop stores to Wal-Mart, sold Tejano, less new material was on the shelves. The well-spring for Tejano dried up as clubs closed and radio stations switched to urban and Mexican regional formats. From 1999 to 2001, I noticed the difference from what producers nostalgically remembered and what an actual consumer might find in San Antonio. Outside of the local circuit of weddings and parties, I had my choice of two major nightclubs. In the first club, Tejano was only one of five different themes in a multiplex setting. On a weekend, I had to squeeze through the techno and disco rooms to make it to the tightly packed dance floor for Tejano aficionados. The second club was bigger but also switched between a Tejano and Mexican regional venue, depending on the booking. Even though the place attracted large crowds some nights, the club still struggled to survive with regular drink specials and low cover charges. In 2000, Ramiro Burr, the most prominent critic of the genre, announced that Tejano, if not dead, was dying.[13]

As workers within the Tejano industry faced these new economic realities, they labored to redefine the genre and its relationship with Mexican American cultures. Should Tejano reflect a certain Mexican American experience or tradition? What are the boundaries for change? These questions were both personal and professional for the more than thirty people I spoke with in all segments of the industry, from songwriters to roadies. They were or once were fans of the accordion and the bajo sexto (bass) strumming to the two-four beat. Hence the future of the music to them communicated something about the future of the community and the visibility of its cultures.

Any industry is diverse in terms of the range of perspectives and predictions that workers within the industry have. In Tejano, workers possessed different forms of training and daily roles in delivering music that would both sell to and represent a cultural community in which they often claimed membership. Although the music has generally been associated with an organic, working-class, Mexican American experience, the workers themselves came from different generations, class backgrounds, and social experiences.[14] It is then outside of the music itself—its lyrics, melodies, and performances—that this chapter focuses on how the production of Tejano music is a negotiated process between real people coming from various backgrounds with often divergent aims.[15] What the people I interviewed shared was the sense of economic and cultural crisis in their field. With few exceptions, people took time out of extremely busy schedules to talk to me as a scribe for a historical moment in the industry. As such, they did not see me as an expert, a colleague, or even a fan. The interviews, ranging between one and two hours, offered an opportunity to record the rapid pace at which their music and livelihood was changing and how they were trying to make sense of it.

This chapter examines how workers involved in all parts of the Tejano industry struggled to produce music and its accompanying products within evolving definitions of what seemed authentic and what seemed marketable. This process—which I am calling a dialectic of authentic marketability—provided spaces for new professionals in the field. Even during the downturn, many people capitalized on their ability to create new trends and scoop the competition. Most important, these new players turned toward young people and Mexican immigrants as the future for the survival of the genre in a transnational music economy. At the same time, others felt marginalized in the new economy for Tejano. Their stories illustrate the cultural tensions in a changing environment for Mexican American mass media, an environment that excluded certain workers and their labor while including others.

The New Tejano Imaginary and the Reorganization of Labor

Around the time that Tejano was booming, Sony Discos executives asked Robert Lopez, a photographer in a local advertising agency, to shoot a music video for the song "Ay Papi." Soon after, he founded Raging Bull Productions, which continued to shoot music videos for the Tejano industry throughout the late 1990s. Lopez gave me a tape of raw footage from the "Ay Papi" video. He had planned to use the footage to make a behind-the-scenes video, though budget and time restrictions eventually condemned the project to a corner of the studio. Although it reflects the height of the industry, the video also shows the fissures in an industry that quickly became reorganized under late capitalism. It is a uniquely self-reflexive document of Tejano as an image and as a profession.

"Ay Papi" became a dance hit for its singer, Stefani Montiel, crossing into Mexican markets with a salsa-inspired beat. In the video, national and ethnic boundaries were a focal point of the narrative, which switched between a nostalgic salsa dance club, a futuristic cyborg rodeo, and Stefani's stage performance. Inspired by postmodern aesthetics of dislocation, the salsa club segment tells a story of a Latino man who, wearing the unmarked suit of middle-class status, passes through a smoky salsa stage. He stops and pauses in front of the camera before joining the sexy choreography of a multiracial dance troupe. The man's gaze, first into the camera, then into a Latina woman's eyes, generates the implicit message of a Tejano audience that has merged into a pan-Latino and multiracial world. This message reverses in the second story, in which racial borders seem fixed. Here, an African American drenched in silver latex rides a mechanical bull under a spotlight. His slow, sexualized movements are objects for a group of Latina women, who are jeering and cheering at him from a balcony above. Even in the futuristic carnival of the story's setting, the women's position and actions reaffirm that the man below is an outsider, an unassimilable "other." All the while, Stefani sings as an icon for Tejano's new ambiguous imaginary.

Behind the scenes, however, Tejano workers in the cultural field told a different story. Strapped for resources, many of the cast and crew were outsourced for the day. The lead male in the dance scene in fact had never acted before and undoubtedly earned less than a professional actor in a general market video. The sets were minimally lit, and, aside from some chairs and a mechanical bull, props were sparse. These measures saved time and money in the production of "Ay Papi," which had to be shot in one day. Even the artist, who might receive star treatment in other genres, had to juggle several tasks that day without staff. She was both the performer in the video and an artist for the behind-the-scenes video. While talking with the interviewer for the latter production, the artist's children wandered into the video frame. Startled, she cut the take to look for her mother, her childcare for the day, before repeating the entire interview.

The video illustrates the challenges Tejano industry workers faced in trying to increase sales globally with less capital locally. In terms of image and music, people in the Tejano industry searched for the crossover, a term with loaded meanings in the industry. Historically, the institutionalization of musical genres categorized artists by race, policing the boundaries of what was an acceptable sound for Mexican Americans.[16] Some veterans in the industry complained that they had to play Spanish-language music in the 1980s if they wanted a contract with the majors. Yet the politics of crossing over to other genres in the United States and Mexico were equally problematic in the 1990s. The emergence of pan-Latino pop stars, such as Ricky Martin, Christina Aguilera, and Enrique Iglesias, promoted a dehistoricized "otherness" that sold Latinos as the "spicier" and sexier counterparts of white pop stars.[17] At the same time, industry workers looked toward Mexico, with the largest market in close proximity to Texas, as the place where Tejano could boost its sales. Mexican *norteño* music promoted a more modest aesthetic of men dressed in identical Western wear. Trying to produce both aesthetics within those genres, while not leaving loyal consumers of the music behind, generated anxieties in the industry.

These anxieties grew in the following years as budgets tightened and Tejano professionals tried to achieve their target markets with fewer resources. In the late capitalist economy, record labels adopted primarily two strategies: international outsourcing and local in-housing.[18] These strategies reorganized labor within the industry, reflecting both the ways capital circulated in the industry and the changing ways that people saw their roles in the new organizational hierarchies.

THE MAJORS AND INTERNATIONAL OUTSOURCING

Major labels poured money into the Tejano market almost as quickly as they pulled it out. By 2000, BMG had little presence in the Tejano market. The Texas offices for Sony and EMI pared down corporate staff and relied on a short list of professionals who worked for the parent companies in Los Angeles, Miami, and New York. In a period of flexible capital and mobile resources, executives with the major labels looked to these professionals to produce the crossover Latin hit that usually traveled to Mexico before leaving Texas. The increasing monopolization of radio stations and media airing Spanish-language music in the United States meant that record labels faced increased competition from outside of Tejano to become part of a radio format, a satellite music line-up, or a video music program. Lupe Rosales, then of EMI-Latin, said he sometimes visited radio stations three times a day, offering DVD-player giveaways and other promotions to enter singles into the program. Yet in the globalized music economy, Mexico became the linchpin for creating the buzz to attract U.S. media, who were then also focused on Mexican regional and U.S. Latin markets. At Sony Discos' Texas headquarters, former executive Robert de la Garza said he learned this lesson early in his career, when, as a promoter for the band La Mafia, he realized that a successful tour in Mexico generated airplay in the United States. Rosales added that success in Mexico also signaled a captured market of Mexican immigrants, who executives had already foreseen as the next wave of Tejano consumers. Perhaps with this synergy in mind, Univision developed its own Spanish-language music label in 2001.[19] Vertically integrated with television stations in the United States and with close ties to media giant Televisa in Mexico, Univision would be able to sell to both sides of the border while drawing on the network's vast resources in urban cities throughout the country.

The focus on Mexico and international networks of professionals changed the ways that the major record labels interacted with workers, both in the production and the promotion of their products. Although the total budgets for Tejano production fell, label executives still felt they needed to spend as much as possible to compete with those general market labels. For example, executives wanted videos and graphics to use the latest digital technologies or the best film quality to try to break into the decreasing number of Spanish-language video programs in the United States. Technological demands cost money that often resulted in smaller cuts for the artists they promoted. Many times, this meant working with professionals outside of San Antonio and south Texas because the parent company already had a contract with a professional who could work in Tejano, rock, salsa, or country. The explosion of the Latin market in the 1990s brought many Mexican Americans working in Tejano in closer contact with other Latinos and Latin Americans. For de la Garza and others, Tejano's entrance into those markets meant, in practical terms, becoming more fluent in Spanish to better manage and promote their music, some of which was in English. In the push for the crossover hit, the majors

internationalized Tejano with the hopes that it might integrate further into
the mainstream in the United States.

THE INDEPENDENTS AND LOCAL IN-HOUSING

The term *independent* was generally used to refer to all other Tejano record
labels, though they were each unique in their own right. Some independents,
such as Joey Records and Freddie Records, had long histories in Tejano music.[20] Other labels started at the crest of Tejano's popularity or just after. Musicians and producers alike started these labels. Just as the major labels took
some artists from smaller labels, the smaller labels learned lessons, if nothing
else, from the majors. Of them, Abraham Quintanilla's Q Productions was perhaps the most successful in maintaining independence from major labels while
using alliances with them to his benefit. Q Productions signed a licensing
agreement with EMI-Latin to distribute its artists, hence opening its stars to
national audiences. Meanwhile, Quintanilla reserved all creative control over
their artists and stipulated that Q received licensing rights for any artist after
five years. This ensured that the label could market artists who succeeded nationally.[21] Similarly, longtime Tejano musician Ruben Ramos distributed
through Virgin Records, but, in his case, he used a small independent label,
Barb Wire, to help build his own studio in Austin and eventually sign their
own group in 2001. After working with RCA (later CBS and then Sony Discos), and "a half-dozen record labels that never paid him a dime after issuing
a slab of vinyl," Ramos said the arrangement left him more creative control.[22]
Other labels stayed clear of major labels altogether but learned valuable tricks
of the trade. Tejas Records, for example, started in 1993 after co-owners Chris
Leick and John Whipple produced for the major labels in their studio. Their
focus on image and promotions resembled marketing plans with the majors,
but they secured their own distribution through megastores such as Wal-Mart.
In eight years, Tejas signed nine groups formerly associated with major labels.

The independents differed from the majors in their attempts to cover all
parts of the production process in-house and cut nonessential expenditures.
Q Productions built an impressive complex in Corpus Christi, complete with
a television studio, graphics and video computers, and a silk-screening machine. Sixteen staffers worked in the complex in 2001. Tejas's building had
primarily a recording studio, but they also operated a publishing house, signed
merchandizing agreements, and encouraged artists to write their own songs.
Only six people worked out of the main facility. Still, independents worked
harder to get radio airplay and store distribution because they did not have as
much capital to invest in promotions. To spend money on promotions often
meant cutting other expenditures for professionals in the industry. "We don't

waste money," Whipple explained, adding that the additional costs would result in less profit for the artists. Like all recording labels, independents struggled to promote record sales while still recouping their added expenditures on videos, graphics, songwriters, and so on.

WORKING WITHIN STRATEGIES

The reorganization of Tejano labor shaped discourses in the field, stressing professionalism as cultural capital in global music marketplaces. Songwriting was one example where shrinking budgets and divergence between major and independent record labels' production strategies created a new competitive environment with its own language of achievement. Whereas a number-one Tejano song in the mid–1990s might garner $10,000–$20,000 per quarter, the same song might earn only $7,000–$9,000 in 2000. Songwriters competed for exclusivity contracts with record labels at the same time that major labels looked outside of Texas and independents looked to their own artists. In addition, many Mexican writers migrated to Texas during the Tejano boom looking for better opportunities. Given these circumstances, professionalism became a way for writers to assert their skills in the market for freelancers.

Professionalism was a way of creating distinctions in a cultural field.[23] In the past, popular songwriters in Tejano were often self-taught or learned from a family member how to write lyrics.[24] For them, talent came from within a particular experience as a working-class Mexican American. For example, Beto Ramon, a Laredo native, prided himself as "an independent writer from the barrio." Although a high school Spanish teacher prepared his linguistic abilities, he said his mother and neighborhood had the strongest influence on his gifts: "I was really self-taught and I had a lot of exposure through my family, through my mom basically. My mom is from Mexico and we always listened to the Mexican records. Then, if I may add how I learned. Basically, in my neighborhood we had corner musicians. They got together and drank a beer on a corner or by a car. Actually, it was a little house with a swing and they were a little bit older than I was. I used to hang around and I was attracted to the music." Ramon, age forty-two, remembered breaking into the industry in 1989, just before the industry took off. Afterward, the stakes changed. Record labels sought songwriters with either prior track records or more formal credentials. Hector Escamilla, a winner of the prestigious BMI Award and an inductee into the Tejano Hall of Fame, attributed his success to a master's degree in Spanish and his literary skills as an English teacher in Crystal City, Texas. One afternoon at my house, he told me that education in a literary canon had expanded Tejano as a whole. "I develop phrases and poetry into songs. For example, I could use Dylan Thomas's *The Force that Through the Green*

Fuse Drives the Flower. . . . No one had ever done that in Tejano before," he said. His training and awards classified him as a contender both among the major and independent record labels where he had been contracted. In the language of professionalism, education became as important as location, if not more so.

In an international music marketplace, songwriters who were not Mexican American or from Texas challenged the fragile ties between location, ethnicity, and talent in Tejano. Cuban-born Jorge Luis Borrego wrote Tejano music exclusively for Warner Brothers from his residence in Miami. His new DirecTV system, which had a digital Tejano channel, kept him abreast of the latest developments in the genre. As a longtime writer of salsa and other Latin music genres, Tejano was just another style he could apply his crafts to.

> When you write for a specific artist, it's like a tailor. He can make a suit, but we're going to see that when he's doing it; he can take your measurements before and that makes the suit fit even better. Do you see? When it's like this, it's better. It's a lot better because you are more specific in what you know that artist has done. You know his/her voice, you know what he/she records, the type of lyrics and the music he/she likes. The other type of composition is the one done for whomever. I try to make it more generic so that many times, both women and men can use it. I have learned this along the way. I try to make my music as adaptable as possible so that it can be played in various rhythms.

Borrego used much of the same language as the other writers, speaking of their trade as part craft and part inspiration. His mobility both inside and outside of the Tejano market, however, illustrated the barriers that Texas-based Mexican American songwriters still faced. They were limited to the genre they claimed to know best, but Borrego could cross genres as part of the short list of EMI-Latin's music professionals. In addition, the professionalization of Tejano songwriters might have safeguarded those already in the market, but it also established barriers to Mexican Americans without access to higher education or private tutoring. Borrego's status showed that the discourse of professionalism was bittersweet, emphasizing new hierarchies in the place of old ones.

TRANSNATIONAL HIERARCHIES

Record label executives saw crossover hits as being both necessary and increasingly difficult in the globalized market for pop, rap, country, and norteño. In all of these markets, Tejano struggled from a position of less status and less capital. Tejano workers were aware of these transnational hierarchies and yet embraced the need to climb them. Under late capitalism, corporations easily moved capital to cultural producers who could tap niche markets. This reshaped the international division of labor, rewarding those who had specialized knowledge, corporate connections, and technological know-how.[25] The upsurge in the corporate production of world music indicated that workers in specialized fields such as zydeco and Celtic stood to profit from globalization while still continuing to work locally. In other words, if Tejano workers wanted local investment, technological resources, and professional connections, then they had to integrate into the global hierarchies that marginalized them.

Yet the need to compete in transnational hierarchies cannot be reduced to economistic analyses either. Producers' needs were both professionally driven, as workers in a capitalist bureaucracy, and personally motivated, as Mexican Americans who had grown up with Tejano and its musical predecessors. The language of product development, professionalization, and networking did not eradicate personal attachments to the music. Lopez, and nearly everyone I talked with, said they continued to work for less money in Tejano because it meant something to them as Mexican Americans who grew up with the music. In this sense, the new Tejano imaginary and its reorganization of labor were extremely awkward to them because, as much as they wanted the music to become more marketable to Mexicans and non–Mexican Americans, it was a music they still identified as their own.

The Dialectic of Authentic Marketability

It seemed odd to me at first that whenever I asked about the decline of the Tejano industry after 1995, the response was often to answer who the next Selena would be. Indeed, it did not matter who I talked with, their role in the production process or their preference for the music, the quest for another young Tejano icon seemed insatiable. Selena Quintanilla's tragic death in 1995, at the age of twenty-four, not only coincided with the industry's downturn but also left a huge young Mexican American fan base without an icon. Even six years after her death, young Mexican Americans still visited the Selena museum in the Q Productions complex. One afternoon, I watched no fewer than twenty Mexican American children from throughout Texas come to see her personally designed outfits, customized car, and fan mail from as far away as Europe and East Asia. Selena had become a metaphor for an entire industry in crisis—one that was intimately related to their own children's interest in the genre.

No one could compare to Selena in the discourse of Tejano producers. Emilio and other Tejano singers had achieved star status in country music, but they did not capture a multigenerational consumer market the same way that Selena's pop-inspired image did. Singers who had switched to Mexican regional music tapped into another market, but culturally the music seemed as foreign to Mexican Americans as Puerto Rican salsa or Cuban son. Selena embodied everything that Mexican American adults in the industry wanted. She was both marketable and authentic. Postmortem, the "Selena package" still sold thousands of compact discs, videos, posters, pins, and other memorabilia.[26] On the fifth anniversary of her death, Mexican Americans throughout San Antonio lined up for blocks to get a collectible pin produced by the Hard Rock Cafe. The next year, a re-release of one of her songs stayed in the top ten of the Tejano charts for weeks. Q Productions planned a collector's video for the following year.

Most important, Selena had the loyal support of thousands of young Mexican Americans who otherwise did not like Tejano. Without Selena, Tejano professionals worried that an entire generation of Mexican Americans would abandon the genre. Club owner Jesse Carvajal said he saw the downturn in the industry first reflected in the declining number of young people in his club. Although he allowed people ages eighteen and up, attendance for most young people dropped from a regular habit to only one night per week. Carvajal said, "The young people are not really tuning to Tejano. They are tuning to hip-hop, R&B bands, country, and areas other than Tejano. There are a few out there that [say], "'Hey, Mom and Dad used to go out to Desperados so we'll probably go out there.' Like I said, they only come out one night."

This anxiety extended to many of the interviewees' own children. De la Garza worried deeply that "it may not be cool to be Tejano right now." Whereas producers counted on older fans for loyalty to the music, younger Mexican American listeners' fickle tastes in an oversaturated media environment evaded their entreaties. De la Garza added:

> I think we're losing the youth market. We still have some of them but
> again being as diverse as we are, you know. . . . If in my household I
> grew up listening to Tejano music, but here's my, you know, nine-year-
> old son and he's listening to rap music, or he's listening to R&B
> music, or he's listening to English music, but he doesn't like Spanish
> at all. So there goes my son. . . . What's gonna bring him back and say,
> "Hey my dad used to listen to this music, so I'm going to listen to it
> also, because I like it, because he liked it." So it's kind of hard because
> you know they're going off into somewhere else where they have
> Nintendo and Sony Playstations.

In de la Garza's words, his son represented an entire generation of Mexican Americans "lost" in the technological world of other consumer products. As his father, he asks who will bring his son back to his roots. As a recording label executive, he answers that he must sign more young acts. He described one of his premiere bands as the "Tejano Spice Girls," presumably alluding to the success the band had in attracting a young female demographic of record buyers.

In an office down the highway, Rosales echoed de la Garza's sentiments. Although he did not see his own family reflected in the downsized market, he felt the Tejano industry needed not only young performers but also youth icons to maintain the genre.

> Four- and five-year-olds can relate to Christina Aguilera, Britney Spears, *NSYNC, Backstreet Boys, and so on. If someone at that age begins to like those, they are obviously gonna ask Mom and Dad, "Hey can I have that CD?" Through the years they will probably like it until, obviously, they outgrow it. However, they could be a fan for the next ten to twelve years, and so the same thing goes for Tejano singers. . . . People that liked the Tejano music when they were younger are older now. They own homes. They have kids. Some of them have grandkids already. They're not as apt to go out anymore, to be responsive to calling radio stations. So I think that the new generation that's coming has got to fill that void. That's the next group of people that, once they embrace it, I think Tejano music will begin to flourish again and there'll be a new breed of artists.

Rosales feared that in a world saturated with global pop icons, Mexican American young people would break with not only their roots but also their consumer habits. As such, he had to work harder than ever to bring teens into the consumer fold. That meant signing more youthful bands, flashier image development, pyrotechnic shows, and merging the music more with global youth genres, such as rap and pop. The young Tejano singer could signify at one time a commodity for Mexican American consumption and a bridge to the cultural past—one that for the producers re-created images of familial unity. The process of producing a Tejano artist or group that was at one time authentic and marketable was dialectical, meaning that different people involved in different stages of the process constantly tinkered with what would make a group more authentic or more marketable. The dual consciousness of creating a product for Mexican Americans like themselves and a general market departs strongly from the notion that Tejano was once "authentic" and became "commercial."[27] This perspective also counters the idea that the terms are mutually exclusive, though many people within the industry often saw them as such.[28] Rather, the actual production of each song and its artist was a negotiating process between what would sell and what would seem real. Songs had to be carefully selected and arranged. Images had to be groomed and maintained. Managers and sponsors had to conform to an overall marketing strategy for a "true Tejano" product.

MARKETING THE TRUE TEJANO

Definitions of authenticity in Tejano mythologized performers, if not all industry workers, as members of a close-knit community of Mexican Americans in south Texas. Neither completely true nor false, the myth provided a set of codes that industry workers argued for and against in the marketing of new stars. In this myth, Tejano artists came from the same place and time as their fans, establishing an organic connection that the artist cultivated throughout his career. Always Mexican American and almost always male, the mythological Tejano learned to play from his immersion in a working-class world of family celebrations and local dances. Family played a large role in helping the young artist and may have helped the formation or management of his band. The band signed with an independent record label and distributed through mom-and-pop record stores, but their success relied ultimately on the local circuit of live performances that put artists in direct contact with their community again. This myth, repeated by people in the industry, defined Tejanos in opposition to workers in other musical fields, who by definition were detached from their roots, alienated from their families, and cared little about the personal lives of their fans. It was a story of resistance to those who supported the myth and a story of nostalgia to those who wanted to rewrite it. Either way, the story and its mythic codes held value both in connecting with Tejano fans and in marketing to them.

By all accounts, David Lee Garza and his band Los Musicales upheld the codes of authenticity for Tejano music and yet also attributed their success to a strong marketing strategy. Hailing from the small farm town of Poteet, Garza formed the band with his two uncles and a cousin in the late 1970s. He played accordion across the state for faithful fans, whom he had gotten to know personally over the years. Garza considered his band part of an extended family; they used to go on vacations together and gather at his father's house for barbecues. His history contributed to his authenticity as a Tejano musician, but he needed marketing principles to help sell his band as a dance band, a band that people would pay money to dance to. Their first step was to create a theme—in their case, identical Western outfits—that would help listeners identify the group more easily. Garza said, "There were a lot of bands out there. . . . We were more uniformed in our company and it has been one of our trademarks. All the time we dress in uniform." From there, the group created a logo. Ruben Cubillos designed a cowboy hat drawn from three single lines to top off the word "Musicales" in the group's name. The logo was an enormous success, helping to sell assorted merchandise. Garza's manager, Joey Rodriguez, affirmed: "We sell a lot of merchandise. We're talking a lot of merchandising. We have everything from key-chains, t-shirts, caps, window decals that go on the back of the vehicle. We just have everything that you could think of. We try to market everything there is. People go out and buy their own jackets and bring it to us to put our logo on them. The merchandising has been very good for us. It's the trademark everybody wants to have on their vehicles." What Rodriguez could not generate in direct sales he tried to make up in sponsorship. Miller Lite, Ford, Auto Zone, and Havoline Motor Oil endorsed Garza, making him one of the most successful artists in the industry.[29] Garza said he felt lucky to have the endorsements because they meant that the band was good enough to hire and would continue playing in the future: "We're lucky to be noticed by these big companies. But being in such a small market and being noticed by these companies like motor parts and car dealers, it says something about the industry. It's not dying out; we're here and we're going to be here."

Products that featured Tejano artists helped produce them as Tejanos in two ways. First, money from car dealers and auto parts stores offset rising production costs. Being authentic took capital investment not only to put on a better show but also to better reach the community at home, many of which were increasingly outside of Texas. Second, sponsorship and endorsements reinforced Tejanos' authenticity visually, condensing images of an autonomous Mexican American culture in products associated with American masculinity. For example, automobile and beer products simultaneously affirmed the diversity of American masculinity while reinforcing Garza's image as a cowboy Tejano unafraid of hands-on labor and male bonding. In these senses, authentic images had high exchange value because they not only sold the artist but also an array of ancillary products that ultimately helped sell the music genre itself.

Other Tejanos, particularly young people, worked harder to construct themselves as both marketable and authentic. Caught between their own desires and the desires of an adult-managed industry who needed young people to advance the entire Tejano industry, they broke the boundaries between what had formerly been known as the division between "hats," or country-styled Tejanos, and "non-hats," or rock and pop-styled Tejanos. Grupo Vida borrowed glam rock elements of sequined outfits and face makeup. Kumbia Kings adopted a homeboy hip hop image for their urban sounds. Hearkening to the past, Los Garcia Brothers wore zoot suits when playing an updated conjunto mix. With their hybrid images, the new groups often adopted codes of authenticity in the other musical genres. Kumbia Kings, for example, dressed, performed, and spoke in the same ways that inner-city adults do when they claim to be authentic or "keepin' it real."[30] In this new constellation of identities, authenticity had to be carefully managed from the studio to the stage if these new artists were going to be both real Tejanos and crossover stars.

IN THE STUDIO

The trio of female singers in Brillante was happy but apprehensive when I met them outside of Studio M. They had been driving all day from their small west Texas town to come record their second album in four years. During that time, Sony Discos decided to rework the band's image from a hip pop group such as Destiny's Child to a traditional Mexican regional band. This album would determine whether they would keep their contract or would look for another label as part of their two-and-three agreement with the label.[31] As the first "girl group" in Tejano, they knew they were breaking barriers in a largely male-dominated industry, and this in itself was exciting. Still, Krystal, Brandi, and Sonia had mixed feelings about embodying a Mexican regional image as a group of teenage Mexican American girls.

Like other young Tejano bands, Brillante followed many of the codes of authenticity. They were a family and community affair; two of the girls were sisters, and Sonia was their neighbor and friend. The girls' fathers were their financial managers, and their mothers did their hair, makeup, and the other important accoutrements to the girls' look. Although the girls attended school most of the year, they sang for local festivals and events. In the studio, one of the mothers had brought a video camera with a recording of the band on stage. Everyone took pleasure recalling who was at the concert, who got on stage, and, especially, a shy boy who became Krystal's fan. Together, all of the families and their local fans participated in the production of Brillante's image and its promotion as an authentic Tejano group.

During the recording, Morales worked to bring out the singers' personalities. He told jokes, many times speaking to Brandi in a heavy Mexican accent to make her laugh. He tossed imaginary treats to the girls through the sound glass when they did well. Brandi received tacos; Sonia got chocolates. Finally, he labored to make them sound authentically Mexican. For this, he enlisted the help of the fathers, whom I sat with, to check whether the Spanish lyrics sounded correct. These details emphasized the differences between the girls' identities as Mexican American teenagers who ate tacos but spoke English, and the girls' image. After nearly twelve hours, everyone went home.

Morales had captured the vocals for two songs, and they needed to rest up before returning for six more long days of recording. The girls had to be back in school by the next week.

Image-construction became a balancing act for Tejano producers as they tried to elicit what sounded good to them while satisfying the overall marketing strategy of the record label. For Morales, this meant creating a total marketing package to fit each song with the album's image. "We really spend a long time choosing songs, determining the direction of the album and deciding exactly what you're going to do to make every song palatable and support the overall direction of the record," he said, adding that this was a recent development in Tejano. In the case of Brillante, Morales's role entailed choosing songs that would seem credible for young females to sing and authentic to listeners on both sides of the border. He favored *cumbias* over *rancheras* because of their generic appeal. Then he regendered the songs, changing the lyrics written by men for men to more ambiguous and, in one case, less sexist lyrics. Picking out "El Gordito," he said that the song originally envisioned a man singing about a woman who betrayed him. "We changed the concept on that one; it seemed too macho. We made it more abstract and less direct." In the final version, Morales changed the words from "The saying that 'dogs dance for money' really fits you" to "People don't appreciate something until they lose it."[32] The new ambiguity of the line allowed him to create the girl group as females less interested in attacking men as gold-diggers than in reprimanding their bad choices. In order to create Brillante's image as a girl group in Tejano, Morales needed to inject feminine symbols into the genre—right down to the lyrics.

Changing Tejano by altering lyrics and expanding genres could be fun, but it also enforced constraints on music producers who saw artists' images becoming more important than their musical skills. David Velasquez, of Velasquez Productions, lamented that he had resorted to hiring outside musicians to achieve quality sounds. "They'll come in and play a part and get paid," he explained. Few bands performed together in the studio anymore, he said. Instead, the process was very structured. First, he decided which song the artist could comfortably sing in key, since the emphasis on image downgraded the importance of singing talent. Then he decided whether to make the song a cumbia or a ranchera "or whatever beat we are going to give to the song." From there, an arranger sits with Velasquez to set the beat to a keyboard and a guitar: "We'll figure out a little intro and then we'll say here's the first verse and the second verse and then the bridge comes in here. We'll figure it out on a piece of paper . . . and then we'll just follow our road map from there. We start with a piano and bass and just keep adding parts until we hear what we want to hear." The image of the road map, a way to get from point A to point B, created a metaphor for a formulaic construction of Tejano music in an era of making the artist more marketable.

Formulas helped since there was no time to waste. Those involved in the production of artists' images worked with several accounts or clients at once, frequently under tight deadlines, Whereas Cubillos remembered spending a day brainstorming and then another day shooting to get a good album cover, a contemporary graphic artist usually performed the same tasks in less than half the time to complete more than fifty album covers per year. One graphic artist, who was working on seven covers when I talked with him, said that he saw some bands yearly, but only in three-hour increments for the meetings and shoots. These time restrictions limited the kinds of images workers could create. David Villareal, a video producer, said he rarely shot for Tejano artists in the late 1990s because he could not tell the stories he wanted to anymore. Villareal worked in high sixteen-millimeter film, a medium that relied on well-developed storyboards and achieved a letterbox look in a music video.[33] He also preferred to shoot in picturesque, natural settings, a look that depended heavily on weather conditions. Without the time to do these things, Villareal, like Cubillos and others, drifted toward advertising where he felt he could express himself more.

ON STAGE

Tejano image construction took center stage at the concerts, which made up most of the bands' revenues. At a Grupo Vida concert, I waited thirty minutes to ensure my front-row spot. Still, once the smoke filled the stage, I had to plant myself firmly not to be mobbed. The show crossed Tejano with heavy metal, rock, and a little Chippendales. Each band member looked different, signaling a break with the traditional uniforms. The drummer wore a backward baseball cap with TAZ sewn in sequins above his face. A silver lamé shirt covered his otherwise black outfit. The acoustic guitarist dressed more punk, complete with a bandana, a pierced eyebrow, and several earrings with rhinestones. He had a KISS tattoo on his arm and braces that seemed to make his whole face glitter when he smiled. A sax, cowbell, and conga player wore a maroon guayabera with rhinestones sewn on. The lead singer sported a leather vest, half-buttoned, and black jeans covered in leather chaps. The lead guitarist donned a red cowboy shirt with cut-off sleeves and a straw hat topped in black felt, conveying a modified cowboy look. In contrast, the bajo sexto (bass player) wore a leopard shirt and vinyl pants. He painted his face black with white circles around his eyes, and his arms were covered in tattoos. Finally, Sunny Sauceda, the accordionist and leader of the band, was the most decked out—and he was very proud of this costume in his interview. His pants were both glittered and fringed. He cut out the back pockets and replaced them with stuffed sequin patches. His aqua blue cowboy cut-off shirt matched the blue leopard pattern he airbrushed onto his cowboy hat, along with the number thirteen, his lucky number. To top it off, he wore bright aqua contacts. When we talked before the show, he called each of these looks the band members' "trademarks."

Image was as important as the music on stage. For two hours, the men in the band performed complicated dance choreography and sexual hip thrusts more associated with boy bands than with the family-targeted shows I was used to in Tejano. They jumped in the air and swayed in opposite time like a drill team at the big game. The men took turns sexualizing the moves, treating their instruments like lovers while gyrating around the stage. According to the band leader, Sunny Sauceda, "People say we're like strippers on stage without really stripping. . . . The women just go crazy." Apparently the mix was appealing that night. Young women screamed throughout the concert and the group toured with the Dixie Chicks in 2001.[34] "We're not that good yet," said Sauceda. "But we're like a Backstreet or *NSYNC meets Limp Bizkit meets Texas Tornadoes."

Despite their desire to be famous, Vida still balanced their boundary-crossing looks and sounds with the need to be authentic. After the performance, the distant-but-sexual rocker image that had taken front stage faded to the image of respectable local boys. They became accessible and clean, both physically and emotionally. They changed their clothes and wiped off the makeup and signed autographs. No longer "bad boys" of Tejano, Vida members stayed for an extra hour, waiting until every fan had hugged them, received an autograph, and chatted a bit. The personal contact between Tejano stars and their fans, a marker of authenticity, continued to be important, but it took a new meaning in the space of the Tejano show, where it contradicted the group's image as teen idols.

In the new politics of image control, Tejano image had to be preserved to keep up market value and shared as an authentic representative of the fans. Bill Angelini, promoter for Paramount Enterprises, said bands and clubs negotiated exclusive performances to drive up ticket prices and, hence, profits: "Now there are some groups that just keep themselves out of the market to keep their price up, like Mafia, Michael Salgado, and Luis Garcia. They understand that oversaturating the market causes their value to decrease." By being selective, Angelini preserved bands' marketability in Texas while selling

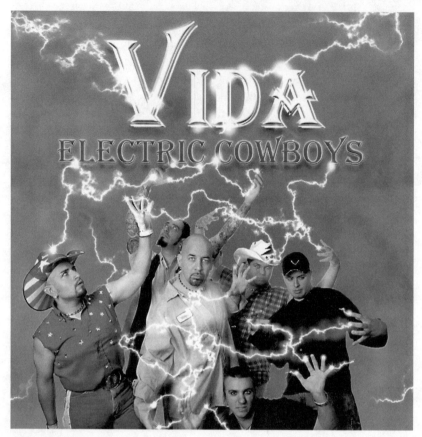

Figure 3. Grupo Vida. *Reprinted with permission of Tejas Records.*

them to nightclubs outside the state. Two weeks before we talked, Angelini booked Grupo Vida in Mexico through an alliance with Universal Latin, a company founded by the William Morris Agency in Nashville. The network helped Vida find large venues in Monterrey, hence keeping up their booking value. Infrequently booked bands risked losing their connection with their listeners. Dan Flores, who was a road manager for several groups, interpreted the economic shift as a cultural issue for Mexican Americans:

> The artists are going back to their roots. A lot of artists forgot where they came from. Now artists are realizing the decline in Tejano music and the only way that we're going to be doing it is to go back on the road. . . . [In its heyday,] a lot of the artists didn't want to do this stuff. "Oh I'm so and so, they know who I am, they're going to buy my CD anyway." They forgot where they came from. That's where a lot of the decline came from there. The artists just got too big for it also. I say

the industry is too small for that. Our market is way too small for people to get big-headed.

Flores portrayed Tejano stars as humble, hard-working people connected to their community who somehow lost these attributes when market imperatives took artists away from their audiences. Even Sauceda admitted he would have trouble giving his fans—some of whom e-mail him daily—individual attention if the band really did become a Limp Bizkit or *NSYNC. So while singers felt image maintenance was key to financial success, it implied a danger to the rituals that tied the music to their fans.

THE LIMITS OF IMAGE CONSTRUCTION

Based on binary oppositions, the mythological Tejano coded musicians within an imagined community of Mexican Americans, protecting who could become Tejano and under what terms. For women, body image was everything. Whereas men could be sexy with their instruments, like the members of Grupo Vida, women achieved sexiness only through strict diet and exercise routines. Both men's and women's bodies were implicitly Mexican American. By including those who maintained the codes of the mythologized Tejano, the industry also policed borders for exclusion, marginalizing musicians outside of the community as inauthentic, alienated, and detached from their roots. This was particularly apparent for Tejano musicians whose bodies diverged from the standard images of Tejano stars, prototypically Mexican American and either male or young and female.

The focus on the body associated slenderness with self-management, a trend present in much of popular culture in the 1990s.[35] Record labels regularly created biographies for female artists that referred to their bodies as part of their image. A rising star in Tejano, Miraeya, age twenty-one, said her body and personality communicated her image: "I'm taking my bio [to radio stations] with me and its says, 'This is Miraeya, new Q Productions artist.' They have a picture of me and they say 'new' and they say 'sexy' in there and that's what I need to portray, because that's my bio. If I show up to a radio station like this and I hand them my bio and I give them the word 'sexy,' they're going to be like, 'This is not true, they're not being too honest with us.' So I try." After Selena's passing, Tejano female singers stressed that thinness and flat stomachs factored into contract negotiations because so many mainstream artists popularized midriff-bearing images. Although she worked in a fitness club, Miraeya harbored anxiety that her body might have too many curves for the market, "It's very difficult for me to do that. A lot of the ones in the industry right now are very fortunate in that they do have that. I think I'm not as attractive as some of those." To compensate, she said she worked on dance routines and "being sexy with your eyes and being sexy with certain things covered up."

Sexiness, however, was limited to the young. Although many men sang well into their senior years, women over age thirty-five had trouble securing recording contracts in Tejano. An aspiring artist, Aurelia Gonzalez said that recording labels held women to a double standard. "A man could be up there and be almost thirty to forty pounds overweight, but they're not going to see a woman anywhere forty to fifty pounds overweight on the stage. Unless she is singing, bashing against the male agenda, you're not going to see an over-sized girl up there singing. They want these Latinas, big derrières and sexy images. . . . They always try to project new blood, new little girls, new little this, new little that." Gonzalez said she was proud of her age and body be-cause it was much like the bodies of the women she sang to. Label execu-tives, however, perceived their audience as too "moral and conservative" to accept a Mexican American "woman who's over forty to fifty years old, who's a grandmother," and who's dressed provocatively. Gonzalez's insight regularly revealed itself at concerts, where announcers and Tejano industry profession-als referenced the perfect Tejano female body. At one concert I attended, Elida, a female singer in her twenties, performed in a tight denim jumpsuit to a largely female audience. The announcer praised her svelte figure for "looking so goooood after having a baby," reaffirming the value of the youthful, thin body in Tejano.

Non–Mexican Americans have been rare in Tejano, perhaps exemplify-ing the limits that the myth will allow. In many ways, Dee Burleson, an Afri-can American, shared many of the same experiences as the other Tejano musicians. Born in San Antonio, he reminisced what drew him to Tejano:

> [My neighborhood] no longer exists. It was a little stretch called
> Paradise along Culebra Road here in San Antonio. It was about a
> block wide and half a mile long, and that's where all the Black people
> in this area lived. It was just a little tiny community. It was sand-
> wiched between what is now Culebra Park and Loma Terras. There
> were Mexican American families that lived all around us and there
> was a little family down the street, the Garcias, who ran a little illegal
> bar on the weekends. They'd have beer and whatever else and they'd
> have a live band, little cumbia bands playing. Well, we called them
> "tunda" bands back then because, "Tunda, tunda, tunda," that's all we
> could hear from a distance. We were warned that people were
> drinking—these were Baptists in this neighborhood, so no drinking
> allowed, no smoking, no gambling. So when there's something like
> this on the outskirts, "You can't go there because there's drinking and
> carousing and people carrying weapons and stuff like that." So at 11

o'clock at night I would sneak out and peer over the fence on the weekends, and I liked what I heard. I saw all these people—it's called *allegria*; I didn't know it then. I had it explained to me by my wife later on. It's just where people have this overwhelming sense of joy except they are able to cut loose. I enjoyed that that was how music was able to affect people.

Despite his homegrown credentials, Burleson confronted vocal, even violent, reactions to his stage presence as one of the only African Americans to break into the Tejano music charts. "I'm still surprised by people who can go, 'Man, I can't believe a Black dude singing Spanish. Wow man, where'd you learn, how'd you learn Spanish?' I say, 'The same way you learn English. You just grow up learning it I guess.' There've been mixed reactions. My most dismal moment was when a little old lady came to me after a performance and she says, 'No matter what you do, you'll never be one of us.' To this day, that statement still gets to me." Although most Tejano fans did not discriminate, he explained, race was a subtext for his image. Record labels structured fan reception to his music by representing Burleson's "Africanness," including long dreadlocks, hip-hop-inspired outfits, and reggae and R&B influenced songs. Although Burleson hoped the image would attract a younger audience, it also marked him as different from other performers, thus reinforcing the industry's construction of Tejano as Mexican American.

Race and gender formed significant parts of the discourse of what Tejano either could be or could not be. African Americans and women stood a better chance of success with record labels if they contributed exotic elements that enhanced their crossover to teen markets. The regulation of cultural images was particularly acute when negotiating which people could be Tejanos and on what terms. Otherwise, race and gender were invisible, maintaining some workers' beliefs that anyone could be Tejano.

The Pervasiveness of the Authentic

Tejano professionals labored to produce music that was both authentic and profitable, but the definition of "authentic" relied on a host of other professionals charged with defining the music for consumers. By booking the bands, choosing the singles, and publicizing what was considered noteworthy, various professionals—including disc jockeys, reporters, music store representatives, and club owners—played integral roles in deciding which music could be classified as "authentically Tejano" and thus marketed to their consumers. Although these professionals often did not agree with definitions of authentic music proposed by record labels, they shared the recording industry's interests in "find[ing] a material or symbolic profit in reading it, classifying it, commenting on it, combating it, knowing it, possessing it."[36] Authenticity was thus more than an internal measure of Tejano's marketability among producers and artists. Authenticity was also a well-publicized rhetoric that often opposed the economic conditions that helped produce it.

The self-conscious definition of Tejano happened almost daily on the radio, where disc jockeys, callers, and musicians discussed how the music was or should be. Authenticity stood in contrast here to a rhetoric of "co-optation," in which the music had assimilated into mainstream culture or "sold-out" to cultureless corporations.[37] I sat in on one of these dialogues in the weeks before the 2001 Texas Tejano Music Association (TTMA) Awards, which yearly has drawn between twenty thousand and thirty thousand attendees. This event not only celebrated the music but also generated revenue for the industry, including the radio station, which could raise money both through direct advertising and nontraditional revenue.[38] KXTN promoted the TTMA Awards Show by inviting nominees from the various record labels to talk on the morning show with their disc jockeys "Jon," "Di," and "Petey." In the course of talking with the nominees on the air, they and the staff opposed Tejano's authenticity and the corporations that profited from the music and exploited its listeners.

On the morning I observed the show, Ruben Ramos, a longtime Tejano singer who played in the 1950s *orquesta* tradition, was the invited guest with his trumpet player Alberto "Skeeter" Amesquita. Johnny Ramirez, or "Jon" on the air, introduced Ramos as a legend, comparable to Mick Jagger in rock music, and a man who helped bring Tejano to the outside world when he appeared on Jay Leno and Conan O'Brien. "You're now going to meet a man who's been thirty years in the industry," Ramirez began. "He started with his brother. The majors forgot about him but he just keeps coming up from nowhere. And now he's been nominated for five awards." Turning to Ramos, he added, "Look who just walked in with some *pan dulce!*" Ramirez instantly established Ramos's authenticity as the reason behind his return to the limelight in the upcoming awards program. In their ensuing chat, Ramos talked about his new album, one he produced himself in his own recording studio under his own label. This narrative separated him from corporate actors who just wanted to turn out a Tejano product. Ramirez told listeners: "Ruben is making the major record weenies quake. They complain—the EMIs and Sonys—that we need younger performers. So you had to open your own studio. You had to mortgage your house [*Ruben:* And my car], and all your ex-wives . . . [*laughter*] to put it on your own label. But the record weenies are just kidding themselves. You got five nominations. And now they have their tail between their legs right now." Without dwelling on how Ramos became successful, his nominations demonstrated his achievement. Ramirez compared Ramos to Sunny and the Sunliners, whose appearance on *American Bandstand* generated positive recognition for the musical talents of all Mexican Americans in Texas. In this sense, commercial success was not bad in itself, but authentic success represented a positive picture of the entire community, one that stressed hard work, dedication, independence, and respect for the community.

In contrast, the radio personalities and Ramos constructed people who made profit-motivated decisions in the industry as inauthentic. This included the "major record weenies," but also the producers of the TTMA Awards Show. Off-air Ramos shared his disappointment that the event planners were eliminating live performances that year, right down to the orchestra that played for the winners as they came on stage. This conversation carried through to the airwaves, becoming a parable for what happened when profit motives replaced respect for the community of Mexican American listeners. "Why can't you play live?" Ramirez asked. "I guess they think it will make the show run too long," Ramos answered. In an age of broadcasting schedules when overtime cost advertising revenues, Ramos had not revealed much, but the statement broke the boundary between the authentic and the overly commercial. This became a rallying call for all of the studio crew who chanted for the next hour that they wanted their music "live" and urged listeners to call the TTMA in protest. Approximately ten callers responded to the station directly. A female complained, "For seventy-five dollars a ticket they're [TTMA] going to play tracks? That's ridiculous. We bought a whole table!" For her, the show's offensiveness stemmed from the sense that she had been tricked; she had paid for the "real" thing but would not hear the live music. Callers became part of an imagined community that could distinguish real Tejano from a huckster product. Ramirez responded before hanging up, "That's right. But why are you calling me? Call them." For Ramos and the crew, crass commercialism sold out authentic Tejano when it severed the bonds between producers and their audiences. Ramos said, "It's like they don't understand that this is our Grammys *vato*. Can you see the Grammys doing tracks?" Together, the disc jockeys, artists, and callers that morning wove a narrative of authenticity that tied Tejano to its community.

THE MORNING AFTER THE MORNING SHOW

As much as individuals in the Tejano industry valued their definitions of authenticity, the classification of the genre also served professional needs. Those who could not set boundaries between Tejano and other genres had difficulty selling their market as a specific demographic share. For example, KXTN considered its loyal listener base, called "P–1"s, its top priority when programming music for the station. Other listeners, "P–2"s, could not be counted on to listen to the station all day, everyday, and thus were not as valuable to sell to advertisers. According to Ramirez, the station's success at maintaining the P–1 base regularly paid off with the highest advertising rates in San Antonio. Furthermore, KXTN shared its listener demographics with other Clear Channel stations (all located in the same building) to better sell cross-promotions to large clients, such as grocery store chains, car dealers, and a weight-loss company. Promotions director for all five stations, Lupe Contreras said that the combined audience data helped create the stations' annual calendars, including live remotes and charity events. In other words, the definition of authenticity through the Tejano station's programming identified an audience for sale to advertisers, who then sponsored events that further identified a Tejano community.

Divergent definitions of authenticity reflected different conceptions of both a Tejano community and a consumer market. In San Antonio, *Que Onda*, a free Houston-based weekly, and the *San Antonio Express-News*, the city's daily newspaper, were the only publications that regularly covered the Tejano industry. Both played a large role in defining Tejano and its boundaries through their articles and advertising. At the *Express-News*, "Latin Notes" columnist Ramiro Burr gave authoritative information on who was Tejano and in what ways, leading eventually to the publication of a book that defined the genre and its musicians. Burr likened the process of writing the book to creating a history for an entire style of music: "There was no guideline, and unlike American rock and country, where you could read articles about George Jones, who later spawned Merle Haggard, who was part of a tradition with Randy Travis, and later became rock. . . . That's what I was looking for, because it was in the rock world, but I couldn't see it here [in Tejano]. I realized I was so far out here in the grass that I would have to come up with my own terms." Burr's work created distinctions between what was Tejano and what was not for a niche, book-and-newspaper-reading market. *Que Onda*, on the other hand, tried to be as inclusive as possible to sell a general market to the largest number of advertisers and the widest numbers of distributors. This meant eschewing criticism that would limit the genre's definition, the labels' profit margins, and, ultimately, the Tejano community. As publisher Gabriel Esparza explained: "One of the things about the paper is that I do not talk negative about any artist. It reflects a red flag with the label and stops them from producing revenues. . . . If I do that [print negative stories], then you won't buy records and that will hurt my revenue." For a general market that did not buy newspapers, *Que Onda* defined Tejano positively as a consumer democracy, where articles encouraged consumption to perpetuate the entire industry and thus the community as well.

Professionals who attempted to contest the classification of the music faced difficulties both in terms of revenue and ultimately symbolic status. For example, longtime Tejano workers around San Antonio knew KEDA as the "library," because it was a storehouse of objects and knowledge based on the history of Mexican American music. Disc jockey Güero Polcas chose his own singles to play across genres because the idea of Tejano was arbitrary to begin with: "The basic roots of conjunto, Tejano, and *banda* all come from the same place." Yet resistance came at a price. Without demographic data that commodified one audience, the station had difficulty selling advertising. Without advertising, the station could not upgrade its transmitter, a move that prevented them from reaching much of the city and allowed competitor stations to further define Tejano in their absence.

Constructions of Tejano authenticity were symbolically important in maintaining the status of Tejano professionals and the communities they claimed to represent. The "expert-status" of the people working in places such as *Que Onda* and the *Express-News* ensured their readers that they were part of a Tejano community that was "in the know" about new releases, upcoming shows, and trade secrets.[39] In return, the experts profited from their authority, especially since there was little competition in their fields. As of 2001, nine newspapers published Burr's syndicated column.[40] He received book royalties and traveled throughout Texas to give speeches to general audiences and professionals. Esparza sold 105 front covers on the magazine in three Texas cities to approximately thirteen record labels in 2001. His economy of scale allowed him to service record labels exclusively with access to major Tejano markets at reduced rates. Esparza reinvested the capital from *Que Onda* to develop its cross-promotional activities, from a Tejano club in Houston to sponsorships that led to more advertising accounts or public exposure. Both professionals' achievements in their respective areas ensured their continued authority over the definition of Tejano, shaping what information could be received about Tejano in print. The fact that many people read both publications suggested that as much as professionals needed to define the limits of the Tejano genre, the actual listeners either accepted both definitions or neither, creating their own ideas of what Tejano means.

What Is Tejano? Who Is Tejano?

The 2001 TTMA Awards Show attracted fewer people than in years past, but that did not matter to the thousands who did come. Officially, this was the night to reward individuals who had achieved sales and popularity in their fields. Overall, though, the night celebrated the economic survival of the Tejano industry during its hardest times. After the cash flow from the major labels ended and the spotlight on a few major icons faded, Tejano professionals from the late 1990s until the beginning of the millennium needed to find new ways to attract global capital, resources, and sales. Market anxieties were intensely personalized as workers in the industry wondered if their children would continue supporting the music, thus keeping the traditions alive. In this sense, cultural concerns and profit motives were always intertwined as production networks became more flexible, money became scarce, and professionals worked to produce music that was marketable yet authentic.

The dialectic of authentic marketability ensured creative change in the Tejano industry because professionals did not agree what formula was to make the next authentic star. The bands performing on the TTMA stage that night illustrated the multidirectionality of the genre as it moved toward country, pop, rap, Latin, and Mexican regional. Kontrol bounced to a cumbia, while three dancers jumped gracefully to Jay Perez's tropical "Balia Morena." Donning their zoot suits, Los Garcia Brothers "played it conjunto carnal," referencing a Mexican American genre of the past that had been updated to play in the United States and Mexico. Referencing the future of Tejano, several girl groups sang pop- and salsa-inspired tunes in an energetic medley before Jennifer Peña, the current young female diva, crooned a romantic duet with A. B. Quintanilla. For the grand finale, Quintanilla returned with the Kumbia Kings to shout out the hip-hop smash "Boom Boom" through the smoke and fireworks. In the new politics of Tejano, crossover was not only a desirable marketing strategy but also a growing matrix of possibilities for some Mexican Americans in music industries who now had greater mobility.[41] Only time will tell whether their new products break into mainstream markets and on what terms.

While the Tejano genre expanded, however, it was clear that not everyone could be Tejano. The exclusion of bodies and labor that did not fit into a new Tejano economy modeled on transnational markets demonstrated the limits of the industry's power to define itself in contrast to mainstream industries. When the TTMA host for that year, Tony Ayala (of Showtime's *Resurrection Boulevard*) slowly exchanged his gray business attire for a cowboy jacket and hat and joked, "I'm a Cuban from Miami turning Tejano," the punch line was double-voiced. On one hand, Ayala seemed silly. The hat and jacket had become meaningless when mixed with the remnants of his cosmopolitan image. Whereas the Kumbia Kings found it easy to turn Tejano into Top 40, a Cuban American from Florida could not turn Tejano. On the other hand,

Ayala had raised the specter of assimilation. Now that Tejano was hot, Latinos everywhere could capitalize on it. For some Mexican Americans, laughter, in this case, leaked the uncomfortable reality that Tejano was no longer "their music." The differences between the two transformations belied the tensions embodied in commodities that claimed to represent a cultural community.

Another possibility, though, was that the audience did not care one way or another. Professionals needed to categorize Tejano for sales and prestige, but in reality, Mexican Americans enjoyed a variety of musical styles, only some of which might be accessible in any one venue or medium. Even Contreras, an audience expert, said, "I know that everybody has to have a classification. I know that I understand the business part of it, but for the most part, music is, you know . . . How do you classify something that in my eyes has no classification?" His question pointed to the contradictions involved in building economic power from a cultural identity. In Tejano, cultural identities were always ideals, based on ideas of Mexican American culture that frequently did not match the diversity of real Mexican Americans' lived experiences.[42]

Chapter 4

Representations of Kids
and *La Familia*

I<small>N</small> 1998 <small>AND</small> 1999 <small>TWO</small> M<small>EXICAN</small> A<small>MERICAN</small>–produced short films took honors at CineFestival, San Antonio's premiere Latino film festival.[1] *Barbacoa*, by San Antonians Mike and Gibby Cevallos, showed in 1998 as both a short film and a pilot for a Hispanic-themed television series. One year later, Lourdes Portillo, a celebrated documentary maker from California, released *Corpus* but retracted the film at the last minute, despite the documentary's prominent scheduling on Saturday night.[2] On the surface these two media texts might appear very different. One is a fictional day in the life of a Mexican American family. The other is a realistic account of Mexican American fan culture after the death of Selena. Taken together, these texts reveal some prevalent ways that Mexican American media producers represented Mexican American culture in San Antonio.

Both of these films focused on Mexican American young people and their families. This in itself departed from the stereotypical representations of Mexican Americans that ignited protests in the 1960s and 1970s. Targeting such controlling images as the "Frito Bandito," the chip-gobbling villain in a sombrero, many Mexican American protestors successfully spotlighted the need for more Mexican Americans working in film, broadcast, and other media industries to make Mexican Americans more visible.[3] The media producers I spoke with, particularly those in the first generation, still carried these aims with them. Packaged in the rhetoric of citizenship, their position was that

Mexican Americans should be represented as equals in a multicultural society according to the producers. The films *Barbacoa* and *Corpus* foregrounded equality and multiculturalism through the representations of young people as culturally different from Anglo Americans but still respectful of the American institutions of the family, the home, and the consumer market. And they were not alone.

That is, despite the goals to diversify mass media images of Mexican Americans, the family—or *la familia*—became a common trope in the 1990s to display cultural differences and similarities in the United States.[4] Advertising often displayed happy families, both nuclear and extended, who achieved the American Dream by buying their favorite brand-name products. Men spoke with authority; women did gender-specific activities. Young people, now visible in mass media, were the drivers in a push to redefine Mexican American middle-class family values while also being the cutting-edge ethnic consumers for white middle-class suburbia. Through the family, Mexican American producers could represent paradoxes of being Mexican American while still containing all the potential ways that Mexican Americans could be represented within certain limits. Mexican American media constructed a new norm that interpreted Mexican American culture in a narrow manner that is still visible today. This final chapter on Mexican American media production thus ends with a conundrum that continues to shape representations of Mexican Americans. How do Mexican Americans represent the diversity of Mexican American cultures while still working in industries where the norm may not be as white as in the past, but almost exclusively middle-class?

Corpus *and* Barbacoa: *Girls and Boys*

Mike and Gibby Cevallos released *Barbacoa* in San Antonio's Hard Rock Cafe amid a flurry of media reviews that promoted the local producers.[5] The twenty-five-minute film presents a series of rituals in the Camacho family on a typical Sunday. The family of six gets up early. The three boys deliver the Sunday paper and buy *barbacoa* meat tacos with their father. When they return home, the mother and daughter entertain female neighbors in the house. The father retreats to the backyard to play cards and drink beer with his friends. The boys play baseball in the street. In the late afternoon, the family attends church and eats together in the dining room. At night, everyone goes to bed except the father, who drinks beer on the front porch. Each of these rituals unfolds with specific plot points and from differing points of view, but together they present a narrative for regularity within the Camacho family's average Sunday. Like one of the film's inspirations, *The Wonder Years, Barbacoa* presents a singular family that many families could potentially relate to. At the same time, the Camacho family is specifically Mexican American, a departure from the Anglo Americans that often represent the "all-American" family.

Similarly, *Corpus* focuses specifically on Mexican American culture, but through the real-life story of Mexican American singer Selena Quintanilla. The forty-five-minute documentary describes both the events and fan culture surrounding Selena after her untimely death at the hands of her fan club president. Important themes in Selena's life, such as her training, her physical appearance, and her favorite foods, loosely organize the documentary. The mixture of video footage depicts different Mexican American cultural spaces: home videos, music videos, and first-person accounts about what Selena means to them and to Mexican Americans as a whole. These accounts move between overt praise and critique of Selena's contradictory persona as sexy bombshell and as a family-oriented role model for young Mexican American women. Between the vignettes, the documentary reconstructs the events in Selena's life leading to her death. The detailed description of her murder opens the documentary, pointing to the tragedy as the framework for understanding her transcendent popularity after death.

The preeminence of Mexican American imagery already marks these films as important contributions to Mexican American media that are different from mainstream mass media. Historically, Mexican Americans have been notoriously absent from mass media except in the forms of stereotypes. The "Latin lover," the "criminal bandito," and the "gang member" have been among the stock roles that identified Mexican Americans as contradictorily alluring and despicable.[6] The 1990s did not show much improvement in the number or types of representations, especially considering the dramatic increase in the sheer number of television stations and media productions. Content analyses of U.S.-made films and television programs revealed few identifiable Mexican Americans, and few Latinos in general, in prominent on-camera roles.[7] In the late-twentieth century, the proportion of Latinos dropped from 2 percent to 1 percent of the total roles on network television programs.[8] Most of these roles could be interpreted as negative portrayals: "Set in Latino communities, these movies often had as central to their themes, or as the unspoken backdrop, crime, drugs, and violence."[9] The invisibility and negativity of Mexican American characters in mass media led one prominent industry official to declare that pigs and bugs had more positive media representation than Latinos in 1998 and 1999 with the movies *Babe, A Bug's Life,* and *Ants.*

Given the dearth of representations, Cevallos and Portillo chose modes that would represent Mexican American cultures in credible and accessible ways. Both films spotlighted the vernacular and biculturalism in Mexican Americans' language and daily life. Portillo's use of the documentary form validated the diversity of Mexican Americans' real experiences in relation to Selena. Like in her other documentaries, Portillo used social realist techniques to represent "people who are ignored or underrepresented in the dominant media" while avoiding the tendency to exoticize people of color for the benefit of cultural outsiders.[10] In addition, the documentary reflects a very personal sensibility as a Mexican American woman filming perspectives on Mexican Americans in south Texas. The subtitle of the film, "A Home Movie for Selena," localizes the movie in south Texas as not only Selena's home but also a cultural home for Portillo and her imagined audience. As such, the film is steeped in references to Mexican American culture both past and present. The film's title, *Corpus*, is both a local nickname for Corpus Christi, the Gulf Coast Texas town where Selena was born and raised, and a reference to her body of work there. From Corpus Christi, the documentary travels to San Antonio, both literally, in scenes set on the road and in both cities, and figuratively, in showing Selena's expanding popularity in the largest Mexican American market in the region. Subtitles with names and dates punctuate the locales for viewers who do not recognize the places as signs of working-class, Mexican American daily life in this area. For example, the film presents outdoor murals, a *botánica* (curative shop), and a Mexican restaurant as sites of Mexican American culture. In these sites, Portillo's interviewees create a sense of place for the lived experiences of Mexican Americans in the San Antonio–Corpus Christi region.

Similarly, the Cevallos brothers drew on signs of local Mexican American culture in presenting the Camachos, although they approached their subject through mainstream Hollywood television techniques. *Barbacoa* refers to the ritual barbecued meal that the family eats together each Sunday. Along with the other rituals in the film—backyard poker games, afternoon women's coffee meetings, and church services—the family meal indicates the real rituals of many Mexican American families in San Antonio and south Texas. Like in *The Wonder Years*, these rituals are addressed with some nostalgia, suggesting that they are less evident in the present day. Yet the presence of other local sites around San Antonio and the theme music, a Chicano blues song by the late local artist Randy Garibay, contribute to the credibility of the narrative, both aesthetically and emotionally. In this sense, the fact that the Cevallos brothers did not detour formally from Hollywood techniques may have made the film all the more realistic to viewers who found the film more accessible in a mainstream form. Indeed, I found this strategy worked when I screened the film for young Mexican Americans who otherwise were bored or uninterested in other independently made Mexican American films and videos.

More important, these films also spotlighted the bicultural voices of Mexican American young people. In *Barbacoa*, Juanito Camacho, the youngest boy in the family, both narrates the story and subjectively comments on the other characters, including his seemingly omniscient father. In *Corpus*, it is the young girls who are central to the narrative. Their singing performances, visits to the grave site, and other fan rituals communicate their adoration for a Mexican American female star in a sea of largely Anglo and African American musical performers. Through their eyes and ears, young people offer alternative points of view from adults in the films, reflecting what some Chicana feminists call "standpoints," or perspectives that arise from different social locations.[11] These standpoints are perhaps most evident through the young characters' desires. In *Barbacoa*, the active dream-life of "Baby Ray," the eldest son in the Camacho family, is a synecdoche for young boys' fantasies, even though he does not speak during the entire movie. Instead, we see him imagining his own success as the "Indiana Jones" of newspaper delivery and the home-run star of the neighborhood baseball game. In these dreams, he is a "Don Juan" that women go crazy for, but he saves his strongest emotions for a blond-haired girl whom he quietly adores in his conscious life. His desire for both fame in his Mexican American neighborhood and an Anglo American girl are not so unlike the girls in *Corpus* who desire a Mexican American star who crossed over into Anglo American popular culture. Both demonstrate the bicultural mixing of Mexican Americans and Anglo Americans in south Texas culture. In these films, Mexican American children are not islands segregated from Anglo American life. Rather they are members of a society that is both race conscious and bicultural.

The complex intertwinings of young people's identities motivates adults throughout both films. In *Corpus*, the Quintanilla family and a group of Chicana intellectuals, including Cherríe Moraga, Rosa Linda Fregoso, and Sandra Cisneros, talk about Selena and her impact on Mexican American girls. For the family, the youngest daughter Selena had to be protected from jealous outsiders, a poignant fact given that her fan club president eventually murdered her. Yet to the intellectuals, Selena belongs to a larger community as well. Although they do not agree on every point, the intellectuals act as both chorus and narrators in Portillo's argument, raising issues for debate and then commenting on the opinions of other interviewees in the documentary. From these debates, Selena becomes a metaphor for other Mexican American girls torn between private family and public recognition, culturally specific values

Figure 4. "Baby Ray" and "Juanito" in *Barbacoa. Reprinted with permission of Mike Cevallos.*

and mainstream standards for female visibility. The adults' concern and support in *Corpus* is similarly present in *Barbacoa,* though these sentiments are localized in the roles of the mother and father of the family. In the Camacho household, the adults do everything for their children. Unlike in *Corpus,* however, the parents' culture is strikingly more traditional than their sons' biculturalism. The father plays the patriarch. He not only works hard during the week, he gets up on the weekends to make the boys deliver newspapers. Inevitably, when Baby Ray daydreams too much, his father brings him to his senses, usually by yelling at him. The father is not all bad in these scenes. When the sports car that belongs to the blond-haired girl's father breaks down, Mr. Camacho helps fix it, to the delight of Baby Ray, who flirts shyly with the girl. Their mother, a veritable "angel of the household," also contributes to her sons' well-being. In one scene, she examines the men of the household carefully before going to church, noticing Juanito's dirty sneakers. Instead of scolding like the father, however, the mother leaves the frame only to return with a pair of shiny, white, patent-leather shoes, thrilled that she can, literally, provide the shoes on her children's feet. The rigidity of the parents' gender roles holds the children's biculturalism in high relief: they are not macho like their father nor traditional like their mother. They are "Mexican" and "American," two identities woven together in images and voices of the young.

The important contributions that *Barbacoa* and *Corpus* make to both images of Mexican Americans and images made by Mexican Americans cannot be underestimated. Few, if any films, have been credible and accessible reflections of the diversity of Mexican American experiences in south Texas. The focus on girls' and boys' subjectivities not only validates alternative points of view in Mexican American communities but also illustrates how those communities are sources of support to those young people. To push the analysis further, however, requires understanding of why children are the locus and impetus behind the films' narratives. The centrality of young people opens a question: what did they stand for at this particular moment in the history of Mexican American media production? To answer this begs deeper analysis into both the representations and realities of Mexican American young people in relation to their families and communities in the 1990s.

All in the Families: Real and Representations

Barbacoa director and co-producer Mike Cevallos felt that by focusing on youths he could encourage Mexican Americans to reflect on their communities and experiences in more positive ways. In a personal interview with me at a coffee shop, Cevallos said he wanted to layer the film with different positive messages about Mexican American culture. For non–Mexican Americans, the film could be entertaining, presenting Mexican American culture in a humorous yet touching way. For Mexican Americans, the film would have more subtle messages:

> We have two ways of looking at things, you know? You could say,
> "Oh, we don't even have curbs in our streets and I hate this neighbor-
> hood." Or you can look at it as, "This is where I live and this is what
> I'm proud of. Let me make it look beautiful. Let me find the beauty in
> it." We tried to incorporate different layers so it's not just one theme
> of "Hey, that's good and everything's okay." That's how we walk away
> from it, but between the lines, there's more messages of family,
> reflection, and perspective.

By focusing on the family in particular, Cevallos said he wanted to validate the experiences of Mexican Americans who may have once disregarded their culture as ugly or unimportant.

Similarly, director Portillo asserted that representations of Mexican American youths are empowering visions of Mexican American culture that usually are absent in mass media. In her introduction to the PBS debut of *Corpus* in July 1999, Portillo said that she wanted to make three points in the piece. First, she wanted to show the Quintanilla family, "because they had a story that was important to tell." Second, she wanted to focus on Selena as a role model for Mexican American women, particularly young girls: "[They] saw in her who they could be because they couldn't be like the blond Barbie. So they could be like Selena." Third, Portillo said she chose Selena to make Mexican American experiences visible and validated in the media. "We need to see ourselves in the media," she reflected. These assertions echo Cevallos's attention, both to the positive aspects of Mexican American cultures and to the family as a site where stories about young people can be told.

The heavy reliance on the family as the medium for understanding and resolving issues around young people in the films raises problems as well. Frequently shown with their parents, the young girls in *Corpus* rarely speak without a parent's guidance or protective presence. The typical Sunday in *Barbacoa* is family time and the boys inevitably get into trouble when they are away from their parents' watchful eyes. In these representations, parents shoulder the burden of protecting their children and raising them "in the right ways." These ways tend to support a familial ideology that can be easily recognized in the two-parent, middle-class, hetero-normative ideal that has existed throughout mainstream media since the late 1940s.[12] Displayed through print, broadcast, and celluloid, familial ideology frames social problems as personal problems, which are generally resolved only when family members comply with their gender-specific roles. Familial ideology not only tends to erase the real conditions of families, but also, in the case of Mexican Americans, has become the primary way to comment positively on young people. The Mexican American family thus becomes the place to read Mexican American youths as members of the nation and, paradoxically, as different.

THE GOOD FAMILY AND COMMUNITY

The representations of Mexican American families and communities surround young people in *Corpus* and *Barbacoa* with love and support. In Portillo's film, members of the Quintanilla family narrate one story of Selena, her humble beginnings, her vivacious spirit, and the sadness of her death. Local members of the community, particularly women who also loved Selena, reaffirm this story. Together, the family and community come together to share their different knowledge of Selena and her memories. For example, Selena's sister knows and speaks about Selena's private aspirations, but a local restaurant owner knows and speaks about her diet. Similarly, fans in the documentary know about Selena's public persona and stardom, while intellectuals know about Selena's public legacy in mass culture. These contrasting viewpoints create a constellation of Mexican American voices that comment on Selena's importance to a cultural community.

In Cevallos's film, the Camachos as a family are the synecdoche for a Mexican American community who support their children through a form of tough love. When the boys oversleep in the morning, the father screams at them to wake up. When they act lazy or daydream on their paper route, the father scolds them. Yet when Juanito nervously says grace before the family's church congregation instead of a sermon, the family cheers, elated and supportive of the boy's effort. The daily system of discipline and rewards ends when the family gathers to eat the barbacoa that the father buys from the local *tacqueria*. In this story about the average Mexican American family on Sunday, the meal signifies reunification, loyalty, and peace. All of these traits then also stand in for the community, which may have internal conflicts or be torn by differences but still come together for what is really important. The film's nostalgia—also an important element in *The Wonder Years*—also reinforces the message that family togetherness was an important, if not the essential, bedrock for a unified Mexican American community.

Barbacoa and *Corpus* explicitly critique the negative and racist determinism of stereotypes about the Mexican American family. The championing of the Mexican American family in the 1990s "fought against Latinos being perceived as a poor subculture," according to media critics Santiago Nieves and Frank Algarin.[13] Stereotypes of the Mexican American family date to the 1930s, when elite fears of juvenile delinquency focused on Mexican American children as a social problem and threat.[14] Using pseudoscientific research to back their claims, scholars and other institutionally based elites blamed the problem youth on the unassimilated Mexican American family.[15] In these accounts, the Mexican American family was feudally organized, an extended group of kin headed by the patriarchal father who demanded respect and submission from his clan.[16] The literature concludes that this organization "propagates the subordination of women, impedes individual achievement, engenders passivity and dependence, stifles normal personality development, and on occasion can even give rise to incestuous feelings among siblings."[17] According to this literature, Mexican American families, bordering on the pathological, could not assimilate because they were by nature undemocratic and unindividualistic; their family values could not compete with American values. From deviancy to difference, the Mexican American family represented everything that the presumably white, middle-class norm was not. In contrast, the families in *Corpus* and *Barbacoa* not only embody American family values but have also achieved the American Dream because of their strong kinship ties.

Neither film celebrates only positive aspects of the family, but each film's nostalgia sediments an idealized Mexican American family by clearly juxtaposing the family and community of the past and those of the present. In *Barbacoa*, it is not that Mexican Americans do not eat tacos anymore, it is that they rarely eat them together as a family. In *Corpus*, it is not known what Selena would have achieved under the guidance of her family, because an outsider took her life. The ethereal nostalgia portrayed by the Quintanilla family and the community gives way to the real television coverage of Yolanda Saldívar's standoff with police after shooting Selena. By comparing the ideal past with the messier present, the films can still point to an earlier time when

Mexican American families and communities supposedly harmonized. According to Henry Jenkins, who wrote on the sentimental value of stories about childhood, nostalgia is sadness for a past that never existed except in people's memories. Nostalgia for the family, manifest through myths, reveals present anxieties over real changes in Mexican American communities. As Jenkins reminds us, "Things are not the same. They never were."[18]

THE GAPS BETWEEN THE REAL AND IDEAL

Throughout this discussion, it should be remembered that the ideal representation of the Mexican American *family* never encompassed the reality of Mexican American *families*. A growing body of scholarship in this area reveals that Mexican American families are as different from each other as Anglo American families are presumed to be. At the same time, myths about Mexican American families and familial ideology are still prevalent, both among Mexican Americans and non–Mexican Americans. While these myths at times provide comfort, with nostalgic ideas about an imagined past, they also obscure other realities, particularly economic conditions, that create familial strife and struggle. *Barbacoa* and *Corpus* illustrate one type of Mexican American family in which family members occupy specific, gendered roles. Everyone is loyal and loving. Nonconformity is tolerated but ends in a fatalistic punishment. In representations, this has been the ideal.

In reality, Mexican American families have been very diverse, flexibly adapting to the specific historical conditions through which they formed. Since 1850, Mexican American families in San Antonio and the Southwest have differed widely depending on their socioeconomic class, region, and the decades in which they lived. Much like Irish American and African American families at the end of the nineteenth century, Mexican American, matriarchal-led and patriarchal-led families during that period coexisted in equal numbers within the working class.[19] Fathers in many families left in search of work; many mothers died in childbirth. Many couples never married but had children. Like working-class people of other ethnic groups, Mexican American families frequently accepted boarders and temporary live-in visitors into the household to generate revenue and share resources.[20] Census takers often confused these boarders as "family," perpetuating a myth that all Mexican Americans lived with extended families.[21] In general, only elite Mexican American families could maintain extended families, forcing most families to fragment. Intermarriage was prevalent. By the early twentieth century, exogamy between Mexican Americans and other ethnic groups matched other immigrant families in cities with increasingly diverse populations.[22] It was not that Mexican American families were the same as all other families, but that they responded flexibly to the same processes of industrialization and urbanization as other families in the United States.

In the period after World War II, more Mexicans came to the United States than in the previous hundred years. Sunbelt states such as Texas and California relied on Mexican American labor exactly at a time when Mexico increased its dependence on U.S. foreign aid.[23] Mexican Americans became the fastest urbanizing group in San Antonio, Los Angeles, and other large cities. Like previous generations, real families looked little like the mythological ones. Only perhaps four percent lived with extended families.[24] About one-third of families had single-parent homes. Recent immigrants could expect little financial help from their kin, except from families that already had high social status.[25] In this sense, myths about the Mexican American family could never account for the different experiences that real Mexican American families encountered when undergoing such large-scale economic and social changes.

Despite the discrepancies, family continues to be one of the primary metaphors for organizing knowledge about Mexican American identity within middle-class Mexican American communities. Often referenced in Spanish as *la familia*, the family is often a trope for a traditional identity. Alfredo Mirandé and Evangelina Enriquez, for example, accept sex role differences among family members as remnants of the division of labor in Aztec society. In their mythical family, fathers are patriarchs and mothers are the "backbone of the culture."[26] Although this myth reinforces many of the same stereotypes of an earlier Anglo American literature, the primacy of the family and its associated strengths resonates with many middle-class Mexican Americans as an ideal. Chicana research into family roles illustrates how Mexican American women working outside of the home frequently justified their labor by saying that they worked *for the well-being of their families*. This position was strongest among professional women whose social standing often did not require an additional salary.[27] In this construction, *la familia* supplants the reality of middle-class Mexican American families, creating an ideal that both parents attempt to achieve through work, consumption, and traditional values. These three elements are central to the representation of family in *Corpus* and *Barbacoa*.

THE REVISED IDEAL FAMILY

Barbacoa and *Corpus* construct the ideal Mexican American family. Both films place young people's identities in relation to traditional nuclear families. Both films feature patriarchs—Mr. Camacho and Mr. Quintanilla—and gender-segregated spheres. Women in the narratives gossip in the private sphere of the home, while men are more often pictured in public spaces, at work or in the neighborhood. Although children in the films seem to occupy diverse roles, their parents appear more traditional, reaffirming the myth that an ideal really did once exist. As a result, the films replace traditional family ideals with a modern family ideal, one that is integrated into labor and consumer markets.

At the same time, both films deconstruct certain traditional aspects of its associations through humor and commentary. The Sunday trials of the Camachos continuously illustrate the pitfalls of their traditional family values. Outsiders rebuff the father's authority directly, through the white father's racist dismissal, or indirectly. In one scene, he has to stand in a long line to wait for barbacoa when the restaurant owners refuse to let him step to the front. Frustrated at the slight, he proceeds to ignore his family in the car while he tries to entertain the other people in line with a joke he always tells. The father's inability to occupy a status role in the eyes of both his sons and the community belittles his role as the manager of the family. In *Corpus*, the roles of Mexican American women as angels of the household comes into question when discussing Selena as both an object of desire and a good daughter. Selena's ambiguous role as what the popular press called a "Tex-Mex Madonna" made her a repository of explicitly sexual meanings and a "devoted and respectful daughter" who had to be protected from an exploitative world.[28] This contradiction becomes the central problematic of the documentary, which replaces patriarchal readings of Selena as a sinner or saint with the portrait of a sexual woman who is nonetheless a moral force in her family.

In separate interviews, Portillo and Cevallos expressed the desire to rescue the idea of the Mexican American family by critiquing it. According to Portillo: "There is a whole mythification of the family in our culture. What I do, and I think it's the most transgressive of all things . . . I go into the family and kind of scrutinize it, investigate it, deconstruct it, in order to strengthen it in a different way."[29] Whereas Portillo wanted to reinterpret positive forces in Mexican American families, Cevallos told me that he wanted Mexican Americans to recognize that, although traditions change, family is still an important part of the culture: "You recognize, 'Hey, man, we used to do that every Sunday. It was great. . . . Sunday was a day for us to be together. Dad didn't work. We all hung around the house. The cousins came over. It was a very magical time.' Maybe it didn't feel like that then, but it does now because we don't get together anymore. We don't go to church together anymore, but we still kind of go on our own. So it's just the kind of thing, trying to strike a chord that 'Hey, we're still a family.'" Following the directors' intentions, *Barbacoa* and *Corpus* deconstruct the family as homogeneously positive forces in Mexican Americans' lives. By presenting the ups and downs of the past, the Camachos encourage viewers to value their present familial realities. Similarly, the contradictions of Selena's persona—for example, her natural beauty versus plastic surgery, her obedience to her family versus her inability to finish formal schooling—introduces modern interpretations of Mexican American family life. Through these juxtapositions, both films reimagine a Mexican American family against a fragmented, individualistic, and assimilated mainstream American society.

The representation of the Mexican American family, in short, is not the same as the myths of the past, but it is also different from an Anglo American family. This difference is key to representing Mexican Americans as both Americans and particular kinds of Americans. The Mexican American interlocutors and characters in Corpus and Barbacoa are acculturated Americans, but they are also more communal and less individualistic. In the late 1990s, these portrayals were familiar, literally and figuratively. Spanish-language advertising had long used the family as a vehicle for communicating Mexican Americans' "supposed nostalgia for the past, sense of rootlessness over family separations or relatives left behind, or fixed gender roles within the family."[30] Those advertisements also pushed products aimed at Mexican American consumers as a different segment of a general market. Family representations are thus double-voiced; they show Mexican Americans as unique members of a pluralistic American consumer society.

The Mexican American Consumer and Citizen

Barbacoa and Corpus may have their antecedents in other Mexican American films, but they also share common cause with other contemporary media that focus on the family. In his book on Hispanic advertising, San Antonian Lionel Sosa compares successful and failed mainstream advertising campaigns in terms of Mexican American reception: "Ads for McDonalds, which stress the emotional world of family values over the 'benefit' of good food at a low price are particularly effective in a Latino market; 'you deserve a break today' also has a particular resonance. So are ads for Coke (world harmony over the 'benefit' of refreshment), Kodak (happy memories over clear pictures), Nike (personal achievement over performance), and Hallmark ('care enough to send the very best' over an easy way to send greetings)."[31] In short, mainstream advertisements resonated with Mexican American audiences when they stressed family and collective values, themes interwoven in Corpus and Barbacoa. Although these media, independent film and advertising, had very different aims, together they mark the historical development of the repre-

sentations of Mexican Americans. No longer confined to "adobe houses, se-
rapes and mariachis," in the words of advertising executive Aldolfo Aguilar,
Mexican Americans emerged in positive representations that reconfirmed the
values of mainstream America and the story of the American Dream. *Barbacoa*
and *Corpus* thus contributed to a larger paradigm in which Mexican Americans show their "Americanness" through their family values and collective
consumption.

The use of families in advertising Mexican Americanness in San Antonio dates to the 1980s, when Spanish-language advertising agencies adjusted
general market campaigns toward a Mexican American audience that they
presumed spoke Spanish. Aguilar related how he helped create a Western
Union campaign for Spanish-language audiences. The general campaign
emphasized the speed of the wire transfer service in times of emergency or
when someone got in trouble—for example, when someone you know lands
in jail. In contrast, Aguilar said, "with the Hispanic market, wire services have
nothing to do with emergency situations, but it has everything to do with a
regular and consistent way of sending money back home. It's not about speed
of service; it's about trust—*la confianza.*" Two aspects of this advertisement
are noteworthy. First, the Mexican American family is a more loyal consumer
unit in this portrayal than the Anglo American family. The Mexican American family saves their money to send regularly, rather than hoarding it or
spending it all at once. Second, the Mexican American family uses the wire
transfer to hold the family together in spite of the psychical damage caused
by immigration. The Western Union campaign makes no mention of the
wounds that a wire transfer could not possibly heal, especially ones that might
fragment the family forever. The warm and supportive family members in these
advertisements purchase products that foster their togetherness when social
forces may tear them apart. Advertisements like these spoke miles about Mexican American consumers. For more than a decade, advertisers marketed the
Spanish-speaking family as *the* metonym of Mexican American culture.

In my conversations with advertisers in the 1990s, the family was not only
an alibi for a collective Mexican American past but also a motivation for sacrifice in the present and a future goal to attain. When asked about Mexican
American consumers, executive Luis Garcia envisioned an immigrant family
that works hard to improve the lot of their children: "I think the most important similarity [among Mexican Americans] is family, the importance of family, the family unity . . . The fact we came here for a better life, and that we
want to leave our kids a bit better off than the way we had it. There's this
tremendous and almost all-encompassing dedication to the next generation
and this really close-knit family unit that drives every decision." In Garcia's

words, parents invest in their children for the future of the whole. This articulation of the American Dream finds its way into *Barbacoa* and *Corpus* ironically through the focus on young people as the products of their parents' upbringing. The Camachos, the Quintanillas, and other parents in the documentary invest heavily in the future of their children to be capable citizens, talented individuals, and good consumers.

Investment in one's children included spending money on the goods advertisers promoted. The new Mexican American family in advertisements attempted to blend idealized visions of the family from Mexico with the consumer family in the United States. Together, they created an imagined Mexican American utopia for cultural uniqueness and economic assimilation. It was no coincidence that Mexican American advertisers promoted family unity, dedication, and sacrifice at the same time that they promoted consumer happiness and satisfaction. Narratives about the family have long invested consumer products with the emotional qualities that Americans seek in social relationships.[32] Ethnic integration into an imagined "melting pot" of modern American consumers frequently has been the subtext of television programs that could erase social problems with the purchase of a new television.[33] As viewers watched the representations of ethnic families consuming, they too could be sold to advertisers in the form of ratings and audience measurements. Once integrated into the general market, the ethnic consumer could be represented in more diverse ways; ethnicity gave way to assimilation.

For Mexican Americans, the representation of ethnicity has wavered between difference and acculturation, reflecting both the uniqueness of Mexican American identity and changing aspects of consumer markets. On one hand, the perpetuation of the American Dream narrative reflected the continuing flow of Mexican immigrants into the United States. Unlike European immigrant groups, who supposedly assimilated in two generations, Mexican Americans remained in an "immigrant audience paradigm" that must continually re-present their ability to blend into American society.[34] Generational differences between Mexican Americans were less visible than their presumed homogeneity. On the other hand, commercial industries in the 1990s began targeting cultural differences to define and develop niche markets. According to marketers, "Hispanic youth," for example, would be not only one of the fastest growing markets in the first decade of the twenty-first century, second only to Asian youth, but also the trendsetters for all other youth markets.[35] This market definition relied on images of young Mexican Americans as urban hipsters and already-acculturated insiders, a far cry from the immigrant outsiders who look to just fit in. The new Mexican American ideal family must contain both these representations. Neither insiders nor outsiders, the

Mexican American family in contemporary media celebrated consumption as a way to show they are achieving the American Dream but have maintained their distinctive cultural differences.

Consumption is collectively soothing and self-affirming for members of the Mexican American family in many Mexican American media productions. In *Barbacoa*, it is the meal shared with family that defines the members as a unit and as Mexican American individuals. In advertising, it is the product that helps the young people obey their parents and define themselves. In a 1998 AT&T advertisement, the phone's auto-redial feature ultimately helps a suitor ask his girlfriend's father for her hand.[36] The father accepts, affirming the suitor's worthiness and the value of the family patriarch. According to Kathy Sosa, creative director for Garcia LKS, these kinds of ads target teens with messages of family authority that they can relate to. However, family roles have changed, too. Sosa said the days have gone when Mexican American women in advertisements were only portrayed as passive mothers in the kitchen exclaiming, "¡Que rica! [Delicious!]" Women more often affirm their roles as buyers for the family, thus promoting unity of the group. Laura Barbarena, who worked part time with a small Spanish-language advertising agency, asserted that advertisers framed direct appeals to women in terms of their consumer power and knowledge of their children. "The reality is that a lot of the products like food are aimed at women because women make those kinds of purchasing decisions. So they're conscious of showing women in a positive light," she said. In the new scenario for Mexican American families, gender and age roles remain fixed but can be interpreted as empowering through consumer decisions.

Consumption as a soothing cure for the collectivity and empowering for the self is also present in *Corpus*, where Mexican American girls are both daughters and fans. For all the questions the film raises around Selena's celebrity, it does not critique Selena fan consumption. Even Sandra Cisneros, who is most critical of other aspects about Selena, exclaims, "I'm not a Selena fan. But I do have a Selena keychain. . . . I went to the Stop and Shop here, the little gas station there, and it's the first time I saw a Chicana on a key chain that wasn't the Virgin of Guadalupe. And I had to buy it." Intellectuals uniformly praise girls' adoration of Selena, a love expressed through buying posters, pins, compact discs and other fan memorabilia. "Selena did indeed become a fetish for Tejanos," writes Raúl Coronado Jr., referring to the cult of fans who bought Selena objects as an assertion of a social identity.[37] Although, in this case, consumption expressed resistance to Anglo American cultural idols, it never challenged the capitalist system that promotes cultural divisions in commodities. By centering on Selena's sexuality versus her family,

Corpus nevertheless accepts that girls need Selena to define themselves as Mexican Americans in a consumer society.

Through cultural difference and consumer equality, these Mexican American media represent the world as a middle-class multicultural playland. It is a place where rights are defined by consumer styles and political demands are rendered invisible. Most important, the playland is reserved for children: those who represent the future Mexican American citizen. In Baby Ray's final dream sequence, he fantasizes about himself and the blond girl running toward each other in an open field, their outstretched arms aimed at a union. A visual cliché, the scene does not so much romanticize exogamy as the desire for unity, to be part of the middle-class lifestyle that the blond girl embodies with her continuous carefree smile. As his father snaps at him, disrupting his dream, Baby Ray represents the future Mexican American citizen, one who, unlike his father, can dream.

Both family members and independent consumers, Mexican American young people in these representations embodied the paradoxes underlining Mexican American producers' conceptions of citizenship. Tied to traditions and cultural values, the young people in their productions did not lose their heritage, their cultural differences, or an organic connection to a larger community. At the same time, they adopted what John Hartley calls a "do-it-yourself" version of citizenship. Referring to his own daughter, Hartley writes that British girls selectively "Americanized" themselves by choosing which cultural attitudes, dress styles, daily rituals, fan cultures, and viewing habits they cared to appropriate. In a manner that seemed to parallel shopping in a mall of cultural values, Hartley concludes that while his daughter may not become "American," she has remade her identity selectively to be British in a different way.[38] Similarly, the youths in *Barbacoa* and *Corpus* were American in a different way. They were Catholic and revered Indiana Jones. They looked different but dressed the same. They ate pizza and tacos. In the mediated postmodern world, Mexican American identity has become a set of interchangeable symbols, able to be mixed and recombined in the sea of commodities available. It is a vision of Mexican American young people that projected both consumer values and middle-class disposable incomes while leaving their foundation, the family, unshaken and untouched by the markets that demand youths' values and income.

The Invisible Mexican American Citizen and Noncitizen

It perhaps goes without saying that the representation of the new Mexican American family excluded as much as it included real Mexican Americans.

After all, Anglo American families in 1990s sitcoms were distinctively different from the majority of Americans who grew up in single-parent households. Similarly, few Mexican Americans could boast the emotionally warm and financially supportive families that dominated the representational worlds of Mexican American mass media. Whereas Anglo Americans were present in all types of media and their respective genres, the small sample of Mexican American media productions made the lack of diversity most visible. Who was left out of optimistic representation of the middle-class Mexican American family? What kinds of citizenship became invisible?

Two aspects that have become central to representing Mexican American citizens—social class and nationality—mediate friendships in *Corpus* and *Barbacoa*. Neighbors meet with neighbors. Intellectuals meet with intellectuals. Selena's friendship with Saldívar is transgressive from the beginning, not only because she is not family but also because she is positioned as low class, someone using Selena to get ahead. In fact, Selena's friendship with Saldívar ultimately becomes the reason why the family cannot achieve the American Dream. Saldívar—described in the documentary by Abraham Quintanilla as "a person who is not popular at school. Does not have friends. Physically is not a good-looking person"—is the unassimilable ethnic immigrant, a childless, lonely, and unattractive woman who destroys a family. If, like advertising messages, *Barbacoa* reaffirms the positive future of the family, then *Corpus* identifies the family's binary "other" as those who do not have families, capital, or know their place.

The real demographics of Mexican American families during the 1990s were quite different from those celebrated in media. Among Hispanic citizens, the number of single-parent families increased nationally from one-third to more than one-half of total households between 1980 and 1995.[39] Women led the majority of these homes. In Texas, more Mexican American citizens reported being married in the 1990 Census, but women still headed over one-fourth of these homes.[40] Even with significant gains in the late 1980s, Mexican American families still earned and saved approximately half of what Anglo American families earned and saved.[41] Some of those who made the strongest earnings leaps during this time, wealthy Mexican American families benefited much like wealthy Anglo American families during the same time period. None of these figures include noncitizens, Mexican Americans who have lived sometimes decades in the south Texas region.

In addition, to be middle class in the United States has often meant to be represented as someone who succeeds without effort. Shown as professionals or managers, middle-class Americans are rarely shown doing the chores of everyday life, often outsourcing the unpleasant or unglamorous to an assistant or a domestic worker.[42] In *Barbacoa* and *Corpus*, labor integrates the Mexican American family and yet it is nearly invisible. It must be assumed, for example, that some family members must work to buy Juanito his new shoes and to purchase Selena songs for the girls. In both cases, familism obscures economic needs with emotionalism. The father in *Barbacoa* is a heroic breadwinner at the end of the film. He sits up alone at night drinking a beer as the narrator ponders if he does so because "he was dead tired from working so hard that he just couldn't sleep." This touching moment both naturalizes the father's role while ignoring the labor of other family members, from the mother's domestic chores to the boys' paper route. Rather than showing the family's cooperation as an economic unit, it is sentimentalized for the benefit of the boy's nostalgia. Similarly, the families of the young fans of Selena represent their own sacrifices as "labors of love." As mothers describe their daughters' fan activities, they fail to mention their own work to support these consumer habits. Modes of fan dress and object collection require disposable income. Driving girls to and from dance classes, singing lessons, and even Selena memorials not only presupposes that someone in the family must be the chauffeur, but also that someone must pay for their child's leisure. Just as the Quintanilla family members do not discuss their efforts to make Selena a star, the families in *Corpus* do not discuss the expenditures or labor implicated in fan cultures.

Labor becomes even more important when one considers the population of Mexican Americans who are not citizens but are a vital part of the U.S. workforce. The rapid expansion of new immigrant communities of urban workers in construction, factories, and domestic labor includes Mexican American families that are neither citizens nor migrants. Some of these women work as nannies and caretakers in middle-class homes, providing the means for other Americans to maintain a traditional family unit by paying someone else to "mother."[43] The caretakers, especially live-ins, may have difficulty making ends meet and complying with their own familial duties.[44] Their children frequently work alongside their mothers in new family arrangements that look little like the families they work for. In a new economy that demands a new transnational class of women and children workers, it is safe to say there is no normative Mexican American family. As if there ever were.

With all the Mexican American media texts examined here, the representation of cultural differences has come at the expense of exposing class differences among Mexican Americans. The tensions involved in representing Mexican American families should be taken as a symptom of this larger dilemma. How can one represent Mexican American families as culturally different without alienating those who have not had similar experiences? Positive representation is one strategy, but it relies on the assumption that Mexican

Americans will recognize the working, consuming, happy family as *positive* in relation to their own lives. If cultural affirmation replaces criticism of an economic system that exploits Mexican American labor and cultural productions as commodities, then the representation of Mexican American cultural membership is limited to a bourgeois acceptance of economic inequality.

Postscript: *The Mexican American Family Goes to Hollywood*

Although *Corpus* and *Barbacoa* reached relatively small audiences in comparison with commercially sponsored mass media, their legacy lives on in two mainstream television programs that focus on Mexican American families. *Barbacoa* became a pilot for a future television program, *The Brothers Garcia.* Produced and promoted by the Cevallos brothers through Sí TV, the program occupied the Sunday early evening time slot on Nickelodeon in the early 2000s. Similar to the original movie, *The Brothers Garcia,* the program features the voice and subjectivity of the youngest son, who nostalgically remembers his "familia." Since the making of *Corpus,* Portillo went on to make other documentaries, most recently a feature on the mysterious murders of women in Juarez, Mexico. Yet a weekly fictional program bears striking resemblance in terms of its audience and messages. Created by Gregory Nava, *American Family* receives external commercial funding but airs on PBS, attempting to attract roughly a similarly educated, upper-middle-class audience to those who might have seen *Corpus* either on PBS or at a film festival. Like the former, the serial weaves different perspectives of Mexican American men and women in addressing a particular topic of interest to the community. Within the confines of the family, narratives on the program have dealt with immigration, cultural traditions, and identity. Although there are many differences between the new television programs and their film predecessors, the focus on Mexican American families suggests the continuity of the new familial ideal.[45]

Mainstreaming has brought new homogenizing images of Mexican Americans. The new programs are set in what looks like Los Angeles, a city with not only a larger Mexican American population than south Texas but also a more affluent Mexican American viewing base. Just as labor disappears in the representation of Mexican American families, so does the south Texas family, which as a unit earns less and receives fewer social benefits than the urban California family. The Camachos and the Quintanillas are now the Garcias and the Gonzalezes, two last names easily recognizable as Hispanic to a mainstream public that is always presumed to be non-Hispanic. The Garcias and the Gonzalezes live comfortable, middle-class lifestyles. They are homeowners and stylish consumers. As in earlier Mexican American media representations of the family, the children are the ambassadors of the new technologies in the home, playing video games, programming the computer, and shooting digital video. The shows' Internet sites further reinforce the divide between cool kids and traditional parents with activities and film clips featuring the ingenuity of young people. Meanwhile, the elders in the programs maintain traditional family values. *The Brothers Garcia* ends each episode with the mantra "Everything for the family."

Family values here not only coincide with consumer values but also directly mirror the family images presented in advertising around the programs. The Garcias think about consumption on nearly a weekly basis. When they think they have won the lottery, the program is dedicated to spending the money. When Lent comes, family members fail to give up their consumer vices. In *American Family*, major sponsor Johnson & Johnson every week "celebrat[es] the tapestry of the Great American family" with a collage of black and white family photographs. The racial diversity of each family clearly transmits the idea that the Gonzalezes are just one of America's new images of multiculturalism. "The series is about an American family living in Los Angeles that happens to be Latino," says Nava on the program's Web site. "I wanted to create a show that will make the audience laugh and cry as it chronicles the daily struggles and triumphs of a family. *American Family* is about everyone's family."

Of course not every family is like the Gonzalezes or the Garcias, but with so few broadcast television programs produced by Mexican Americans, these programs have done double duty: representing the work of Mexican American producers trying to break into an industrial hierarchy and representing Mexican American cultures. This "burden of representation" seldom extends to media producers who are not people of color.[46] It leaves open the question of what Mexican American media production might look like if there was more access to financing, resources, and personal networks of power. In 1998 the National Association of Latino Independent Producers (NALIP) formed to lobby for access while contending with pressures within industries that perpetuated isomorphic visions of families in the general market. Corporate sponsors, including ABC, CBS, Disney, HBO Latino, Showtime, and AOL Time Warner, support NALIP, suggesting that Mexican American media producers have made their voices heard, but only within the corporate constraints that sponsor family values, conceal labor, and promote consumption. Given the present environment, there might well be more representations of Mexican Americans in the future, but we should not be surprised if these images look little like the majority of Mexican Americans who might see them.

Chapter 5

Mexican American
Alternative Media

NOT ALL MEDIA REPRESENTATIONS of Mexican Americans are broadcast or meant for mass distribution. In fact, many Mexican American media producers traced their own practices back to places outside of mainstream media. Several San Antonio Tejano professionals, for example, got their start in Rudy Treviño's art class at Lanier High School in the early 1980s. In an inner-city classroom, they learned, unwittingly perhaps, how to design and promote for the Tejano Music Awards in an extracurricular school activity that kept them off the streets. These forms of alternative media production were an important introduction to the skills and personal networks they would later need coming into mainstream industries, where they would work with people with more formal training and cultural capital as members of the middle class. For those who did go into the mass media mainstream, alternative media production provided an important stepping stone. For those who did not, however, alternative media production was just that: an alternative to the mainstream representations Mexican Americans encounter every day.

Media and alternative artistic productions have long been part of Mexican American public culture in San Antonio. Public art, theater, dance, and music are as old as the city itself, inscribed into its buildings, plazas, and markets. Throughout the 1960s and into the 1970s, activists of all ethnic backgrounds targeted mass media not just as producers of stereotypes but also as potential spaces for self-representation. Media activism peaked in the late

1970s, when the Intracity Urban Communication Coalition, a group composed of Mexican Americans, Anglo Americans, and African Americans, repeatedly protested for the right to a public access station within the city's first cable television franchise.[1] Under the banner of access for all, activists claimed the right of all of its citizens to make their own broadcast images. The eventual franchise in 1978 fell short of achieving all of the coalition's wishes, resulting in a tightly regulated public access station located far away from areas with high concentrations of working-class people of color. Nevertheless, they successfully put media access in the spotlight as a defining demand of a citizenship that would allow Mexican Americans to represent themselves in a noncommercial space. Two decades later, a public magnet school and several nonprofits in San Antonio continued to dedicate video resources to outreach in Mexican American communities. Video had become a public medium of alternative cultural expression in San Antonio.

In the city's historic west side, one such alternative arts project began in 1993 to use video to give local Mexican Americans, particularly teenagers, the power to represent themselves. Although San Anto Cultural Arts (SACA) never promoted itself as a place for making citizens, it shared common cause with its activist predecessors in struggling for resources to provide public access. This chapter documents the ways in which this struggle manifested during two years I spent with the organization. Theoretically, SACA challenged mainstream mass media by promoting local identities, preserving local histories, and generating alternative artistic creations in an almost exclusively Mexican American neighborhood. In practice, this was a daily process of negotiation, working with heterogeneous individuals to produce alternative visions of Mexican Americanness and to create an inclusive space that opens at least the potential for a different interpretation of Mexican American citizenship.

San Anto Cultural Arts and West Side Identities

The SACA grassroots video project was composed of a coalition of artists, musicians, intellectuals, and activists in the heart of San Antonio's west side, an almost completely Mexican American community. Many of these founders were Mexican Americans themselves who had grown up in this community. According to the mission statement of the group, SACA provides a space for people to have open and creative access to video and other cultural arts, particularly people from the oft-neglected Mexican American working-class areas surrounding the Alazán-Apache housing projects. To achieve this goal, SACA members have tried to create an emergent culture within the project that validates but departs from residual and contemporary cultures in the community. In particular, Chicano and Catholic cultures have framed SACA's history as a west side institution and SACA's volunteers as members of these two cultural identities in the west side. These cultures have given SACA life, but they have also provided the video project with an uncertain path in being able to represent the diversity of its citizen members.

THE WEST SIDE

SACA has been an integral part of San Antonio's west side. As such, the organization is embedded in the ethnic, political, and religious history of its locale. This space has been as much imagined as real; to say one was from the west side automatically established allegiances to a working-class Mexican American structure of feeling that defined the area to outsiders as much as its residents. Shifting in its physical location over time, the west side became coded as such between 1920 and 1930, when the Mexican American population of the city doubled, expanding exponentially in an enclave located west of downtown. Poor and overcrowded, this area often flooded and was plagued by diseases due to a lack of sanitation services.[2] Most workers occupied manual positions, particularly in railroads, construction, and factories that performed piecework, such as sewing, rolling cigars, and shelling pecans. As the neighborhood grew, reinforced by segregationist policies of an Anglo American city government, the west side developed its own institutions and small-scale operations along with a political consciousness that since the 1930s made the neighborhood a hotbed for labor strikes and class-based movements.[3] To this day, the west side shoulders the contradictions of a poor Mexican American community with a vibrant activist tradition.

While the associations between class and ethnicity date to the west side's beginnings, Chicano and Catholic social justice movements formed integral parts of the west side's more recent past, making them "residual cultures" in SACA's space.[4] Since the 1960s, Chicano and Catholic social justice movements forged cultural identities through political activism and social struggle. Chicano activist and founder of the Southwest Voter Education and Registration Project, Willie Velasquez registered west side residents while La Raza Unida organized them to vote for a third, Chicano political party.[5] At the same time and in the same region, Catholic priests and their clergies from the post–Vatican II era supported antipoverty programs, antiwar protests, and human rights organizations. San Antonio Archbishop Robert Lucey began the first Catholic social justice programs for immigrants in the west side; his successor, Patricio Flores, became the first Mexican American archbishop in the United States.[6] Combining both Catholic archdioceses and Chicano activists, Communities Organized for Public Service (COPS) started in 1973 as a direct-action means to improve west side living and working conditions.[7] COPS's neighborhood-based leadership demonstrates the rich interconnections between Chicano and Catholic cultures in the area where SACA has operated.

In the late 1990s, the west side continued to be place-marked by class, ethnicity, and strong political activity. The 1990 U.S. Census designated over 90 percent of the zip code area around SACA as Mexican American, and, on the average, the per capita income for Mexican Americans in this area was less than $4,500 yearly, one of the lowest in the city.[8] During this time, Mexican Americans in COPS, Metro Alliance, and city government rallied around living wages and job training to challenge future urban development and tax breaks for new corporate investors.[9] School dropout rates, ranging from 2 to 60 percent in some schools, and some of the highest teenage pregnancy rates in the country ensured the continuing cycle of poverty in the west side.[10] These statistics were etched into the landscape of the one-mile radius around SACA, located literally across the railroad tracks from the heart of the downtown tourism areas. Traveling west on Guadalupe Street, one passed a series of social service agencies and nonprofits as well as bars, convenience stores, and an old dance hall transformed into a restaurant where one could find a full meal for three dollars. In all directions at all times, there was movement, from the transients with shopping carts to the basketball games at the local courts. Those who lived nearby knew families who had lived in the west side for generations. They knew the deep contradictions that surrounded a neighborhood that was economically disfranchised but politically and culturally rich at the same time.

SAN ANTO CULTURAL ARTS

According to one of SACA's founders, Executive Director Manuel ("Manny") Castillo, the organization began primarily to give these area residents access to cultural arts programming: "The original goal was to fill a void of accessibility to arts programs for people that traditionally don't have access to arts programs outside of school. . . . Well a lot of times you have to look beyond that. When you talk about community development and uplifting the dignity of the community, you have to look beyond the walls of high school and academia." Art classes and cultural education historically were elite activities in San Antonio. Beginning in the 1920s, the city's Mexican American middle class had created arts programs to cultivate and preserve a bourgeois Mexican national culture in opposition to hybrid Mexican American and lowbrow working-class cultures.[11] Working-class Mexican Americans could consume culture and the arts through free, public performances and shows, but they could not join a formal institution to produce cultural arts. This cultural segregation was still evident when SACA began. The Guadalupe Cultural Arts Center and the Southwest School of Arts and Crafts, the city's two primary cultural arts institutions, charged from fifty dollars to three hundred dollars for art courses, effectively barring west side residents from participating. When some publicly funded arts programs began opening doors to west side residents, the programs focused narrowly on one or another west side group, such as housing project residents, women, or children. In contrast, SACA aimed to serve west side residents but also adopted an open-door policy that resulted in a multicultural and multiclass membership.

Class, ethnic, and religious histories thus provided a background for SACA's activities without limiting its membership. I began studying SACA largely because the group did not exclude middle-class Anglo Americans. In 1998, I attempted to participate in another Mexican American cultural arts group but failed to gain any meaningful entrance because I was neither Mexican American nor working class.[12] This experience illustrated the polarized state of ethnic and class relations in San Antonio, a legacy of both Anglo American discrimination and middle-class segregation against working-class Mexican Americans in south Texas. At SACA, staff members and volunteers tried to create a space that actively opposed this legacy. Although most of SACA's original founders and members were working-class Mexican Americans, Anglo Americans and middle-class volunteers participated in all stages of the organization's growth.

THE RESIDUAL AND THE EMERGENT

While SACA members worked to create their own culture based on a tolerance for diversity and respect for differences, the residual cultures of the west side were also present in SACA's emergent culture. A Chicano sensibility, for example, was visible in SACA's cultural arts projects both as a historical and contemporary force in the west side. There was no doubt that when a local resident read the newspaper's masthead and subheading, "El Placazo: A Creative and Soulful Outlet of the People—c/s," that "the people" derived from the inherited language of Chicano nationalism.[13] The notation "c/s" stood for *con safos*, a common phrase in south Texas signaling a Chicano author and a warning against violating authorship through graffiti or plagiarism.[14] Murals that flanked SACA's east wall documented the "Eight Stages in the Life of a Chicana," and other murals drew heavily on folkloric aesthetics and an Aztec symbology. The catalog of video footage was a record of countless mural blessings, street fiestas, and oral histories, themes that also emphasized a

Figure 5. Mural "Educación," completed by San Anto Cultural Arts. *Photo taken by Carole Mayer.*

Mexican American common culture. In this way, SACA incorporated aspects of Chicano cultural arts discourses that became embedded in public sphere productions.

Meanwhile, SACA's organizational structure followed in the footsteps of Catholic humanist traditions. San Antonio's Catholic Church advocated grassroots organizing based on Paulo Freire's methods of nonauthoritarian teaching.[15] These methods interlaced with SACA's own goals. SACA tried to develop the community by developing people first. For this reason, the interpersonal developmental process was more important than the content of the art itself. Regular group meetings and long decision-making processes set the stage for consensus building, while arts activities stressed cooperation and patience. Although SACA encouraged respect of elders, the group discouraged gender and racial hierarchies. These internal rules were reminiscent of the liberational theological movements across Latin America in order to raise political awareness through self-empowerment in the 1960s.[16] Like these consciousness-raising movements, SACA posited that personal development could occur in educational settings in which group members contributed knowledge based on their experience, not on their social authority. In SACA, everyone was a volunteer teacher and learner. Even SACA's three staff positions—one each for murals, the newspaper, and video—were often VISTA volunteers, part of a national service program started in the 1960s under President Lyndon B. Johnson.[17] Volunteers entered SACA with the expectation that they would become facilitators who did not impose their will on others. The spirit of the process was grounded in Christian teachings, though anti-authoritarianism has characterized other leftist social movements, including feminist and nuclear arms movements.[18] In SACA, the secular use of Christian teachings stressing humanitarian good works and inclusiveness were reminiscent of earlier Catholic programs in San Antonio that adapted liberation theology to local conditions.

The intermixing of Chicano and Catholic cultures in informing SACA's structuring became apparent to me in my initial interview with Manny in November 1997. He was, in his own words, a west side homeboy. He attended Catholic schools, went to college in Austin, and traveled the country with a rock band before coming back to the west side. Manny said he learned he could call himself a "Chicano" while immersed in college life at St. Edwards University. "I didn't realize I was a Chicano till I was in college, you know. I went to college in Austin. That was the first time I'd ever been out of the west side, except for going to Mexico. Then I became very Chicano, you know, surrounded by white people. I was a very big minority on campus at the university. So I was lonely and was wondering who I am, and that's where it starts." Manny said that learning about the Chicano movement in Austin made him highly aware of his connection to other Chicanos. When he returned to the west side, he volunteered with Inner City Development, a social works organization that provided basic necessities to anyone who knocked on their door. Founded by a charitable and hard-working Anglo American Catholic couple in 1968, the organization gave Manny "his second education." In his words: "I knew I wanted to learn from other people in the community, from the drug addicts and the prostitutes, to the kids and their families, to the administrators and the Board. . . . I would recommend that anyone do the same thing. That for me made the difference." In 1993, the social works organization gave Manny a room, rent-free, in their house to set up SACA's offices. Four years later, SACA gained its nonprofit status and became an incorporated entity, allowing Manny to apply for independent funding so that SACA could grow.

These two experiences, college and the social works organization, were still present in SACA's physical environment and yet did not define the group exclusively. SACA's office walls were a testament to residual and lived Chicano cultures and politics, from pro-UAW farm-worker banners to anti–Proposition 187 placards. Next door, Inner City Development was a visible presence on SACA's executive board and the numerous volunteers who have worked at both institutions. In its practices, though, SACA strove to define its own identity. Manny said that by talking to Chicano artists and members of the movement, he became aware of problems with Chicano arts movements in the past, including the risk of alienating both Mexican American and Anglo American community members. On the west side, even the term *Chicano* has become increasingly rare; most people prefer to call themselves "Hispanic," "Mexican American," or "Mexicano." SACA thus broke with the essentialism that preceded explicitly Chicano arts projects while adapting prosocial discourses that emphasized self-improvement in a working-class community.[19] In Manny's words: "Cultural arts are an alternative to drug use, substance abuse, teen pregnancy—to everything from mental health to physical health. That sounds kind of cliché, but that's what's happened serendipitously over the last few years. We realized . . . [that we had to] develop programs not just for video's sake, or literature's sake, or for visual-artistic sake, but for developing people. Rehabilitating people as well." SACA used these self-improvement discourses in applying for grant funding, showing that cultural arts were important tools for community development because they taught job skills or inspired creativity in children. In this way, SACA was neither a Chicano organization nor a Catholic social works organization, but it usefully adopted aspects of those cultures in forming its own.

Catholic and Chicano cultures further supported SACA's goals by imagining a fundamentally communal and spiritual society, a component of communitarian citizenship discourses. In a communitarian society, people feel responsible to contribute to various political projects while the state works to eliminate social inequalities.[20] Citizenship, in this paradigm, depends on a sense of the citizen's and the state's shared responsibility in working toward a common good. For Catholics, communitarianism has been an alternative to a democratic liberalism based on individual achievement and selfishness.[21] The American Catholic bishops concurred in a letter, stating, "Justice begins with a life of recognition of the need to take part in the life of the community in order to be fully human, by being united with one another in mutual activity and, finally, mutual love."[22] The bishops' recognition of mutual love as a Christian basis for human society parallels the mutual respect advocated by Chicano scholars as the basis for a human society "beyond Aztlán."[23] A communitarian society would allow Chicano communities to preserve their unique identity while working together to respect other cultural identities. Chicano and Catholic definitions of communitarianism thus presented SACA utopian visions of a future society in which each person contributed to the community in their own way, whether by writing a poem, helping others with a mural, or videotaping public events.

In addition, Catholic and Chicano cultures contributed a spiritualism that informed SACA's events. After the completion of each mural, for instance,

SACA conducted public blessings as opportunities for the community to come together in celebration, cultural reflection, and prayer. Representing Chicano and Catholic spiritualism, Azteca dancers and Father Marty Elsner blessed the murals. Such public religious rituals represented a Chicano public sphere that created alternatives to an Anglo American liberalism that has dominated political discourse.[24] The mural blessings united the community's Chicano and Catholic cultures behind SACA's arts projects. At the same time, other west side cultures joined in the mural blessings: not only priests and Azteca dancers but also local artists, poets, and musicians. Together, they represented what San Antonio Father Virgilio Elizondo called *mestizaje,* or the mixing of religious and national cultures into a multicultural society.[25] SACA thus presented itself publicly as a fundamentally plural organization, open to the diverse cultural identities of the west side.

Sometimes these cultural identities diverged in prescribing what kind of goals SACA should have. In other words, tolerance of cultural identities did not necessarily mean consensus about group goals and strategies for achieving goals. In Chicano cultural discourses, for example, cultural affirmation has been the platform for politics in the present. From the beginning of the Chicano student movements, poetry and cultural productions were precursors to united political fronts.[26] The cultural renaissance sweeping through Mexican American communities at this time simultaneously activated a Chicano rhetoric for political change.[27] Even if Chicano artists did not consider themselves political radicals, many Chicano cultural arts movements fortified the civil rights movement, emphasizing pride while condemning discrimination.[28] Yet Catholic cultural discourses tended to de-emphasize expressly political aims. Mestizaje implied "partial assimilation" into mainstream society: "Mexican Americans want a better life, want to enter the structures of opportunity. For this, they need a North American education but they also want to retain their cultural and linguistic identity. Is this possible? My hypothesis is that not only is this possible, it is necessary for the future."[29] Catholic cultural goals in San Antonio validated cultural production in the name of pluralism not nationalism. Both approaches offered SACA two competing goals to choose from. The latter, nationalism, stressed the path to an identity politics based on difference. The former, pluralism, stressed the path to an assimilative politics.

SACA refused direct affiliation with powerful west side institutions such as the Catholic Church or Chicano political organizations. Although some of the volunteers who joined were also members of La Raza or church groups, SACA continually reestablished its independence from specific political allegiances or goals. This avoided alienating both potential group members and community leaders responsible for the organization's funding. Yet many of these leaders saw the documentation of Mexican American culture as political in itself, leading to intense political haggling when the city allocated money for the arts budget. Manny said the tension between being an apolitical organization open to the community and being pigeonholed for serving the Mexican American community has been hard to balance: "A long time ago, we decided we would stay clear of that [politics] just because it is public art. . . . Going back to the goals, one of our original goals was to document our history. Not only documenting, but making sure the documentation of history, culture, and heritage was being done by the people that created it and are living it, and not [trails off] . . . and that's political right there. And some people might think it's racist. . . . Depending on how I, the director, often I choose to make that statement heard in the community. But no, I don't do that." As this quotation demonstrates, SACA walked a difficult line between being a voice for its constituents while staying apolitical. In the past, SACA has even refused to affiliate with other cultural arts organizations, for fear of being labeled. In a later interview, Manny said that SACA may begin to build stronger coalitions with other cultural arts groups in order to pursue common goals, making it unclear how other cultural arts groups' political affiliations or goals may influence SACA in the future.

SACA engaged in building an emergent culture that incorporated positive aspects of surrounding Chicano and Catholic cultures while avoiding the divisive implications of these cultures, such as an essentialistic membership or explicitly political agendas. Yet even positive influences of residual cultures embodied tensions. For example, communitarianism counters the idea of a liberal democracy based primarily on individual rights. Similarly, spiritualism creates friction with the idea that the United States is a secular society. This invited conflict over SACA's ultimate goals. For one, how should SACA create a multicultural environment based on tolerance and cooperation without privileging any particular cultural vision? Further, how would this environment help Mexican Americans living on the west side? Before addressing these questions, I want to give more insight into the inner workings of a group dedicated to allowing Mexican Americans to represent themselves using media technologies. By chronicling my own experiences in the group, the next section provides a narrative of the tensions involved in SACA's video project culture when it tries to provide an alternative media space for "the people."

San Anto in Action

I came to SACA as a volunteer and a researcher in September 1997. There, I was heavily involved in working toward a number of the organization's goals, volunteering regularly to work with youth crews, to think about shared goals, and to work for the future sustainability of the project through grant writing or public advocacy. Despite my involvement, my perspective on the project is necessarily couched first in the viewpoint of a volunteer and researcher, not a staff member or a member of the west side community. By virtue of my ethnicity, background, and college credentials, I was in many ways an outsider to the west side, from where SACA drew its participants. After working with the group for more than a year, I interviewed three SACA members after they read an earlier draft of this chapter. These three people—the executive director, a former staff member, and a former video project volunteer—reacted in different ways to the draft, offering me suggestions that I have largely tried to adopt.[30] Although the result has my authorial voice, their input provided a more dialogic definition of SACA and its video project.

MY FIRST SACA MEETING

Prior to my first interview with Manny, I attended my first of many video project meetings. For SACA, this was the first video project meeting that the group had held in months, due to the lack of a staff video coordinator. Manny held the meeting at Inner City Development, where SACA still maintained its office until early 1999. The house showed signs of Inner City's growth since it began in 1968. Former outside windows now formed the inside wall of SACA's rectangular office. From their door, I passed through a large multipurpose room with tables and chairs. At the back wall of the large room sat Inner City's office, a set of industrial restroom stalls, and a commercially equipped kitchen that provides food to anyone in need. Down a narrow hall, there was a children's reading room and room with a bank of aged computer terminals. Our meeting was in the adjoining rooms at the end of the hall, which housed art supplies and a collection of colorful youth paintings on the walls. Soon after, I discovered that Inner City also maintained separate offices for an affordable housing loan program and a two-story volunteer house for people who volunteer at least ten hours with the organization. The combined size of the house and offices was larger than any other structure on the otherwise residential street.

Video project meetings are held to help SACA achieve its goals while introducing cultural influences on the organization. At this meeting, Manny sat at one end of a long table with Pablo, a new VISTA volunteer hired to oversee the project.[31] Directly across from them, Berta, a longtime video crew facilitator, sat with Monica, a sixteen-year-old girl from a downtown arts magnet school. Those less experienced with video or SACA, including myself, sat around the sides of the table. Ana, age fifteen, brought her younger cousin Sara, age fourteen, and their even younger cousin Elsa, twelve, who came in place of her brother, Juan, who had a football game. There was a logic for the way we sat around the room. Everyone could see everyone at the table. By implication, everyone could participate. Though Manny led the meeting's agenda, the atmosphere was social. Pablo had even made Frito pies for us since the meeting occurred close to dinnertime.

We each received a copy of Manny's agenda. It read: history of the program, goals, and brainstorming. He began, "In 1993 me and two other artists and friends from the community thought of San Anto to fill the lack we saw of cultural arts programs in the Alazán-Apache [housing project] area." From there, he said, SACA completed its first mural in 1994 and began El Placazo, a monthly community newspaper. He added that the mural project was running smoothly now and the newspaper staff was working on getting more articles and poetry. Manny mentioned that both Sara and Ana had painted murals in the past and complimented their work in front of the group. He also noted the murals at the Cassiano housing projects painted in the 1970s and the rich oral traditions that predate the poetry in the newspaper. Switching the subject to video, Manny said the video project started because group members wanted to document the mural project as part of the culture around them. They solicited a camera from local production studios, until 1994, when Match Frame donated a professional Sony VHS camera. Three years later, the video project was still getting its wings, according to Manny. He hoped Pablo would revitalize the video project as its first paid coordinator. Manny's oral history situated the video project as the last in a long line of arts projects with clear antecedents in Chicano arts projects, such as poetry and murals. In this history, video was a medium of the future more than of the past, and, while this could be exciting, it was also a burden. When Manny referred to the mural project and the newspaper as the smoothest running programs, he implied that the video project would take a longer time to be self-sufficient.[32]

Next, Manny outlined video project goals. One of Pablo's first goals would be to catalog oral histories and other videotapes so that anyone in the community could watch the tapes to understand their past in a free and accessible west side location. From there, he said, "Our goal is to record hundreds of oral histories with people we know. It could be your grandmother or your neighbor or anyone who has a story that needs to be told." Manny cited people that Ana and Sara knew, again in an attempt to be inclusive. After the oral histories, Manny explained to everyone around the table that once they joined the video project, they had a responsibility to help others learn the production process. Each volunteer would be able to be a leader for newcomers. He explained that, eventually, SACA would give stipends to interns like themselves to organize the program. The production process thus relied on both a spirit of cooperation to foster creativity and a quest for a self-sufficient form of organization to provide access.

When he described the video project, Manny stressed creativity over technical skills. He said video provides volunteers with "an alternative means of communication to express yourself." Although he did not say so explicitly, Manny used the word *alternative* to refer to alternative forms and contents to mass media. He explained, "This is a chance to tell your stories, the ones that you never see on TV." Manny described three ongoing documentary projects that would elicit volunteers' creativity. Berta had started a project on a local break-dancing troupe with four girls between the ages of eight and fourteen.[33] She would continue to work on the project. A second project documented the Chicano boycott of a local bank in 1972 after the owner publicly disparaged Mexican Americans. A third project had begun recording interviews with residents who had altars in front of their homes.

From here, the meeting moved forward to a brainstorming session. Manny opened, "So what would you like to make a movie about?" The room fell silent. For the past fifteen minutes, Manny had been talking while others had listened. Except when Manny referred directly to Ana, Sara, and Elsa, the girls looked around and doodled on their agenda sheets like children in a classroom. Respectfully, they had kept quiet while the adult talked. Now, Manny had directly requested their participation. Berta and Pablo already had projects to work on. Monica and I offered to help in whatever was needed. During the meeting, the three youngest participants ate one serving of Frito pie and did not ask for seconds. Feeling the pressure, they became nervous. Sara giggled shyly every time Manny looked at her. When the girls did not talk, Manny addressed questions to them directly. "Oh, you just want to make a telenovela don't you?" he asked, sending them into nervous laughter. "Something romantic right?" Repeating the question, Manny was clearly teasing the girls to get them talking. The direct questioning had the opposite effect. They blushed, looked down, smiled, and said nothing.

In the absence of discussion, Pablo, the new staff member, said, "Well, I would like to do something that's higher quality." He then detailed what a "higher quality" production would be. It would have a small cast of actors, a lighted set, costumes, scripts, and special effects in a full-length running time plot; basically, he envisioned a feature film made in the classical Hollywood mode. His suggestion was not completely surprising. Over the two years I would participate in similar video project meetings, new volunteers often spoke of their desires to make a video that replicated mass mediated forms and contents. Until Pablo had defined his "movie" idea, mass media was relatively absent from the conversation except in opposition to SACA's oral histories and a lighthearted tease. The suggestion generated some tension. Berta rebuked Pablo, calling the latter's vision unfeasible and unrealistic because of SACA's limited resources and equipment.

Still the girls had not spoken. Finally, Manny described the two video projects that SACA volunteers had started in the past but never finished. Whereas the first video about the bank boycott had a historical focus, the second video about altars had a more cultural focus. Manny asked the girls to think if they would like to be involved in one of these projects. They nodded affirmatively and signed an address list before going home. I left the meeting, too. A week later, I phoned Ana, Sara, Elsa, Juan, and five other teens and preteens to begin working together on what eight months later would become "Altars on the West Side."

Even in this initial meeting with my future video crew, I recognized the collective process by which video contents were decided. With phrases like "your own vision," Manny created a context that encouraged people to think of video contents that represented their own cultural experiences. At the same time, SACA failed to achieve completely collective participation. In the room, the participants' cultural experiences ranged widely. Manny was the oldest member and the group's director. Monica, a Mexican American teenager, had extensive video experience through a program at her magnet school. A theater actor, Pablo was older than Monica, but he was just learning video through his coordinator position. Berta and I were the only Anglo Americans at the table. Both in our twenties, we had some video experience, but whereas I was new, Berta had been with the project since its inception. Finally, there were three working-class, Mexican American girls—Ana, Elsa, and Sara—all first-generation Americans with almost no video experience. Among the members, they occupied the most marginalized social statuses in terms of race, gender, class, and age.[34] Manny tried to overcome the girls' potential marginalization from the meeting in two ways. First, he validated the girls' working-class, Mexican American culture by referencing and praising past west side arts projects. Second, he spoke to them directly and with respect, not as if they were children or inexperienced in video. Even these measures could not tear down social barriers that predated the girls and enforced their cultural oppression. The hierarchies between SACA members did not disappear, as evidenced by the girls' shyness, their nervous giggles, and their silence when it came time for them to participate.

As a result, SACA members had to fill in these gaps with their own ideas for video contents. Inadvertently, SACA members had already promoted certain video contents over others by contextualizing the organization's history and suggesting certain video ideas. For example, Manny's description of past local arts in the west side implied an oppositional stance toward mass media, at least in the past if not in the future.[35] To a new member and ethnographer like myself, contextual clues in members' speech identified SACA with a residual Chicano nationalism. After the meeting, I gathered that locally lived experiences, such as mural painting, conjunto, and break dancing, were preferable to videotaping an imagined telenovela romance. Similarly, I thought that certain cultural forms such as murals, newspapers, and documentaries were preferable to more commercialized forms, such as a Hollywood movie.[36]

The contextual clues were necessary in establishing an invisible schema for acculturating new members, especially since the participatory form of the meeting discouraged direct criticism of volunteers' ideas. Manny's teasing gently guided the volunteers away from mass media materials while not criticizing their love of the genre.[37] These contextual clues served an important educational purpose. For adolescents who only know mass media texts, developing their own vision necessitated adult guidance for at least two reasons. First, SACA did not have the resources to create the flashy professional texts that the young crew members already knew. The project had to operate within the limits of one camera, a tripod, one light, and the few daylight hours remaining after school in the winter months. Second, SACA strove for original visions as a creative cultural arts program. Editing televised video segments with music from a Top 40 rock group may be an acceptable video project in some educational settings, but it would not fit easily in SACA's goals, especially because copyright restrictions would prevent public sharing of the project. Eventually, the young volunteers would be able to develop these contents without assistance, but initially the schema clarified an otherwise ambiguous discourse around video contents.

PRODUCING A VIDEO

"Altars on the West Side" differed from previous video projects in SACA in several ways. First, the ten youth volunteers I worked with ranged in age from twelve to seventeen. They were older than volunteers in other SACA video crews, allowing them to control most aspects of the video production process. Second, youth members had access to editing and postproduction equipment.

Pablo's ties with a nearby arts center and my connections with a local university allowed the teens to work on every stage of the video-making process, an impossible task in the past. Third, my role as a researcher in the video crew fostered the youths' autonomy. I relied on the crew to make their own decisions and then presented them to Manny or Pablo in regular meetings about the project. "Altars on the West Side" thus presents a good example of the negotiations that took place over SACA's video content between the youth volunteers and the adult facilitators and staff.

Although the crew members did not devise the altars topic themselves, they made the project their own through their storyboards, interviews, camerawork, and editing. The video adhered to a documentary format but adapted MTV video aesthetics, such as special effects, mainstream pop music, and a choppy editing style. Their video content drew heavily on mass mediated discourses, worrying some staff members whether the video would still express the youths' cultural identity.

Manny never directly challenged the youths' vision of their video, but he expressed concern over the role mass media would take in it. He envisioned a fifteen- to twenty-minute documentary that showed what altars are, using interviews and a voiceover narration. For example, he imagined two youth narrators talking to each other about the altars in their own colloquial language: "Hey man, did you see the altars?" The participants would ask questions about the altars and their significance, which would be answered in the interviews. When I took these ideas back to the crew members (Ana, Sara, Elsa, Juan, and his friend Carlos), they were unenthusiastic. Carlos said the idea sounded like "just another boring documentary." In particular, the participants said the voiceover narration sounded forced. Elsa said that she would never talk with her friends about altars in real life. These negotiations over video content continued throughout the video-making process.

As a facilitator, I played my own role in determining the video content. In trying to accommodate the video crew's vision of their project with the staff's concern that the video still incorporate local cultural elements and realist styles, I let the participants choose their own music, but I limited the number of compact discs I would buy for the project. This forced them to emphasize the interviews over the music, preventing a possible "rockumentary." In a video screening with nearly all of the volunteers in the spring of 1998, the video crew members noticed that the final project reflected a compromise over the video's content. The girls critiqued the lack of mass media devices, special effects, and music. They claimed that if they had overlaid popular songs with each interview, it would make the video more interesting. Ana disliked the opening, saying, "I think we should hear the song longer in the beginning." This is not to say they did not like the final product. During the screening, they sat mesmerized at what they had helped create and laughed at all of the appropriate junctures. Their documentary was not boring in their view. However, the video content was not the one they initially set out to produce, reflecting the compromises I initiated to make sure the video was still an altars documentary.

My actions fit into an overall structure of negotiation that determined video content in the altars project. The fact that the video crew wanted to include the song in the credits showed the group's attempts to be inclusive in their production. This demonstrated the utility of the humanistic orientation of the project. Everyone who appeared in front of the camera made a cameo appearance in the video, and everyone who shot video footage had at least a few frames included in the final edit. The crew also took care to include footage from the interviews that respected the interviewee's dignity. For example, they allowed neighbors to change their clothes and arrange their hair for interviews. The video crew had adopted an ethic that was aware of their own power to objectify people in their filmed work.[38] As such, the interviewees worked to undermine an objectifying gaze to the extent that volunteers tried to humanize each interviewee.

After the first few weeks of taping, the crew decided not to include altars in the video unless the owners approved. That day Ana had learned in high school that taking a photo without someone's permission is an invasion of privacy. Together with Sara, Elsa, Elsa's friend Nora, and Henry, Ana applied the school lesson to their video, adding that it was immoral to tape an altar without permission. These rules illustrated the flexibility between the youths' cultural contexts, on the one hand, and the moral respect for the community, on the other. Together, they integrated learning and experiences from school and home into a vision of the community as part of the family.[39] Thus the video production rules resulted in content that showed a plurality of working-class Mexican Americans in respectful and dignified ways.

In the editing process, the youths tried to include every volunteer's footage in the video, even if they could not come to the editing room. In the opening sequence, the succession of the fifteen to twenty shots displays the democratic use of each crew member's video footage. As a result, many of the altars shown in the opening shots were not necessarily our best aesthetically.[40] A spotlight glazed over a nativity scene, obscuring Joseph's face, while a dark exposure in another shot gives a Mary statue the appearance of floating on a sea of green. In choosing interview footage, the youths selected the most fluid answers to their questions, illustrating another attempt to be respectful of community neighbors while being cognizant of the desire to include clips from male and female, young and old interviewees. A "mistakes" segment at the end became the repository for displaying footage that did not make it into the preceding ten minutes of tape.

The tensions that surfaced over the video content of "Altars on the West Side" revealed the strength of SACA's participatory process. SACA, in this sense, follows in the footsteps of other social movements in that the co-construction of an egalitarian social sphere did not erase conflicts over participants' end goals. Referring to nonviolent social movements in the 1970s, Barbara Epstein writes, "By requiring that everyone participate actively in decision making, it brings differences to the surface that might otherwise remain unexpressed and provides an arena for persuasion and understanding."[41] Similarly, it was impossible to satisfy everyone's vision of the final project, but compromise ultimately helped the project define itself through members' conflicting ideas of what the video should look like. In the future, Manny said, SACA aimed to give each video crew full autonomy to conceptualize and execute their own videos. At our last meeting in 2001, Manny had dedicated a video camera to the mural project crews to create videos about their art and the process of making murals. For aspiring muralists, video was the perfect medium to express their own visions about their art while maintaining the cooperative spirit that the large paintings demanded.

Video Distribution and Exhibition

If mass media influences created tensions in defining a grassroots video about Mexican American altars, then the decision of whether to translate the video to English generated disagreement over exhibition goals. After seeing one of the final versions of "Altars on the West Side" in March, Manny exclaimed, "This is exactly the kind of videos we ought to be doing." He wanted to send the video to film festivals and exhibit SACA volunteers' work. In April 1998, Manny suggested submitting our video to CineFestival, a local showcase for international, Latino-produced film and video in June. Yet when I asked four of the girls (Sara, Ana, Nora, and Elsa) about the competition, they said they did not want to submit the video. When I told Manny, he said I should stress how film festivals and public exhibitions were part of the process of making the video.

In theory, I agreed with both groups. Public exhibitions would stimulate recognition both of the volunteers' good work and of SACA's general video project. I also sympathized with the girls' reasons for not showing the video. They thought of the video as their property and wanted to decide who would see it. For them, their family and friends could see the video but not a group of complete strangers, such as a film festival audience. These differing views over exhibition surfaced and became more vested in the next few weeks. Pablo was in charge of submitting film festival entries. He called me, sometimes daily, to remind me to make copies of the altars video to submit to CineFestival.

During that time, Pablo stressed that the girls needed to translate the Spanish interviews in their video into English.[42] Translation became a pivotal issue because it determined where the video would be exhibited and who would see it. The female participants were a united front against Spanish-to-English translation of the video. "If they want to understand our video, they should learn Spanish," Sara stated flatly. Her use of the word *they* was somewhat ambiguous, referring to an Anglo viewing public but also including the Mexican American video volunteers who did not understand Spanish. When I pointed this out, the girls then saw translation as an issue of equity. "If we translate the Spanish into English, then we should translate the English into Spanish, too," suggested Ana. By translating both languages, they reasoned, monolingual Spanish speakers in the community would also have access to the entire video. Indeed many of their own family members spoke mostly Spanish, including Nora's mother. In addition, translation took both time and effort outside of the community. Translation forced the video crew to spend more time using digital editing equipment located across town in a north side university library. Although Ana and Sara enjoyed the well-manicured campus, they felt uncomfortable. "We're like the only Mexicans here," Ana observed. To spend another twelve to twenty hours in that environment to make the video more palatable to people who do not speak Spanish was unacceptable to them.

From the first video meeting, Manny and I had told volunteers that the altars video was for them, but we also meant for SACA and the community as a whole. Through exhibitions to different kinds of audiences, the video could speak to the cultural recognition of west side residents, San Antonians, or Mexican Americans as a whole. At the same time, community members constituted a different kind of audience from the people who go to film festival premieres.[43] Whereas the latter audience may be members of an artist or documentary community, the former might use the video for more personal reasons, such as discussions or training sessions. Although SACA did not privilege either audience, film festivals played an important role in SACA's institutionalization.

In the current political economy of cultural arts production, grassroots video projects needed film festival screenings in order to survive. According to Sean Cubitt, "Reformist politics re-emerge as struggles for access clash with an emergent sense of what is 'good' video (and considerations of survival), while funding agencies in the late 1980s reassess their commitments to

community-oriented loss-making projects. The tyranny of 'good taste,' of professional standards, of chasing festivals, prizes, and reviews, become necessary
attributes in the new mixed economy model of video production."[44] SACA
included film festival screenings of their videos in grant applications and sent
copies of the videos themselves to potential donors and granting agencies.
Corporate sponsors noticed SACA in part through the distribution of their
professional-looking videos in film festivals and charity events. SACA received
its first major grant in 1997 from SBC, one of the two largest telecommunications companies in the United States and a powerful force in the San Antonio economy. In this way, exhibitions publicized SACA's ability to accomplish
what they set out to do: provide access to people who would otherwise not be
able to create their own video visions.

As we approached the CineFestival deadline, I tried to make this aspect
of SACA's community more visible to the girls, but ultimately I had to co-
erce them. I refused to give the participants their copy of the video until they
helped me translate. Hence, their parents and friends could not see the video
unless a wider English-speaking public could also see it. Resentful, Sara said
to me, "I thought the video was already done." Ana added, "Yeah, I thought
this video was for us." That year, "Altars on the West Side" premiered at two
film festivals. SACA invited them and their families to both premieres, but
the female participants did not attend either. They said they had family en-
gagements or other commitments. After the video received positive feedback
from other community members, however, the girls seemed more positive toward the screenings. They were more enthusiastic about the video exhibitions
and said they wanted to attend a film festival in the future. For them, the
most important audience still remained their families. I dubbed a copy of the
final translated version for each participant. The girls beamed when they said
how proud their fathers were of them. Despite their critiques of the altars video,
all of the participants were enormously proud of it.

The Successes and Challenges of an Alternative Video Project

SACA's ability to create an emergent culture in which working-class Mexican Americans produced their own videos depended on countless interrelated
factors but coincided with at least two results of the process. First, video content reflected participants' cultural identities to different degrees. Second, some
participants were interested and active in the altars project, and other participants left at different points in the process. These results were not "effects,"
in the traditional empirical sense, but rather indicators of SACA's successes
and challenges for the future in terms of video content and the production

process. In all of these issues, the greatest beneficiaries of the video project were the participants who stayed with the organization the longest, raising questions of sustainability over time for alternative media projects.

The content of "Altars on the West Side" most reflected and reinforced the Mexican American Catholic cultural identities of the three girls who participated in the video project from its first meeting. Ana, Sara, and Elsa proudly displayed their active Christian faith during the video-making process by wearing crosses, "What Would Jesus Do?" bracelets, and even a "Thank You Mom For Not Aborting Me" T-shirt. They reflected constantly on how much the video taught them about "real miracles" that altars could accomplish with the power of faith. As they videotaped miraculous stories about altars, the girls became even more cognizant that Catholic altars were an important part of Mexican American culture.

Specifically, the girls' interview with an elderly woman generated a conversation among them about the need for young Mexican Americans to carry on the altar traditions of the old. After the interview, the woman cried as Elsa and Sara helped tidy the altar. In the car, Ana told us, "She cried 'cause her son died and now nobody fixes up the altar." The emotional outburst generated concern. The story passed through all of the crew members and SACA staff. We spent two afternoons discussing whether we should organize a clean-up crew to protect altars from destruction such as the woman's. Although we decided not to embark on the plan, the girls still regularly walked by the woman's house to check on her altar. This interview, shown as the final one in the video, not only reinforced the tie between Mexican American identity and altars but also spurred the youths to think about how they will carry on the tradition.

For at least one of the video crew members, though, the relationship between altars and Mexican American identity was completely foreign and had to be forged in the video production process. A friendly fifteen-year-old, Henry was raised a Baptist. For him, the altars meant Catholicism, but Catholicism did not necessarily mean Mexican American. "This project was cool because I had no idea that altars were so important to people. Now I know about the miracles and why they have them here," he said to me on the ride home to the east side of the city. Henry grew up near other video participants but had since moved four times around San Antonio. He observed that none of the houses in his current working-class neighborhood had altars, though there were many Mexican Americans there, too. He even hesitated to recommend the ska music he chose for the video. "This doesn't really fit the theme of the video," he said to me in the music store, as if the music he identified with was outside of the video content boundaries. His sentiments illustrated the potential pitfalls of the video's message. Since all of the videotaped interviews introduced aspects of making, having, or venerating altars as Mexican Americans, Mexican Americans who did not have, know about, nor perhaps even like altars may have felt excluded. In this case, the desire to present a unified representation of Mexican American identity on the west side as Catholic overrode the desire to be all-inclusive. This became a representation that at one time was empowering for the imaged Mexican American Catholics and disempowering for the Mexican Americans who were absent.

Henry's sentiments did not negate the importance of the video project to his life. Once a week he still called me enthusiastically to participate in the project. For those who stayed with the project, the video-making process raised participants' self-esteem. The initially shy and quiet girls now spoke out about the new videos they wanted to complete. Manny recognized Ana's ability to come to SACA alone without her friends as a sign of newfound independence generated from her desire to do video. As a former SACA board member and academic colleague of mine explained, grassroots video projects can stimulate "a qualitative shift in . . . self-perception" when the video validates participants' own marginalized identities in contrast to the "televisable" middle-class identities on prime time.[45] Sara, Ana, Elsa, Nora, and Henry could not believe they had continued with the project for an entire school year. "If I had known we were going to stick with it, I would have gotten more dressed up for the video," Sara exclaimed in her first screening. Her desire to use the video as part of her college portfolio demonstrated her quick adaptation of the video project into a positive future profile in which the video would market her cultural identity to the outside world.

I can only speculate why SACA's production process failed to interest those who did not stay with the altars video project. Two of the most experienced members of the video project, Juan and his friend Carlos, left the project after only four months of shooting footage and assisting video crews. I did not realize that the boys quit the project until one day when Ana told me that Juan purposely lied to me when he said he would come to video project meetings. At the time, the boys had enrolled in single-sex extracurricular sports, such as football and basketball. In contrast, SACA emphasized the importance of mixed-sex video crews. In the beginning of the altars project, both teenage boys considered themselves leaders. They had participated on the mural video and expected to do much of the taping and editing for the altars project. Over time, the boys and girls became less cooperative, as evidenced by countless bickering matches. I tried to balance power relations between the genders, but ultimately I played the authority role in these arguments. I suspect, too, that the boys would have felt more comfortable working with a Mexican American, male facilitator. When they left, Henry missed their presence. He said the project was more fun when the boys were around and insisted that we continue calling them to participate. In mixing boy and girl video crews, I can only hypothesize that the pluralistic spirit of the video project may have actually turned some volunteers away. As other video crew members joined then left the project without telling me, I began to recognize the delicate balance SACA struck in trying to include everyone in its video crews.

Recent ethnographies of grassroots video projects portray largely utopian narratives of the cultural transformation of their subjects through the production of a video. For example, the participant-observers in one video project concluded that women of color became more confident from the video-making process: "Given the tools, space, and encouragement, youth are able to construct powerful and engaging representations of their own lives."[46] Looking at my own field notes, I also tended at times to overgeneralize the power of video. On 3 May 1998, I wrote: "We didn't talk about much today, but I realized something Manny had told me a long time ago. Watching the girls see the translated video, knowing that they like and want to see it in two festivals (San Francisco and CineFestival) made me happy. This is about building community on various levels. The adults here today had known each other for ages. They were laughing and joking, even though this is work. Everyone feels a responsibility to be here." Yet this unbridled optimism was just one moment of many. A week later, working with a new video crew, the entire process had to be started from scratch.

Grassroots video projects do not create citizens. Rather, they are places that potentially reinforce the ways that people feel like members of a community. SACA members were aware that they could not work with their participants in a vacuum. At home, parents supported their children's involvement with SACA. In school, volunteers learned that video making could count as an extracurricular credit toward college. These cultural contexts supported SACA's charge and motivated its young members. Many of the volunteers grew up with Inner City Development programs, which equipped them with interpersonal skills, educational tutoring, and basic needs like food and clothing. By the time many volunteers joined SACA, they already practiced working in teams, goal setting, and learning new ideas. They knew that they could come to make a video and have a sandwich next door if they were hungry, for Inner City Development, too, provided SACA's structural support in the community. As long as SACA and Inner City Development were neighbors, residents saw the two as cooperative sites for cultural arts and social services.

These strengths behind SACA's video project were also weaknesses, particularly when SACA depended on extraordinary volunteers to grapple with the west side's daunting social problems. Low incomes, high teenage pregnancy rates, and school dropout rates compounded the challenge of creating a shared video project in the community. In this context, few people were willing and able to balance cultural arts with other social and economic demands. Many volunteers left SACA after a few weeks because a family member was sick, work schedules changed, or the family needed extra income.

The most dedicated young SACA volunteers were or soon became model students. They got good grades and were active in civic life. The video project was one of many activities that occupied their attention. In my own video crew, six of ten volunteers joined extracurricular sports teams in the 1998–99 school year. They and the rest of the volunteers also belonged to academic clubs, mentoring programs, art collectives, and church youth groups. SACA risked losing these volunteers when they decided video was a low priority activity, whether for personal ("my friends do something else") or practical ("this will not help me get a scholarship") reasons. Of the ten volunteers in my video crew, only two participants showed interest in continuing to make videos. The difficulty in retaining video project volunteers endangered the possibility of creating a sustainable circuit for video production in the future and emphasized the fragility involved in the process of creating community around cultural identities. After a few years struggling to keep staff and update technology, SACA eventually abandoned the video project as a separate creative project, using the camera to document murals and street events once again.

Access and Process in
Mexican American Alternative Media Production

For the time that the video project lasted, it offered an alternative infrastructure for the production, distribution, and exhibition of images of Mexican Americans. By providing local residents with the tools and know-how to create their own images, SACA extended public access to an oft-forgotten part of the city. This in itself was an alternative to the rhetoric of equal access that permeated the discourse of Mexican American media producers who defined their rights in terms of consumer markets, business networks, and commercial resources. To SACA, the idea of a "public" rescued the idea of access from an imperative of competition to a means "to educate, to communicate, and to empower local citizens."[47] For the teenagers who came to SACA, the "public" included, first, the video-makers themselves as they worked to collectively imagine the project and, second, the audiences for their videos, who became their families, friends, neighbors, as well as festival attendees, university students, and granting agency workers. Their vision of the public stressed participation over the profit motive that drives commercial mass media. Further, SACA's "public" prioritized Mexican American working-class citizens who in theory may have the same rights as all other citizens but in practice rarely have the means in a city still largely segregated by the combination of ethnicity and class. Albeit on a small scale, the video project assumed access as a necessary condition for all Mexican American citizens to participate in public culture.

Still, equal access did not ensure equal participation. SACA tried to go beyond liberal notions of equality by creating a process based on communitarian values and respect for cultural differences. Over the two and a half years that I volunteered with SACA, Manny, Pablo, and other facilitators repeated the format, style, and discursive content of my initial video meeting approximately every other month. Among veterans, the reiteration of SACA's history and goals reaffirmed each member's role in that history and their commitment to the goals. New volunteers learned this information and, by participating in the group, many began to recognize the history and goals as their own. Hence, within the group, the meetings encouraged volunteers to recognize each other as equals committed to a set of unified but flexible goals. The radical idea that equality should extend beyond access to technological resources to the decision-making process itself produced its own tensions, as members could not help exerting their power over each other. Every decision, from time scheduling to the creation of content, influenced who could participate and on what terms. Some volunteers were uncomfortable voicing their opinions, while other volunteers tended to dominate the process. The tensions involved in the production and exhibition of "Altars on the West Side" illustrated the impossibility of recognizing everyone's cultural identities at all times. Language, age, gender, ethnicity, generation, and religion divided the crew members and staff as they negotiated how to validate each other while representing the community. This resulted in internal hierarchies that the group tried to dismantle with each repetition of the process. When each video was finished, old volunteers left and the new volunteers began the process of training, collecting video footage, and editing all over again.

In the end, the final products were as multicultural as the process itself. "Altars on the West Side"—along with the tens of other videos that were started or finished during the video project's duration—showed more diverse representations of Mexican Americans than have ever emerged through commercial mass media. In the videos, Mexican Americans were old and young, bilingual and monolingual. They liked heavy metal and conjunto music, telenovelas, and talk shows. They imagined themselves through original poetry and television program parody. The videos combined the local history of the west side with the global popular culture of film, television, and radio. In short, the videos' hybrid forms and contents reflected the diverse knowledge and tastes of the producers themselves, citizens who consumed mass media but also desired an alternative to them.

Chapter 6

Searching for Media Consumption and Cultural Identities

ALTHOUGH WE GATHERED to produce our own media, commercial mass media were omnipresent in the daily activities at SACA. Teens talked about media constantly. They scheduled their time around media consumption and created their own spaces to consume alone and with others. They participated in the hype of fan materials, concert tickets, and chat rooms. Much of my own work with the young volunteers at SACA relied on our common media interests; logging video footage did not seem so boring if we could talk about Justin Timberlake or the latest Spanish-language telenovela.

Consumption was, in these ways, productive. In the transnational landscape of mass media products, Mexican American young people used global media texts to define who they were in relation to their friends, family, and community on the west side of San Antonio. Music, films, and television programs mediated relationships. The youths' standards for what was cool and desirable reinforced bonds and hierarchies that replicated social divisions based on age, ethnicity, gender, and class while also sometimes surpassing them. By consuming and then talking about consumption, young people staked the boundaries of entire social worlds, expanding the world they experienced directly to encompass people and cultures that they could only imagine through mass media. These "families of resemblance," to borrow Marshall Berman's phrase, extended the youths' sense of community beyond national borders, creating shared allegiances with other consumers regardless of citizenship.[1]

At the same time, the youths were acutely aware of their differences as Mexican Americans from the west side. Lacking the disposable income and the unrestricted environments of middle-class children, the volunteers at SACA could not consume as much or as freely as other children in the United States. Media reminded them constantly that they were neither Mexicans, like their relatives, nor middle class, like the majority of the smiling faces they watched on television. As one female told me, she was "American" but "poor"—a difficult subject position to occupy when she wanted to buy concert tickets in order to feel like part of her fan community. This chapter aims to demonstrate that media reception is more than just an aggregation of readings based on gender, ethnicity, and class; it is also a dynamic process of interpretations within structural limits.

Mass media texts seem, in many ways, ephemeral. The favorite song of the summer was a memory by fall. A film critique might or might not be developed beyond a simple repartee between two friends. Yet over two years and frequent interaction, sometimes as much as four times a week, I could see how particular texts became more important than others, giving insights into the speaker's identity and social reality. Participant observation and interviews thus form the basis for an analysis that tries to capture the passing comments, the fragmented thoughts, and the short interactions, and tries to narrate their significance. As such, all of the following narratives are only partial, reconstructed through my field notes, which are, as Jean Jackson writes, "betwixt and between—because they are between reality and thesis, between memory and publication, between training and professional life."[2]

Media Consumption in Daily Life

Sara was fourteen years old when I first met her in 1997. Her family (five members in all) lived in a two-bedroom house located in the alleyway of two residential streets. Her parents, both Mexican immigrants, settled in houses within a one-mile radius from the rest of Sara's relatives in the United States. Of the participants I met in the video project, her environment was one of the most media rich. Sara's family had two television sets and the full range of cable stations. Sara possessed many audiotapes and saved money to buy compact discs to play on her family's boom box. She also owned a radio and a portable tape player with headphones, though sometimes she did not save enough money for batteries. Sara recorded music from CDs to tapes for herself and her friends who did not have access to CD players. She did not buy magazines, but she often rented movies with her family or went to the cinema on weekends. An avid media consumer, Sara watched television approximately from the time she woke up in the morning until she left for school. She also watched after school when she did not have extracurricular activities, such as soccer, the video project, or the Society for Latina Engineers. She often told me that she never had homework. At night, she watched telenovelas, talk shows, and sitcom reruns with her family. Her favorite channels were Univision, WB, Fox, and Disney.

Another high media consumer, Henry probably matched the total number of hours Sara spent listening to music and watching television. He was fifteen years old when I met him in 1997. Henry lived on the west side until he was fourteen, and since then he had moved to different houses in San Antonio. First, he lived with his brother on the west side. Then he moved to his sister's house on the east side. In 1998, he spent a short time on the north side before moving into his cousin's house on the south side. The youngest of four children, Henry moved with his handicapped mother each time until she died of a sudden heart attack in 1999. Henry's unstable home life obviously disrupted any fixed pattern of media access. For example, some houses had cable television and others did not. He occasionally read comic books but infrequently bought them. Nevertheless, Henry listened to music daily on his radio and cassette player, and he even attempted to write his own music. He often said he would like to own a CD player. Proudly, he showed me his one heavy metal compact disc that he used to play on other people's stereos. During the day and late at night, Henry watched MTV, ESPN, and television channels with syndicated sitcom programming. However, he reserved prime-time hours for watching telenovelas and Spanish-language movies with his mother. Other times, Henry consumed media alone, particularly heavy metal and classic rock music.

Whereas Sara's environment had high media access and usage, Henry's environment had lower media access but high usage. On the lower end of the spectrum, Monica's home had lower media access than Sara, and she also used media less frequently. Monica was sixteen when I met her in the summer of 1998. Since childhood, she had lived with her grandmother and her four siblings in a housing project apartment located one mile from SACA. With so many youngsters competing for use of the single television set in the house, the grandmother tightly regulated which programs Monica watched and when. She told me she enjoyed reading a paperback series called *The Babysitter's Club* until her younger brother carelessly tore up the books. She also searched out teenage magazines but rarely bought any. Virtually her only regular media consumption was a few television sitcoms after school, prime-time telenovelas, and the single video that her family owned: *Selena*. Monica, like the other teenagers, also enjoyed music that she could listen to privately on a portable radio. Her musical tastes included Tejano and popular rock groups such as Boyz II Men and Janet Jackson.

The variation between Monica, Henry, and Sara in terms of media access and media consumption demonstrates the diversity of preferences among Mexican Americans on the west side, and the ways their social environments restricted access to their favorite media. Despite their differences, all shared certain characteristics. First, all of the teens enjoyed media, not just individually but also in groups. Television viewing, particularly during the prime-time telenovela line-up, tended to involve family, friends, and sometimes neighbors. In these situations, the youths had little control over what they saw at certain times. In contrast, radio listening tended to be an individual activity. Most of the teens had either their own clock radio or a portable radio with headphones, thus they had more control over what they listened to and when. Second, all described using mass media both at home and in other places. In interviews as well as daily talk about media, they spent equal amounts of time discussing television, films, videos, radio programming, and tapes; they wove the topics together in general discussions cataloging everything they "did" last night. Finally, all the teens attended school. As obvious as this might seem, school injected large segments of media-less time into their weekday schedules. Thus media consumption fit into both the personal restrictions of home and the institutional restrictions of school, making SACA a place for studying consumption that was not like either location.

VIEWING SPACES

Teachers took ambiguous positions toward mass media in the classroom. Most forbade "mass media talk" about what they saw last night because they had to be silent while working, said Ana. San Antonio public schools on the west side did not offer a course for media analysis except in a magnet school located downtown. Even so, mass media were part of the curriculum, according to the girls. Documentaries, literary adaptations, and historical movies supplemented textbooks in most classes. Furthermore, schools showed blockbuster Hollywood films as "rewards" after the TAAS tests, which were required in Texas to graduate to the next class in the fifth, eighth, and eleventh grades. "They just show us good movies after the TAAS because we don't have to learn anymore," Ana explained to me.

In the absence of sanctioned conversation about mass media products, the female Mexican American teens wore images of their favorite mass media icons on their bodies. Sara, Ana, and many of their friends spent hours outside of class decorating their notebooks with cutout pictures from teen magazines. Lisa, Lydia, and Cristina, three sisters who worked with another adult volunteer, carried around mounds of *NSYNC paraphernalia with them, including pull-out posters, T-shirts, and baseball caps. The T-shirts could not be worn in class after the school passed a dress code policy in 1998. Still the youths still donned the caps as markers of their personal media preferences and as part of the needed symbolic work to identify themselves within Mexican American youth cultures.[3] Whereas mass media were visually present but never discussed in school, parents sanctioned media at home by allowing their children to watch television and play the radio every day.

Participants cited few restrictions on their media consumption at home. This was different from many middle-class families that strongly regulated their children to protect against the presumed negative effects of watching television.[4] Nora told me her parents preferred her to watch television at home alone after school than being "out on the streets all the time" with the video project. In other words, many parents felt mass media was an effective way of safeguarding their children from potential harm. The use of television as a private technology to control adolescents' entrance into the public sphere is certainly not uncommon, particularly for female children.[5] Parents encouraged their children to stay at home through relatively unregulated media consumption. Nearly all of the youths' parents worked outside of the home, leaving them to choose which television programs they watched and when. Many of the fathers also worked second night jobs or went out at night with friends, leaving their children in charge of their own late-night media patterns. In one case, however, Carlos's father cut the family's cable subscription when Carlos's brother refused to stop watching television—sometimes all night long. Carlos told me that his father, a truck driver, knew this was the only way to control his sons' viewing habits.

The teenagers frequently talked about prime-time viewing as the only other limit that parents enforced on their media consumption. In general, female family members tended to watch telenovelas together, leaving males in the house to either put up or shut up. Some boys, like Henry, learned to enjoy telenovelas, while others, like Juan and Carlos, went out with friends (much as their fathers did). During this time, television viewing was balanced with other family rituals, such as cooking dinner, playing with younger siblings, and doing homework. At the same time, the youths usually talked favorably about the family rituals in front of the television. The duality of watching while passing time with brothers, sisters, and adults in the house made this time special for the video participants. Often, we broke video sessions early because Ana and Elsa had to be home to see a "special event program," such as *The World's Greatest Magic Show* or *Cinderella*, with their mothers and siblings.[6] With so many responsibilities embedded in the act of watching television, the female participants made sure they were home on time for television programs.

The repression of talk about mass media at school and permission to consume mass media at home put a project like SACA in the margins of both school and home. Here, the volunteers could talk about media after school, though probably not as much as at home. Sometimes I "policed" the discussion if it meant excluding others from the group or ignoring some of the group members' goals. Through our interactions, video crew members paid attention to how and when to talk about mass media within the context of our group activities and play.[7] At the same time, I tried to be cognizant of when talk about media unified the group or created factions that made some participants want to go home, where they could watch television either alone or with others. Over time, I realized these factions were unavoidable, as media talk created hierarchies based on taste distinctions.

MEDIA CONSUMPTION AS HIERARCHICAL TACTICS

Driving the car, one of my duties at SACA, proved to be a lesson in media taste hierarchies, revealing who associated with whom and the nature of their bond. As soon as one participant shouted "shotgun," there was a race for the passenger seat. Having ridden with me in the past, video crew members knew I did not care what they chose to play on the radio. So the passenger seat rider controlled the radio de facto. From there, the debates ensued. Ana and Sara derided Henry's heavy metal station as well as Elsa and Nora's preference for Aqua songs. Juan and Carlos insisted on hip hop and rap music, which also validated Henry when the music was hardcore rap. Monica often argued with her sister Nicki and Nicki's friend, Francis, over which R&B song was the best, though all three preferred male singers over females. Sometimes I drove the video participants in Inner City's ten-seat van, making the gender and age differences between participants clearer. Girls tended to sing all the words to the song, teasing those who made up words. Boys did not sing and mocked the girls who did by overacting and using falsetto voices. Younger children, ages seven to thirteen, also preferred the more bubbly pop songs, such as "Barbie Girl," while teenagers preferred slower, more soulful R&B songs, like "End of the Road." If I liked the song, sometimes I would sing, too, garnering laughs from everyone. These van trips, while extremely loud, served an important social function in helping the youths construct social relations. Among video participants who barely knew each other, the songs created allegiances based on a common language.

Divisions among the participants also were apparent in these settings. In particular, Elvis and Ben, ages sixteen and seventeen respectively, often displayed media tastes that exposed their social position as "weirdos" or "nerds" in SACA meetings. Other volunteers ignored them or, worse, laughed when Ben made lofty pronouncements such as, "It is a shame that the youth of to-day do not respect their elders." They talked about video games and Dungeons and Dragons, a role-playing fantasy game, though Ben was more talkative than Elvis. Their favorite movies had extensive special effects and science fiction themes, such as *Star Trek* and *Men in Black*. Ben and Elvis's media preferences and ways of talking about those media reflected their estrangement from the others in their peer group. Even other adults poked fun at their differences. Elvis was also an aspiring artist, admitting he spent more time in the art stu-dio than watching television or listening to the radio. Thus he could not even participate in most of the youths' daily media banter. Instead, Elvis encoded his media tastes in the altars video by editing together scenes that seemed more modeled after a fantasy game than any television program. Shots tended to be dark and ominous, using high impact lighting and dramatic tilts because they looked more "holy." He chose choir singing for nondiegetic emphasis. In his final scene, the choir crescendos to the end note and the video goes silent. He said he wanted the silence to be symbolic: "Like a prayer, when you finish it, there's only silence." Whereas other volunteers spoke openly about their media knowledge, Elvis embedded his knowledge in his art rather than becoming further marginalized by the others.

Over short time segments, cliques and allegiances seemed to spring from both internal negotiations of who was "cool" and what was popularly promoted in media texts at the time. I became aware of these power negotiations dur-ing an adult-supervised activity that called upon the participants to be team players. In an ice-breaker activity, boys and girls of different ages worked to-gether to create drawings of "cool students." Many of these were media-inspired, from "yo quiero" Chihuahua students (based on Taco Bell advertisements) to Godzilla and Chuckie (of *Child's Play*) replicas. A week later, the youth peer groups fragmented; girls and boys did not want to play on the same teams. Likewise, they rarely talked about the same media together. Whereas Mexican American teens socialized together around some media lan-guage or symbols, such as the Taco Bell Chihuahua, their media preferences developed more forcefully around the constitution of more exclusive, gendered age groups. Becoming members of social groups thus replicated the gender and age dynamics for social cliques outside of SACA, in San Antonio, and nationally.

Lay Theories of Media Influence

As the teens jockeyed for position within their own hierarchies of preferences, they drew upon national discourses to reinforce their authority over such matters. These lay theories functioned to assert young people's knowledge about media and their influence in context of their own lives. As such, their theories of what media do, to whom, and with what effect were flexible depending on the circumstances. For example, the participants generally thought films with stereotypical portrayals of people of color were harmless, unless they recognized the image as specifically referring to Mexican Americans in south Texas. In this vein, John Leguizamo's parodies of different ethnic groups in *The Pest*, African American gangbangers in *Boyz in the Hood*, and the Taco Bell Chihuahua were not maligning images worthy of concern. Instead, young people took pride in knowing which portrayals were real or fictional, demonstrating their knowledge of both media conventions and different people's identity. Henry knew, for instance, that the characters on *Seinfeld* were completely realistic, because "that's how people are in New York City." Conversely, Cristina, age ten, knew that the controversial film *187* was only a story and thus could be viewed without harm. She asked me one day if I had seen any good movies lately:

> VM: I saw *GI Jane* on video. It was really cool. Have you seen it?
> C: I don't know about that movie, but I saw *187* for the second time.
> VM: The second time? What is it about?
> C: Well it's about these students who have a gun with one bullet. They all take turns shooting it at the teacher and he dies. The first time I saw it was in the theater and yesterday my dad rented it for us.
> VM: Isn't that too violent for you?
> C: Oh no. [*Smiles*] I don't mind the blood.

In this somewhat typical interaction around age-restricted media, Cristina displayed her knowledge of the movie and her ability to handle the subject matter. Her pleasure with being "in the know" about the film aimed to show me not only her ambivalence around the film's topic but also her maturity in an interaction with an adult such as myself. By mentioning her father, Cristina also pointed to the social context for her viewing pleasures. Her father, whom she did not live with, rented the film, making the content less relevant than the fact of them spending time together. Lay theories of media thus reflected complicated social realities, ones in which young people established their relationships to the national discourses about media through their relationships to the people around them, including me.

When images appeared more relevant to their own realities, the participants seemed more concerned and critical of what they consumed. Unlike films that may be real or fake, many teenagers talked about the film *Selena* as a real story that disappointed with its fake conventions. On one hand, the film, which documented the life of singer Selena Quintanilla, was educational for the youths, many of whom were too young to know much about the singer at the time of her death. For them, Jennifer Lopez drew them to the theater, but they ended up learning a lot about their local culture. Henry said he learned a lot from it:

> H: The Selena movie was good because, you know, I never really heard her music and when I saw her video I was like, "Now I know why people like her so much."
>
> VM: Did you know she was from around here?
>
> H: Yeah, I knew she was from Corpus Christi, but I just, like, I never listened to her music and I never knew why people were so sad and why they liked her so much. But she did sing pretty good.

Like Henry, all of the participants enjoyed the film and claimed to have learned from it. What made it controversial, however, was the fact that it was partially set and filmed in San Antonio. Henry found flaws in the film's details, focusing on the location sets for events in Selena's life:

> It was supposed to take place in Corpus Christi and they had a lot of places that are here in San Antonio. Like there's a place in the movie where she's in Monterrey and she's supposed to sing there and she's doing an interview and it's supposed to be like a courthouse. . . . It's supposed to be like a big place in the city and it turns out it's the library downtown here in San Antonio. . . . And then I saw this—in one part of the movie when she starts singing, when she's a little girl. She starts singing first as Selena and Los Dinos at her first, I guess, place where she found this. Her dad opened up a restaurant and it's supposed to be called, I forgot the name, but it was supposed to be, I think, in I don't know where [Corpus Christi]. But it was not [there].

In a separate conversation with Monica, she echoed Henry's preoccupation with the film showing a San Antonio restaurant instead of a Corpus Christi one. Although they undoubtedly felt empowered by being able to identify false pieces of evidence in the film's argument, they never spent equal attention criticizing texts that were not directly related to their own experiences.

To this end, a Mexican American writer from Dallas penned one of the most inflammatory media texts for the teens. In 1997, freelancer Barbara Renaud González implied in a newspaper editorial that Mexican Americans were physically unsuited to become superstars in professional football, adding that Texas cities should pour fewer resources into a sport that de facto excludes them.[8] The editorial, which became a "news story" in the youths' discourse, caused a complete work stoppage at SACA as Carlos and Juan spent an entire video project meeting complaining about the story's falsity. For Juan, a potential quarterback on his high school team, the newspaper was spreading lies. "We made it to the finals last year over all the white schools. And this lady thinks Mexicans can't play. She's crazy," he argued. Carlos added that the Lanier High School football team would probably make it to the state championship next year, which would prove to him that the news was just trying to hurt the team's self-esteem. Because of the publication of this op-ed essay, all the news became biased in Juan's and Carlos's minds. According to them, the story should have emphasized Mexican Americans' progress in football, instead of criticizing their lack of success at the professional level. To rectify the story's damage, the boys planned to write a counter article in *El Placazo* outlining the success Mexican American sports teams have had on the west side, from football to golf. Their strategy not only reaffirmed their faith in the community paper to tell the truth but also confirmed their general distrust for anyone not from the community to write about something so important to them.

The football editorial was not the first time the teens focused on the ethnic dimensions of the news they heard. Young participants did not have to read the newspaper to identify positive and negative images of Mexican Americans, which could then eliminate or perpetuate societal racism in their eyes. That is, participants generally expressed their concern over representations not for themselves, for they were "in the know," but for others whom they saw as more vulnerable to strong media effects. Often called "third-person effects," children as young as eight presumed that more susceptible readers, including their elders, might be infected by biased media reports, though they knew they themselves were immune. In this way, the children could participate in national discourses about media effects, but with a perspective that honed in on the structural racism underlying news coverage.

After asserting that some people *do* become violent after watching horror movies, Ana and Sara still questioned the validity of a news program that emphasized the ethnicity of a violent perpetrator.

> S: [*To Ana*] Did you know that two Hispanics killed a woman after seeing *Scream 2*?
> A: That's dumb.

S: So now they're gonna say Hispanics get violent at certain movies.

A: Yeah, but we saw it and we're fine.

VM: How did you see it?

S: We snuck in.

VM: Through the back?

A: No. We went there and it was "18 and over" and they were checking IDs. So we got scared. But then we ran into someone Sara knew and he bought us all tickets.

S: And we're fine, and the media made a big deal that the men who killed that woman was Hispanic when anybody could have been affected by the movie, not just Hispanics. And now the woman's parents are going to sue the movie company.

A: That's not right.

S: Yeah, it's sad, but they shouldn't sue the movie.

Although it was impossible to dissect all of the ramifications embedded in a conversation taken out of the context of an entire afternoon, Sara and Ana's remarks about *Scream 2* highlighted a complex lay theory of media effects. Although the girls did not doubt the movie would affect some people in the wrong way, they took issue with the news coverage of the suspect's ethnicity. Reasoning that they could see the film without harm, they criticized the negative light cast on Hispanics in general and feared the consequences, first, in terms of public opinion and, second, in terms of hurting a movie company that gave them pleasure. Their lay theory of media effects thus negotiated a complex intersection of age and ethnicity by balancing their own right to see the adult film versus the news reporters' right to cover media effects in an ethnically charged way.

The youths' media talk played a vital role in constructing the different spheres of cultural identification. By talking about a scary movie, for example, youths adapted popular perceptions to their own circumstances by emphasizing social bonds, hierarchies, and visions of community that extended to all Mexican Americans. Their beliefs in strong media effects replicated the language of adults around them, thus drawing on their authority to criticize media texts in socially condoned ways.[9] This helped the teens talk to me about media in a way that sanctioned their own enjoyment of media texts while defending them against any potential criticisms that they engaged in mindless forms of entertainment. On the contrary, the closer media representations were to their own realities, the more serious and critical the young people became. When they felt a media portrayal maligned some aspect of their identity, the young Mexican Americans quickly became vocal critics of what they saw as unjust or unfair. My presence surely encouraged some of these critiques; children of color could show me they were "in the know" about ageism and racism in a way that I did not personally experience. Yet these commentaries also provided a public sphere for teens to debate the issues they felt were collectively important to them. As such, a discussion of the racialization of media effects could bridge the real disparities that Mexican American adolescents may have felt among themselves.

Imagining the Outside World

In getting to know several Mexican American girls on the west side, I became aware of their diverse media tastes. Although many watched Spanish-language television, they also loved English-language movies, such as *Scream* and *Titanic*, and popular television programs, such as *Ricki Lake*, *The Simpsons*, *Jerry Springer*, and *Seinfeld*. They listened to Mexican music generally with their families and to Top 40 pop music with their friends. Their media preferences were comparable to market research data for all youths and teens in San Antonio in 1998 and 1999,[10] suggesting that understanding these girls' identification with media entails studying both Spanish- and English-language texts across several media. As a result, I began looking at my subjects as fans of multiple media (e.g., magazines, radio, and television), genres (e.g., pop, hip hop, and Tejano), and idols (e.g., Bobby Pulido, Justin Timberlake, and Leonardo di Caprio).

The fluidity of the girls' consumer habits reflected the numerous consumer choices available to them in the media ecology of the late 1990s. Cable stations, specialized magazines, and radio stations competed for youth audiences, enlarging the media "flow" that the girls received in daily life.[11] In one way, the accelerated media flow made their identification more transitory and fragmented. The popular song of the summer of 1998 was a distant memory by the fall. Favorite telenovela characters changed constantly with the end of one story and the start of another. In another way, the different media encouraged different forms of consumption in return for the girls' identification. Radio stations repeatedly played from song lists that studios wanted to promote. Disc jockeys introduced new songs and faded out old songs weekly according to national record sales of a product. Television affiliates rebroadcast telenovelas that had already been successful in Mexico, in hopes that sponsors would invest in the American audience for such programs. Although these industries moved rapidly to sell new media materials, both radio and television used intertextual references to previous successful songs and novelas to provide continuity in the consumer markets for these items. The expansion of both industries thus depended on creating loyal groups of consumers who took pleasure in recognizing borrowed plots, characters, and stories in telenovelas, and verses, rhythms, and melodies in popular music. The girls thus might have liked different media texts from day to day, but those texts also happened to be those most promoted in the political economy of mass media.

In another way, however, Mexican American girls' media preferences reflected deeply personal negotiations over cultural identity in a social space largely ignored by mass media producers. Marked by their gender, age, ethnicity, and socioeconomic status, the participants I met through SACA were off the radar screen of the multinational corporations that created and distributed media with a far more affluent, and often whiter, consumer in mind. Nevertheless, when they consumed the global texts, they counted themselves as members of a much larger community of consumers. This identification was crucial to the girls' socialization into a nation where to be a citizen is to recognize oneself as a particular kind of consumer. In our daily chats, the girls compared themselves to the characters they adored, the stories that felt realistic, and the songs they related to. Their definitions of membership included people generally relegated to its borders: the young, the working class, and the ethnic immigrant. At the same time, their cultural affirmation was fraught with contradictions that exposed their exclusion from other communities, particularly those that were middle class.

WATCHING, LISTENING, AND TALKING

Although the female participants at SACA shared a common interest in telenovelas and pop music, the dimensions of their consumption were quite different. Television was a far more social medium in the girls' houses, located front and center in the living room and often adorned with lace doilies, religious figures, and family photos. On the occasions that I saw people watching television, it was often the children in the house, either accompanied by relatives or friends. Program selections seemed to emerge from a mutual agreement of those viewing. In contrast, listening to the radio could be more privately enjoyed. One teen confided that she sat in bed at night listening to the clock radio while her siblings and parents watched television in the main room. This was her personal time. Nearly all of the girls had a portable radio or boom box to facilitate individual listening. Among the older ones, cassette players and VCRs were central to a system of exchange. Girls recorded favorite songs for each other off the radio or programs off the television, though these practices required some capital. One of the girls had a portable tape player through a free mail offer, but she did not have batteries, rendering the technology useless. The VCR, in this case, was a bigger priority for the family that treated the tape player as individual property but the television as communal.

The social conditions around watching and listening reflected ways in which many of the adults interpreted texts for those media. Adults sanctioned telenovelas as a way of connecting both to a cultural past and a real social network of family and friends. They often introduced telenovelas to the girls who then became fans regardless of their Spanish abilities. One girl knew little Spanish, but between her mother and her own decoding abilities, she claimed to understand everything. By introducing girls to the genre, they became part of a female "common culture" that extended to Mexico.[12] For example, I met Lupe through SACA after she volunteered to help at a fundraising event. We spoke briefly and agreed to meet at a coffeehouse downtown for a taped interview. Her guardian and best friend's mother, Virginia, age forty-eight, also came. In their home, they were part of a longer lineage of Mexican telenovela viewers: "We come from Mexico, and in Mexico that's all that you look at. It just stays in your family and you just get into it," said Virginia. Even though Virginia moved from Mexico two decades earlier, the telenovela established an imagined bond to those she had left behind "who watch telenovelas all day."

For Mexicans living in the United States, telenovelas were a way to connect to women of all ages on both sides of the border, though these networks were maintained privately through relatives and close friends. Ana and Sara found out about new novelas from their parents, or they found out on their own when they traveled to Mexico. Lupe said she learned about novelas through her younger cousins in Monterrey: "A lot of them they'll be like, 'Well, this novela came out over here.' And we'll be like, 'Oh it just started over here.' And they're like 'It just started over there? That was a good one!' And they know what's going to happen, and we won't see that happening until maybe a few more weeks. Like maybe three weeks later, we'll be like, oh, okay, that's what she was talking about. There's a lot of communication." In exchange, Lupe said she might tell her Mexican cousins about Hollywood movies, establishing the basis for an equal information exchange about popular media. For example, she claimed that her cousins wanted to know the English names for movies because often the translated name had nothing to do with the original title. The more distant the network, the more telenovelas provided a stable referent point for females in otherwise very different cultural contexts.

In contrast, pop music fandom implied a far more age-segregated genre. Although parents bought pop music, magazines, and concert tickets for their daughters, they did not share their enthusiasm for the genre. In my car, the girls preferred to listen to KTFM 102.7. It was the only station in 1997 that broadcast a popular Top 40 format in San Antonio, and it was the girls' favorite station until 1999, when Clear Channel Communication opened the city's second Top 40 station.[13] In their parents' cars, the girls said they often listened to Tejano and other Spanish-language-format radio stations. Similarly, Top 40 was teen format at SACA, where the radio often played an oldies-format station when staff were around and KTFM when youths were working alone. Radio's mobility helped young people consume pop in their own spaces, though their favorite songs often infiltrated adult spaces, ingraining the lyrics into their memories, to their chagrin.

Whereas none of the adults complained that girls might watch too many telenovelas, pop music caused more concern. One family worried that pop music fan activities occupied too much of their daughters' time and financial resources. The sisters, Lisa, Lydia, and Cristina, adored boy bands, buying fan magazines and memorabilia with whatever extra money their parents offered them. More disconcerting to the adults around them was the fact that the eldest of the three girls spent her time after school and on weekends alone in the city's public library. Instead of spending time with the family, Lisa went to the free Internet room and logged into Web sites for her favorite pop singer, Justin Timberlake. There, she maintained a network of friends through Hotmail accounts and fan chat rooms. Although adults considered her solitary activity positive at first—the time spent in the library and on the computer seemed to them like a justified use of time for a young female—some of the SACA staff members worried that she had developed an unhealthy obsession. Lisa was first in her class and a leader in several extracurricular clubs. She was an ideal candidate for scholarly achievement. As she grew older, though, her grades slipped, though she still hovered in the top ten of her class. She continued with some extracurricular activities, but the trip to the library to communicate with *NSYNC fans took far more of her time. In the face of other budgetary needs, such as books to study for the SAT, Lisa's pleas with her father for concert tickets and a home computer with dial-up modem access seemed unreasonable to outsiders. In the latter half of 1999, staff volunteers, myself included, tried to convince Lisa to stay away from the Internet terminals at the library and resume her SACA responsibilities. Upon request, I showed her college materials on the Web and offered supportive words as someone who left home for college. When Lisa missed the SAT exam deadline and did not meet a school counselor to discuss scholarship opportunities, adults were frustrated. Lisa had let pop music consumption become an unnecessary distraction, in their estimation. Had telenovelas occupied her time, her fandom might not have been considered so disruptive.

Despite the differences, however, adults and adolescents alike heavily coded both telenovelas and pop music as female forms for consumption. Boys were likely to mimic the girls' favorite songs in falsettos, emphasizing what they saw as ridiculously romantic lyrics and harmonies. Similarly, telenovelas were unworthy of praise. Like daytime soap operas, a genre associated with "waste-of-time women's trash," many local residents associated the telenovela genre with lower-class feminine consumption.[14] Working with Sandra on an *El Placazo* article, we found that men tended to either deny watching or to blame their watching on women in the household. In the estimation of the men we talked to, telenovelas were a female activity unless they featured a very attractive star, such as Thalia. Even at SACA, Henry was the only boy to admit watching telenovelas, and then only "to spend time with my mom." Thus telenovelas locally carried a heavy social stigma, like English-language American soap operas, coding all viewing as feminine.

In these ways, watching telenovelas and listening to pop music were complex activities that implicated the girls' gender, age, and ethnicity in their repeated actions. They could stimulate praise or derision, social bonding or disruptions. Still, the girls enjoyed these two genres and identified with aspects of their texts. The summer months, during which they attended a camp next door to SACA, were full of favorite songs, films, and television characters as children fostered their common interests in the absence of classes. The video project, where I spent the majority of my time, also bred media talk as the same volunteers came back each day after seeing the same episode of the nightly telenovelas. Over time, they mentioned some of these texts and their performers more than others. The next section examines two very popular media products from 1997 to 1999, focusing specifically on how girls interpreted a telenovela and pop singers to express personal parts of their own identities.

Identifying the Outside and Inside: Telenovelas and Pop Music

While music was more or less omnipresent at SACA, either directly through the radio or indirectly through magazine cutouts and conversations, the girls' unique telenovela culture was less visible to me. I only began to realize the importance of the genre to many of them after listening to three girls gossip about *María Isabel* in January 1998. The novela piqued Elsa's, Ana's, and Sara's interest because it filled in some of the gaps in their knowledge about Mexicans, particularly indigenous Mexicans. I heard the girls talking about the "funny Indian language" that María Isabel's parents spoke on the program. "They say 'Quywhatu!' which means '*callate*' [shut up]," said Sara, giggling. Unlike other telenovelas, the indigenous language was the first thing that attracted the girls to *María Isabel* after hearing about the program from their Mexican relatives. Like their favorite pop songs, the telenovela was a ticket to another world, one that was familiar but also very different from their own. By reaffirming the familiar and the strange, Mexican American girls established aspects of their own identities in relation to the world around them. In this way, these transnational commercial products became symbolic in highly local and personal ways. Upon hearing their jests, I began watching *María Isabel*, too, so I could join the conversations.

Telenovelas and pop music cannot express the breadth of media that Mexican American girls consumed in the late 1990s, but these forms expressed the different kinds of pleasure they took in constructing their identities. Telenovelas helped the youths envision past identities. Popular music helped them envision future identities. These past and future identities intersected the present in the form of fantasies, in which, as Ien Ang writes, "alternative, imaginary scenarios for the subject's real life are evoked . . . offering the subject an opportunity to take up positions which she could not assume in real life."[15] Telenovelas and pop music were the media for exploring ethnicity, gender, and sexuality in ways they did not otherwise do around me. Ultimately, these interpretations communicated two different visions of community, even if in fleeting ways. Whereas telenovelas pointed to their cultural differences as girls living in the United States who were from Mexico, pop music heightened the sense that all girls could be the same in their pursuit of the perfect boyfriend.

THE MANY MEANINGS OF MARÍA ISABEL

Although *María Isabel* was not the only telenovela that the girls watched in early 1998, it became one of the most talked about in our group. Broadcast on weeknights at 7 P.M. for three months, *María Isabel* often lagged in ratings behind two other telenovelas on the same station: *Esmeralda* at 6 P.M. and *Pueblo Chico, Infierno Grande* at 8 P.M. All of these telenovelas aired originally in Mexico before appearing on KWEX–41, San Antonio's Univision affiliate. The producer of the programs, Televisa, specialized in the production of modern telenovelas, which it began exporting to the United States in the mid–1960s. According to Argentinean scholar María Soto, "modern" telenovelas contain a determinate series of stories that moves the characters through a part-real and part-fantasy world of contemporary Latin American society.[16]

The characters are transformed through the narrative, both by finding the object of desire and by discovering the truth or falsity of the past. The modern telenovela concludes upon "the constitution of at least one monogamous and heterosexual couple" who demonstrate the proper type of family in contrast to other family types displayed in side-plots.[17] Indeed, all three of the telenovelas airing at that time fit in the narrative structure of the genre. Yet, María Isabel was unique in that the girls said it was the first telenovela they had ever seen with a "real Indian."

Written approximately fifty years earlier by Yolanda Vargas Dulché, the story of María Isabel first appeared in her own serialized periodical, Lágrimas, Risas y Amor. Subsequently, Dulché and René Muñoz at Televisa wrote the popular story into a telenovela script, which eventually starred Adela Noriega and Fernando Carrillo, two rising actors in the industry.[18] Although not indigenous herself, Noriega played the lead role of María Isabel, a native Mexican in the countryside, who eventually becomes an acculturated, cosmopolitan Mexican citizen. Partially set in the lush Mexican countryside, María Isabel, like many other telenovelas, emphasized Mexico's natural beauty.[19] Meanwhile, the telenovela celebrates the protagonist's move into Mexican modernity. Together, the pristine nature and the championing culture make for a telenovela that narrates the parable of the "good Native" who becomes civilized while retaining an inner beauty and simplicity.[20]

This binary is evident through the lives of the two protagonists, who represent the urban and the rural in the plot. Ricardo Mendiola, an accomplished automotive engineer and maquiladora manager from a wealthy family, resides in a Guadalajara mansion with his daughter after his wife and only love dies suddenly. María Isabel Sánchez, his indigenous domestic, is from a small town in Nayarit, Mexico, where she lived in a hut with her argumentative but comical parents, Tata and Chona. María Isabel leaves home when her best friend dies in childbirth and she must hide the baby, Rosa Isela, from her powerful grandfather, Don Felix Pererra. While María Isabel encounters various dysfunctional families in the city, Ricardo falls in love with a seductress bent on stealing his money for her other lover. María Isabel eventually comes to work for Ricardo and they fall in love. They marry, but three intervening families cause problems for the new couple.[21] These families, all in urban settings, successfully separate Ricardo and María Isabel until the finale, when they return to the premodern village to mend all the broken families María Isabel left behind.

María Isabel is distinctly a story about Mexican cultural identities. Geographic settings in Toluca, Guadalajara, and Nayarit show rural and urban areas in Mexico. The closing sequence of the telenovela contrasts these images,

Figure 6. "María Isabel" played by Adela Noriega. *Reprinted with permission of Univision.*

showing maquiladoras and an indigenous village. The central narrative in the telenovela reinforces these contrasting images of Mexico. The indigenous village is fertile but untouched by urban hands. People in colorful costumes happily would work the land if there were no land barons to tax them. They play music, have large families, and speak occasional phrases in an indigenous language (with Spanish subtitles). In contrast, the Ford maquiladora is a symbol of Mexican modernity. Always expanding with Ricardo's guidance and American technology, the maquiladora as transnational assembly plant is only specified at the end of each episode via a few clean shots of the line. Besides that, we see the maquiladora only in scenes of the sparkling executive offices, complete with computers, cellular phones, and smiling blond secretaries. Catholic churches and home altars are also prominent Mexican settings in the telenovela, as they are marked by the iconic image of the Virgin of Guadalupe, Mexico's patron saint. María Isabel appeals to the Virgin throughout the story, representing religious syncretism between indigenous and Roman Catholic belief systems. The telenovela's cultural references made it specifically Mexican, and its social-realist elements mediated specifically national meanings to viewers within national-state boundaries.[22] At a time when the Mexican state still waged a repressive campaign against rebellious indigenous communities in the south of the country, *María Isabel* showed a docile indigenous community that lived peacefully in the social structures of the state.

These national meanings, important in a Mexican context, were not important in a San Antonio context. For although the telenovela had crossed the border each day, the girls I knew who watched *María Isabel* went to Mexico more infrequently. In general, the more removed the teen was from immigration, the less she traveled to Mexico. Monica, whose family had been in Texas for generations, hardly ever went to Mexico. Ana, whose parents immigrated when she was a baby, returned more often for the occasional *quinceañera* (debut party) or family holiday. During these trips, the girls said they visited their relatives' houses in Monterrey or other cities just south of the U.S.-Mexican border. There they remained under the care of their families. Sara said she went to parties, movies, and restaurants only with her cousins. Even in Mexico, girls' experiences were limited to the restrictive conditions of their families and finances. As a result, *María Isabel* became an opportunity to learn about Mexico rather than to reinforce knowledge they already had.

Ana and Sara told me on more than one occasion that they "learned" about Mexican indigenous peoples by watching *María Isabel*. Their comments reflected both on the state of their education system and the authority of the telenovela to educate. On the west side, most girls did not receive even the most rudimentary information about Mexico in their schools. Required to take Texas history in their curriculum, Ana and Sara, who were then fifteen and fourteen, respectively, said that telenovelas taught them where they were from. In *María Isabel*, the girls liked to refer to the cultural differences of the indigenous characters as evidence of their authenticity.

> A: Like in *María Isabel*, they have beads all over them. They have earrings that are beads.
>
> S: So they have *chanclas* [sandals]. And the men have ties.

They also talked about their colorful clothing, their dirt-floor hut, and their weird musical instruments. When I asked them if they had seen other "Mexican Indians," they responded no. I asked again if they ever saw them on the border. Ana responded, "Ohhh, yeah. Remember Sara? They beg for money sometimes in Laredo." When they thought about it, they had seen an indigenous Mexican, but to them, the telenovela's positive portrayal seemed more realistic, more truthful to how they wanted to read indigenous cultures.

When María Isabel acculturated to modern Mexican life, she transcended her identity of an indigenous or a Mexican woman for the girls, who came to relate her story to their own lives. As the weeks passed, María Isabel's transformation from "a real Indian" to a cosmopolitan Mexican became the focal point of the girls' comments and completely necessary to their enjoyment of the telenovela. Monica thought it was natural that María Isabel must learn how to dress, speak, and even play piano like a member of the Mexican upper class in order to marry Ricardo. After all, Monica reasoned the character could not go to live with her parents, adding, "She couldn't go back to her past." By equating living with one's parents with the past and an urban acculturation with the future, Monica's explanation had a local logic. After all, many of their Mexican relatives lived with their parents. Yet the girls saw the heroine as different; she was Mexican, but she was part of their culture, too.

As girls who saw themselves as American but also ethnically Mexican, they identified with María Isabel as a hybrid, a woman living between two cultures. María Isabel was fluent in the folk traditions of her native culture and yet prayed to the Virgin of Guadalupe, Mexico's patron saint. The girls noticed this duality in her clothing. "When she started out, she wore braids tied in ribbons and an all-white dress," said Nora. "Now she has just braids." The girls admired how María Isabel could fit into elite Mexican society while still maintaining some aspects of her original identity. Although Ricardo's relatives used María Isabel's cultural differences as evidence of her inferiority, the girls reinterpreted these signs as symbols of María Isabel's inner superiority. From the beginning of the program, they wanted her to not just become a part of Mexican society but also to preserve her roots.

When the program began in December, the researcher asked Sara what the novela was about. She responded, "It's about Indians and American people, I mean Mexican people . . . from the city. . . . And she [María Isabel] learns her language better so she don't sound like an Indian no more." In describing the novela's plot, Sara automatically focuses on María Isabel's transition into a modern citizen, one who is urban and well spoken in Spanish. Although at first she claims the modern citizen is American, she immediately realizes that the citizen in the novela represents a Mexican identity. The comment reveals the easy elision between a Mexican identity and an identity that is part Mexican, part American. In a later conversation, Ana and Sara said they had to learn how to speak Spanish better, too. "Sometimes our cousins will laugh at us because we don't say it right," explained Ana, adding that they spoke less in Mexico as a result. These words, spoken within the same afternoon, belie the obvious comparison between María Isabel's linguistic struggles and their own. Whereas María Isabel had to practice speaking Spanish to fit into Ricardo's family, Ana and Sara had to lose their regional dialect of Spanish to fit into their own families in Mexico.

As the telenovela continued, Sara and Ana clarified their identification with María Isabel's transformation into a "real Mexican." In doing so, they

projected their feelings toward Mexican society onto their own parents. I asked
Sara if it was bad for María Isabel to marry Ricardo. She responded:

S: No, she should marry who she loves.

VM: Would your parents be angry if you married someone like María
Isabel?

S: No, but it's none of their business who I'm gonna marry. I mean my
parents told me to leave home if I go out with someone who's Black.
But I will if I fall in love.

A: Sara's mom and dad are racist just like Gloria [Ricardo's daughter].

In comparing Gloria's and Sara's parents to racists, the girls saw the telenovela
as indicative of the identity clash between Mexican attitudes toward race and
their own. As Mexican Americans, the girls expressed their dismay that Mexicans, particularly their parents, harbored antiquated racial views that contradicted their own beliefs in a multiracial society. In this way, the girls partially
identified with María Isabel as a woman of color while also designating a Mexican national identity as the inferior "other."

This is not to say María Isabel was a role model for the girls. On one hand,
they admired María Isabel, calling her brave, strong, and deserving. On the
other hand, they knew they were different from her. Elsa spoke less often than
the other girls, but when she did talk in the group, she was more direct than
the others. María Isabel, Elsa said, was "the prettiest." María Isabel's slim figure was a recurrent topic of commentary. Ana said, "María Isabel wears like a
midriff. Her belly shows," referring to the character's body in a revealing indigenous frock during the program's opening sequence. Like other female pop
stars and actresses who displayed their flat stomachs at the time, the girls knew
that María Isabel's unattainable body was a sign of her eventual success.[23] One
day they compared midsections and decided they were "fatter" and "not as
pretty" as María Isabel and me, a clear reference to the shared ethnicity and
socioeconomic mobility of the character and myself. This was the clearest recognition of the representational limits of the program. Although they never
denied María Isabel was a "real Indian," they reproduced the class and gender
stereotypes that tied body image to female social mobility. What was a sign of
María Isabel's positive future became a sign of their own exclusion.

Emblazoned on her body and given the narrative conventions of the genre,
the girls knew María Isabel would achieve happiness at the end of the
telenovela, but they wanted more for their favorite character. Once they identified racism in Ricardo's world, Ana, Sara, Nora, and Elsa wanted María Isabel
to overcome the discrimination she faced, even if she lost her "true love" as a
result. One afternoon, they cheered María Isabel's confrontation with Ricardo's

Aunt Rosaura, whom they described as a "racist" because her overt prejudice forbade her nephew to associate with María Isabel. Similarly, they wanted María Isabel to punish Gloria, who was angry with her father for marrying beneath him. "She's a stuck-up brat. She should let him marry who he wants," asserted Nora, defending Ricardo's rights as an individual over his loyalty to his daughter. Yet the girls thought even Ricardo was racially biased when he said that María Isabel "would always be his Indian":

> s: That's wrong because it makes her seem inferior.
> vm: Well, what do you think will happen?
> s: I don't know. I think they'll break up because he doesn't respect her.

In our talk, María Isabel's struggle for recognition as a woman of color took precedence even over the predestined happy marriage between her and Ricardo. When the heroine eventually accepted Ricardo's paternalistic attitudes, the girls were disappointed.

María Isabel was as much a story of American immigration as it was a story of Mexican national identity. Like Horatio Alger, María Isabel was an ethnic outsider who came to the city to make a new life for herself. She worked hard to acculturate and yet never lost sight of who she was as an individual. This narrative, which the girls read easily into the telenovela, superceded meanings that Mexican viewers might have about a program that championed multicultural harmony at a time when the national government had repressed Zapatista rebellions in the country's southern regions. Instead, the telenovela's ideological charge was strongest in its ability to capture the American Dream while still mediating specific meanings about Mexico. By skillfully reading *María Isabel* in the two registers, the young viewers were capable of relating aspects of the telenovela to their own lives. It became a site for fantasies as well as criticism when the telenovela could not represent all of their own desires. The girls felt satisfied with María Isabel's achievements, and yet they identified with her more distantly at the conclusion of the telenovela than they had before. In the end, María Isabel had succeeded in ways that the girls felt they could not and failed in other ways that the girls could not respect, leaving Elsa to conclude that "that's just how it is there."

DREAMING OF BOY BANDS

Whereas the girls at SACA considered telenovelas specifically Mexican texts that they had to work to decipher, pop music provided fluidly open texts for them to dream about. Most of the time, the favorite song evaded explanation as to why someone liked it. Catchy rhythms and lyrics that were omnipresent on the radio emblazoned themselves in the unconsciousness of the teens who hummed the melodies while doing other activities. When asked why that song, as opposed to others, the teen might say the song was "cool" or "romantic," but she lacked either the forethought or the desire to explain her preferences more fully. The following week, the earlier song usually was forgotten and a new one arose in step with the radio playlist. Yet although the songs came and went, their singers drew upon the girls' fantasies more strongly. Pop stars, and the commercial goods surrounding them, were conscious parts of the girls' social interactions, defining both who they were and what they desired.

Nearly every girl at SACA carried the material evidence of their favorite singers. T-shirts, keychains, and canceled concert tickets helped distinguish *NSYNC aficionados from Ricky Martin fans. Thick binders, filled with pinups, clipped images from teen magazines, and publicity interviews of their favorite singers, accompanied them to school, weighing down their backpacks or oversized purses. Sara's scrapbook had overflowed from the binder to her school notebooks and locker, where favorite views of her favorite stars might be displayed prominently for public consumption. One day she wanted to show me her wallet. She had a school photograph of herself, a photo of her best friend, and several pictures of Bobby Pulido, her favorite Tejano star. She had larger versions of these images in her scrapbook. In the book, repeated images were permissible, even desirable, if something about the image had changed, such as the size of the photo or if a color photo was reproduced in black-and-white. Together with her friend, she shared scrapbooks with meticulous filing systems for knowing where images of Pulido ended and images of Boyz II Men began. The system also helped store knowledge about the stars. If Sara needed to know, for example, Pulido's favorite color, she had the information at her fingertips. The materiality of the girls' preferences identified them and their friends as intelligent consumers, who, with even the smallest weekly allowance, could participate in fan cultures.

These preferences reflected both market choices available to the girls and the symbolic universe that they encompassed. In the late 1990s, the pop industry sold young men as romantic Casanovas, suavely courting teen girls' affections. A well-seasoned music writer described the recipe for a top-ten song at the time: "The winning formula seems to be four or five young lads belting out songs in near-perfect harmony, either with lyrics of the love variety that promise young (and not-so-young) girls everything they've wanted to hear, or upbeat non-ballads encouraging males and females alike to shake their asses, which is exactly what these groups usually do during their polished, well-choreographed live performances."[24] Known as "boy bands," groups such as the Backstreet Boys, Nu Flavor, Boyz II Men, Take That, All For One, 98°, and *NSYNC shared common musical features in composing their romantic songs. Emphasizing vocals, tonal ranges, and harmonies over instrumental or lyrical skills, the groups featured their singers as the objects of fans' desires. For example, the official fan Internet site for *NSYNC (www.nsync.com) devoted a whole page to each singer as an individual part of the band's personality. Yet the site used only one page for all of the other band members together, relegating their importance to the site's margins. The site's subtitle, "Five Guys, One Sound," promoted the singers' ability to meld five voices into a single melodic harmony.

The unity of the music implied cultural melding as well. For all the diverse personalities presented in each boy band, the racial and sexual homogeneity of the groups reinforced the cohesiveness of the groups and their images. Few people of color graced the membership of these bands, which in their absence presented whiteness as the norm. Even a spate of Latin male singers, including Enrique Iglesias, Marc Anthony, and Ricky Martin, embodied whiteness, with their use of "mock Spanish," their "not too Latin looks," and their ability to cross into an "unmarked, white pop norm."[25] Male singers in the late 1990s hence combined many contradictions of cultural marketing. Prepackaged as individual heartthrobs with their own signature looks and moves, they still marketed themselves as members of an undifferentiated mass of whitened products for all girls to consume. Perhaps, for this reason, the girls differentiated the personalities of their favorite singers without ever discussing their race or ethnicity. Rita, age fifteen, simply compared her idol, Enrique Iglesias, to a "flying angel" whose fans worshipped and devoted themselves to "his beautiful breathtaking voice."

The malleability of the pop singers suited the girls, who imagined them in the positive, upbeat narratives of their favorite songs. Girls appropriated the transnational songs and singers to other local images that seemed authentic to their lives. Since many of them did not have access to MTV or other music video forums, they imagined the songs in their own contexts. The radio encouraged "dimensional listening" through which the sounds escaped the confines of a single visual picture.[26] By singing them aloud alone or together, pop songs narrated symbolic escapes from everyday life. This was apparent with two of the most popular songs in the field: "I Believe I Can Fly" by Sugar Ray and "Madly, Truly, Deeply" by Savage Garden. The songs fostered appropriation to the girls' own contexts with open lyrics that did not specify the gender, race, or age of the singers' objects of affection. I knew, for example, Dina as a spunky ten-year-old who often stood in the shadow of her older siblings and their friends. Like many children her age, she eagerly complied with the chores at SACA because she enjoyed the attention she got by being helpful.

During the summer we worked together, Dina's favorite song was "Madly, Truly, Deeply," a tune that touts a romance so deep that it makes the singer want to stand on a mountain and bathe in the sea with his love. When I asked her if she would like to video a short music clip on the song, she jumped at the chance and set about finding the highest mountain and widest sea in San Antonio—two geographical features she had never seen. Rather than searching for the scenery in the flat and arid city, I asked her to imagine a story to fit to the song. That was easy, she sighed. In her dreams, a Backstreet Boy crooned the song to her while she had become a princess on a mountain. In making the music her own, Dina and others appropriated the open lyrics to include their own characters, mise-en-scène, and plot lines.

Hits like "Madly, Truly, Deeply" offered the girls largely positive representations of the future, emphasizing personal happiness despite one's social environment. The girls' favorite songs thus differed sharply from the negative or angst-ridden visions of life as portrayed in grunge, "grrrl," and other alternative music genres that were popular with middle-class suburban girls during the same time period.[27] The boy-bands' songs espoused ideal and utopian visions of human relationships. Songs such as "I Swear," "I Do [Cherish You]," and "God Must Have Spent (A Little More Time on You)" promoted traditional, mainstream conceptions of heterosexual love, courtship, and marriage. Unlike some rap or hip-hop artists who mediated misogynistic messages, the boy bands revered women, putting them on pedestals. However, like some rap and hip-hop songs, the lyrics imagined a utopia where social differences and inequalities disappeared. In rap songs, public racism may be resolved through some political resistance, legal or illegal.[28] In boy band songs, the songs resolved private forms of racial exclusion through romance and acceptance. In the latter, any two people, regardless of their race or class, can fall in love and live happily ever after. To the girls who adored these groups, the songs imagined a safe, secure, and overall loving environment where all their dreams came true.

For three sisters, these dreams were embodied in the visage of Justin Timberlake, a blond, blue-eyed singer with the boy band *NSYNC. At a party in March 1998, they approached me, a rare occurrence, to say they wanted to make a video about *NSYNC. My conversation with Cristina, Lydia, and Lisa confirmed the use of *NSYNC songs to imagine their fantasy boyfriends.

LI: We want to make a video about *NSYNC.

VM: What about them?

LI: There's a song that needs a music video and we wanted to do it. Pleeeeeaaaase?

VM: Why do you want to do this?

LY: 'Cause we love them. We're all going to be their girlfriends.

Lydia then proceeded to explain why each of them selected Timberlake as their "perfect boyfriend." The eighteen-year-old from Memphis was the youngest band member and, like the girls, loved basketball.[29] The girls said they also liked the other singers in the band, Chris, Lance, J.C., and Joey, but occasionally bickered about which one of them would be "Justin's girl."

In previous encounters, I had sat by and watched them weigh the evidence in the debate over who could be "Justin's girl," which included the quality of pinups, articles, and other Justin-specific materials versus the quantity of Internet correspondence. Letters and computer literacy favored Lisa, because she could most easily take the bus alone to the library with free Internet access. As an assistant editor to the newspaper, she also had stronger writing skills to engage in a fast-paced chat room. From my standpoint, the pinup competition seemed relatively equal. Each one saved bits of the family budget to purchase fan literature, a major investment since the house did not have a telephone. The material comparisons, though, seemed less important than the emotional investment in Justin's suitability as a mate. Lydia thought she was the most dedicated to Justin, while she accused Cristina of liking some of the other boys as well. Disloyalty was a measure of a girl's unworthiness to be Justin's girl, though this did not mean they could not continue to adore him.

Though these debates could be intense, the conflict over their favorite idol displaced other conflicts among the girls. A week after the aforementioned party, Lydia and Lisa told me the group united them as sisters:

VM: Why is *NSYNC important to you?

LI: Well, they brought us together as a family. We used to fight all the time, and now me and Lydia hardly fight at all.

LY: We collect pictures together.

LI: Yeah, our whole room is decorated with *NSYNC.

Here, Lydia and Lisa explained that the shared activities of collecting posters and decorating their room eased the tensions they sometimes felt as three preteen girls growing up together.[30] Meanwhile, the fan culture between them was also a collective bond. Some of the sisters often went to live with their father, breaking them up among different homes. There, the images of Timberlake, along with other popular actors and singers, spilled out of the bedroom onto the living room walls, where they had been glued over the wallpaper. The shared activities of collecting, cutting, and pasting marked the family's unity despite other forces that pulled them apart.

The sisters sought a communal refuge in Timberlake that was not controlled by adults. Lisa, in particular, immersed herself in online *NSYNC fan culture at the time the adults around her wanted her to think about college and her future. The library became a refuge. She told me: "I'm not even sure I want to go to college. I think I just want to take some time off. The library is a great place. I know lots of people there who are *NSYNC fans, too. We got in the same chat room and have learned to design our own Web sites. Wanna see mine sometime?" Whereas college seemed hard to fathom and far away, Lisa felt safe in the small community of library users, many of whom could understand how great Timberlake really was. Besides, Lisa reasoned she had already traveled the world online. "I've met lots of people on the Net. I've chatted with people all over the world." Lisa's fanship allowed her to stay home with a group of sympathetic friends.

When I asked Lisa what made Timberlake so desirable, she compared him to other boys she knew. "The boys around here are stupid. They drink and do drugs and make fun of us. The guys in *NSYNC are clean and polite. They would never be mean," she said. Timberlake embodied marketers' image of teen idols since the 1950s, in which "all pain and deprivation and dangerous habits dropped away; all performers became bright-eyed, personable and polite."[31] Like past stars, Timberlake was squeaky clean, drug-free, and polite. Pop stars accepted Lisa for who she was: a gifted girl who could easily leave the neighborhood on a scholarship. Like her fan friends at the library, they would have understood her fears of leaving home and her family. In contrast, Lisa saw the local boys as macho toward women and as substance abusers. "They all think the *NSYNC thing is stupid, but I don't care what they think," she said. Lisa's reference to "they" in this case was male, given developments at home. In 1997, her older sister had a baby; Lisa shared responsibilities for the absentee father as well as cared for her younger siblings at her own father's house. These real men increasingly determined Lisa future. As the year continued, she decided to stay at home to help care for her sister's soon-to-arrive second baby. She put on hold a dream to go to art school in Chicago. In a changing world, Timberlake was a constant source of support.

Four years after I met her, Lisa had graduated from high school—already an achievement in her family—but had not started college. In this sense, even if the dichotomy between the imaginary boy band and local boys was a fantasy, Lisa needed the fantasy to envision a life far superior to her own reality. Her desire, though, supports the hegemony of white males in a Mexican American female imaginary. As noted previously, whiteness distinguished the boy bands from popular rap and Latino artists both physically and symbolically. Aside from the part-Hispanic member of *NSYNC, a background singer, Lisa and her sisters could not identify another Latino in the boy bands they liked. Hence Lisa, left with few other options, translated whiteness from her fantasy boyfriend, one who was sensitive, polite, and undoubtedly middle class.

Valerie Walkerdine explains that working-class girls' discourses sometimes re-produce bourgeois fantasies that construct their own class as an unruly and uncivilized force to be contained and controlled.[32] Unable to control other aspects of her life, Lisa's attraction to Timberlake presented an impossible chal-lenge for Mexican American girls who wanted something that represented everything that they could not possibly have.

The Cultural Politics of Transnational Consumption

Fantasies are ways of cutting out different cultural identities and trying them on for size. The Mexican American females who adored telenovelas and pop music did so to express both who they were and who they would like to be. Given the choices, girls preferred pop stars to telenovela actors as their imag-ined soul mates. Nora, who liked Ricardo originally in the telenovela *María Isabel*, told me a month later that he had become just a caricature. "I don't like him so much anymore because he gets all these strange looks on his face. Then I laugh at him." Ricardo and other leading men of the telenovelas were interesting to the girls. They learned from them and at times nostalgically iden-tified with them, but ultimately they were too culturally remote to really be their idealized mates. Pop stars, on the other hand, were global superstars who embodied individual achievement and surpassed cultural divisions. Introduc-ing Enrique Iglesias as her favorite icon, Rita wrote he had "achieved his own goals through music and performance," whereas, "at the age of 23, the most people [sic] imagine themselves being in college, married and perhaps raising a family." Rita constructed Iglesias as the perfect male, one who croons to her but also succeeds in the public eye. This balance between romance and per-sonal achievement made pop stars more desirable as they embodied dreams that girls had for their own futures.

Telenovelas and pop music inspired divergent fantasies, ones that were highly personal while reinforcing the cultural politics of these media's transnational distribution. Since the mid–1980s, Televisa has tried to aggre-gate a pan-Latino market by selling telenovelas throughout the Americas, a strategy strengthened by the company purchasing 20 percent of Univision in 1992.[33] For the girls who liked telenovelas, the strategy was very effective. The genre's exposition of cultural difference stirred the memories of an entire generation that found evidence in the texts of their own cultural pasts and explanations for differences in the present.[34] Yet their positioning as pan-Latino consumers in front of the television differed sharply from their positions as global youth consumers in the market for pop. In the pop industry, the sym-bolic ambiguity of the pop stars helped sustain the economic value of the commodities that circulated with the music internationally.[35] Dreamy and romantic stars might have been largely Anglo American, but their whiteness symbolized more a cultural homogeneity, unified through a generalized level of middle class consumption, than cultural difference. According to Phillip Brian Harper, the social access to and identification with whiteness cannot be separated from the material gains that being white has historically implied in our country.[36] In other words, for Mexican American girls who dreamed of going to college and securing middle-class careers, pop stars' whiteness encapsulated the social mobility they wanted for themselves. In these ways, the girls' class identities not only helped them decide what to consume but also provided the structuring absence for their fantasies for the future.

This chapter has demonstrated some of the ways mass media consumption was both a material practice and a platform for Mexican American young people to construct communities based around personal tastes and cultural identities. Participating in cultural markets, adolescents could actively engage in a politics of inclusion and exclusion that they could not in other spheres of their daily lives. Their competencies replicated adult rhetorics of media effects and mainstream discourses of power and privilege while also creating their own common language that addressed inequalities they saw in terms of ethnicity, class, gender, and age. Although they could not change these inequalities, they used media texts to construe alternative realities based on shared desires. By listening to these realities, adults might better understand how, given the chance, Mexican American youths might represent themselves in a public sphere that encourages their participation.

Chapter 7

Videotaping the Future?

THE VIDEO PROJECT WAS fertile ground for studying Mexican American young people as media consumers and producers. That is, Mexican American adolescents living on the west side of San Antonio did not just talk about, wear around, tote along, and consume mass media; mass media also found their way into the videos that teens made about themselves. Though the videos were very much their own—their ideas and labor—they were also mediated by the mass media texts they consumed.[1] With their storehouses of knowledge about popular music, television, and films, activities involved in producing a video—such as brainstorming, storyboarding, shooting, and editing—called upon participants to use their media knowledge in a creative way. Throughout the process, mass media established guidelines for separating good video from bad video, as well as standards for their own productions. Mass media imagery was flexible and relevant, two important aspects in a community project that asked youths to create their own visions. Ultimately, the videos reflected the complicated ways that mass media consumption was productive, helping young people express themselves through media technologies similar to the ones they consumed.

At the same time, the applicability of mass media contents to student-produced videos exposed the political economy of mass media industries that potentially alienated the young producers. The technological gaps that once bifurcated community from commercial productions in the 1970s, and "quality" television from "trash" in the 1980s, were irrelevant in the 1990s, when community video could approximate some of the techniques of their favorite programs. For teenagers raised on television images that emphasized spontaneity and cheaper video technologies, their own videos lacked appeal if they did not appropriate these images, even if they did not have the means to replicate these images directly and became frustrated as a result. As much as mass media aesthetics sparked their interests in community video, they also illustrated their integration into political and economic structures that supported mainstream mass media.

In this chapter, mass media play ambiguous roles for working-class Mexican Americans wanting to represent themselves. Mass media gave teens a tool kit, a set of aesthetics, genres, narrative structures, and production practices. These could be manipulated to support, alter, or resist mainstream representations of Mexican Americans. Sometimes they incorporated mass media elements to legitimate their own productions. At other times the producers wanted to create videos that replaced mass media productions, thus de-legitimating the power of the media to define their lives. Both of these strategies reveal the complex relationships between producers and their texts, what Shaun Moores calls the tension between "creativity and constraint."[2] Mass media aesthetics enabled and stifled the youths' creative visual expressions, making the politics of mass media appropriation always uneven.

Community Video: Technology and Aesthetics

Mexican American youths at SACA were highly aware that the economic power of mass media industries enabled their use of technologies and aesthetics that the participants themselves did not have access to within the confines of a community video project. This awareness would not be so problematic in the video production process if it were not also true that the volunteers wanted access to the same technologies and aesthetics as they watched on television. Their desires departed from those of participants in other alternative video projects who categorically rejected mass media technologies and aesthetics as signifiers of commodification and the alienation of citizens. Creating a binary—themselves as video producers versus television industry producers—video activists in the 1970s did not take into account the technological and aesthetic convergence in postmodern television forms that the 1990s adolescents enjoyed and identified with. It is useful, though, to understand this past binary, because it still existed to a large degree in schools and institutions that told young people what community video is.

Historically, alternative video practitioners saw their medium as ontologically different from television. Beginning with Michael Shamberg and Raindance's publication of *Guerrilla Television* in 1971, video activists in North America adopted a McLuhan-esque optimism toward the democratic potential of video technologies.[3] Unlike film and television production, video production was cheaper and more flexible. By the mid–1970s, several alternative video cooperatives and production groups touted video as a medium of the people for different reasons.[4] For guerrilla television producers, such as TVTV, video could invent a new media economy, challenging television networks' dominance over information dissemination. For community video producers, such as University Community Video in Minnesota and Broadside Television in Tennessee, video's portability and simplicity could foster popular dialogue on local issues. Together these groups saw video's democratic potential opposing television as a medium of the mainstream and status quo.

In community-based video organizations, members emphasized a grassroots production process that would create new and personalized visions of one's culture and identity. Grassroots producers, these organizations assumed, could better communicate with the communities they hailed from and would address issues important to their local area. Based on a binary opposition between nonprofit video production for a local audience and commercial television production for a mass audience, community video would break the visual molds that sold television audiences to advertisers. Alexandra Juhasz contrasts video audiences as members of "'minority,' 'disenfranchised' and 'marginal' communities" to television's "vast audience of 'middle of the road spectators'—usually imagined to be the straight, white, middle-class members of intact families who so few Americans actually are."[5] Supported by universities, philanthropic institutions, and government agencies, community video activists and video festival juries helped institutionalize community video aesthetics by the mid–1970s, solidifying the videos as radical in and of themselves.

Soon these "radical" aesthetics became familiar. Although video artists have always crossed film and television aesthetics in their products, community video producers usually followed a few dominant aesthetic tropes, such as talking-head interviews and group discussions. These aesthetics emphasized the honesty and mirrorlike qualities of video, as opposed to the manipulated or excessive qualities of television.[6] In addition, community video images served to directly quote their subject matter. Unlike radical or avant-garde cinema that sought to destabilize signifiers from one intended meaning, community video aesthetics tended to stabilize the meaning of the "community" through a set of realist conventions.[7] By presenting the faces and voices of people within a community, community video aesthetics operationalized recognition of distinct communities *as they really are*, differentiating them from television or other forms of art or experimental video. Janine Marchessault explains, "Video was the antidote to indeterminacy; the more ordinary and transparent, the more authentic."[8] This transparency in community video corresponded to Lukacsian notions that by presenting to the working class their real life conditions, they would revolt against the bourgeoisie.[9] In practice, though, these pictures of real life became commonplace, reinforcing community-based video's embrace of documentary styles rather than an arsenal of other styles and formats.

In these ways, video activists distinguished video from television in the 1970s, much in the same way that television professionals distinguished television from film in the 1950s.[10] Both discourses argued that their technology was intrinsically more popular than the preceding one and served to delineate cultural production fields, both in terms of workers and product. The separation of video and television revealed the political economy of their separate technological uses. Community video activists developed a technological use that could match the live and portable spontaneity of radical activism in the 1960s.[11] Meanwhile, television producers continued to use technology in ways that secured their economic stability with networks and political security with federal regulators. In a time when three network broadcasters dominated television programming, these uses reinforced differences between video and television in terms of production and aesthetics.

Within a decade, the boundaries between television and video production blurred as television industry professionals began to incorporate video production methods and aesthetics into their own programming. Following their search for new audiences, cheaper production modes, and alternative aesthetic styles, video technology became a staple feature in 1980s television production.[12] Live-remote programming in sports helped decentralize television programs away from Hollywood studios. Music videos acclimated viewers to short, videotaped clips they could not only purchase but also produce themselves. In the 1990s, television programs based on amateur videos, such as *America's Funniest Home Videos*, celebrated viewers as producers, while news programs' use of home videos to capture news events validated video surveillance as a citizenship-enhancing activity. The separation between television, film, and video aesthetics dissolved as television producers freely adopted grainy video footage and shaky, handheld camerawork into mainstream programs. These changes marked the transformation of video's "radicality . . . into a marketing strategy" for niche audiences.[13] The very characteristics that seemed to distinguish video as an oppositional medium—for example, its spontaneity, accessibility, and transparency—became staples in television. By the 1980s, community video technology and aesthetics were neither radical nor on the periphery of commercial production industries.

This is to say that by the time I met my video members, they were already keen to television's use of video technology. Some of their favorite television programs were based on videotaped footage, such as music videos, *Lente Loco*, and *Placas*.[14] These programs fostered the old populist rhetoric surrounding video, emphasizing that anyone with a camera and an idea can make a video program for television. Amateur videos thus blended with other television contents in the range of acceptable television programs and standards. Beyond these boundaries, the video participants had difficulty imagining what kinds of videos they would produce. For example, the Mexican American volunteers generally brainstormed music videos and reality programming clips: two television formats that generally rely on video technology and aesthetics already. For this reason, community video producers may have had technological access but "seem constrained to produce the patterns of textual production which the medium seems to demand."[15] Whereas community video producers may have drawn from a few standard video aesthetics in the 1970s, the SACA video producers looked to television's heterogeneous uses of video aesthetics in the 1990s to draw their inspirations.

The youths' desire to reproduce already existing video formats was not an aberration, but rather evidenced the television culture that the youths understood and could adapt to their own contexts. They were "digital thinkers," having been exposed to a television environment that stressed interactive connectivity.[16] More important, SACA's participants could actively apply their digital knowledge to videos in which the television aesthetics could resignify interactions with each other and connections to an imagined audience. Using mimicry, pastiche, and appropriation, the volunteers' videos became postmodern tributes to the community that they lived in.[17] This meant that the television aesthetics were inherently neither conservative nor radical, but rather served as conceptual tools for the actualization of the youths' creative visions, ones that resulted in a video about altars.

Negotiating Video Aesthetics

Despite the hybridization of mass media genres over the past two decades, mass media scholars and teachers today still privilege documentary and nonfictional media genres as more important to the development of an informed citizenry. Whereas teachers often dismiss fictional genres as merely pleasurable, nonfictional genres may "organize and disseminate knowledge into the public sphere."[18] In academic terms, documentary creates a "love of looking" by empowering viewers to view their subjects in a detached, hence rational, way.[19] In this vein, media literacy courses in the United States have generally encouraged students to make nonfictional representations that will increase their knowledge as citizens, but have ignored the potential use-value of fiction in young people's lives. Working with Mexican American teenagers showed the opposite to be true. The video project volunteers' "distanciation" from their own images made them disinterested. The binaries between fiction and nonfiction genres alienated the youths, who associated documentaries directly with schooling and in opposition to "good" or entertaining media. In their own videos, they worked hard to subvert these oppositions.

"GOOD" VS. "BORING" VIDEO

In late 1997 and early 1998, I gathered between two and six volunteers at a time from the crew to storyboard a video based on our footage of community altars and interviews with altar owners. I had drawn some blank squares on a piece of paper and copied it for the group. We also talked about different ideas they had for the video. Although my video crew knew that we were making a documentary about altars, the group quickly developed a consensus that their video would not be a standard community video that focused on dialogue, nor a standard documentary that focused on an argument. Rather, the participants tended toward mass media aesthetics, stressing imagery over argument, music over dialogue, and the excessive use of special effects over realism. Carlos imagined what he called "MTV style animation," complete with quivering cartoon letters and flashing arrows pointing to participants in the video. Sara likened her introduction to the *Power Rangers*, insisting that each crew member parade into the video frame and pose in an authoritative stance. Her ending, she said, was more akin to Jackie Chan movies, "where they show all the mistakes afterwards." Nora compared her storyboard's ideal beginning to the checkerboard-style opening of the *Brady Bunch* and suggested adding footage from San Fernando Cathedral's Sunday mass, which is broadcast weekly on a local cable station. Finally, Henry envisioned a full-fledged heavy metal music video, where interviews were intercut with altars and surrounded with actors dressed as angels and devils. He told me excitedly that the angels and devils chased each other in beat with the music. While all of the youths had integrated their own video footage into their storyboards, their quotation of mass media aesthetics in the storyboards made the footage more interesting to them.

Conversely, documentaries and interviews were not interesting to many of the young Mexican American participants involved in SACA. This became more obvious after a field trip in April 1998 to the KLRN Youth Video Festival. Organized by video educators from public schools countywide and local PBS affiliate (KLRN) programming staff, the festival attracted more than two hundred high school students to participate in workshops and view student work. I helped organize workshops in anticipation of SACA members' attendance. On that day, Ana, Sara, Lisa, and her two sisters, Lydia and Cristina, went to the festival with two SACA staff members. I saw them later that day.

> VM: How was it?
> A: It was boring.
> VM: Why?
> A: All the videos had just talk.
> S: They needed more music.
> A: The best part was the free pizza, but they ran out.

Lisa and her sisters also expressed disappointment in the videos. To them, their video entry—a thirty-second video poem—was one of the only "fun" entries in the flow of mock advertisements, educational programs, oral histories, news programs, public service announcements, and staged dramatic scenes. As for the workshops, Cristina said that the only interesting session was "editing in camera" because the teacher did not just talk to them but let them play with the equipment. The instructor, a well-seasoned Mexican American media professional, had the highest-rated workshop in student evaluations.

Comparing the youths' collective reactions to these different types of video contents, the Mexican American youths at SACA seemed to have a hierarchy of what they thought were interesting videos. At the top were videos like the ones they saw on television: the storyboarded mass media elements, followed by the altars footage and the video poem. At the bottom of the hierarchy were the student-produced videos that other students like themselves made. For various possible reasons, the SACA participants saw their own use of mass media aesthetics in the storyboarding activity as more interesting than other youth-produced video shorts at the Youth Video Festival or even their own interview footage. Three issues pointed to a hierarchy between mass media and amateur video productions. First, the attendees associated mass media aesthetics with more status than their own footage and productions. Second, they associated the youth-produced videos with an educational context, making their viewing into more of a chore than leisure or entertainment. Third, the youths did not associate the content of the latter videos with topics that were relevant to their world—which made them boring.

AIMING FOR A "QUALITY" VIDEO

The associated status of mass media aesthetics relates to questions of quality that have burdened the medium since the 1950s. The definition of quality television programming traditionally excluded genres enjoyed by women, people of color, or people from lower socioeconomic classes.[20] In the age of niche audiences and the hybridization of genre borders, however, the definition of quality television has been somewhat more flexible. "Quality" television in the 1990s operated according to an "ideology of stylistic excess," which emphasized stylized performance, images over text, and technological prowess.[21] Although television sometimes featured "low-budget" styles, even these aesthetics connoted televisual prestige. Mike Wayne explains, "A fictional piece made on a fraction of an average drama budget would simply look cheap because it would have no compensatory ideology of 'authencity' to legitimise it."[22] In other words, the youths wanted to integrate mass media aesthetics into their own video footage to make it look more prestigious. Yet the student video entries did not and could not connote such prestige. The straight cuts and scenes shot with an immobile, single camera in the student videos revealed the amateurishness of the production compared with television's high-tech styles. In short, the video festival attendees preferred video aesthetics that they associated with the professionalism of mainstream television.

The participants saw the video genres in the Youth Video Festival as educational, a category that schools helped impose, rather than as entertainment, categories that viewers believed they chose. In the Youth Video Festival, the relationship between student videos and the educational workshops was explicit. Schools imposed the generic categories of the festival and also oversaw production of most festival entries. When the volunteers replicated these generic traits in their own documentary footage, they talked about them in the same way they did the festival entries, using the phrases "boring" or "not fun." The standard genre categories communicated a type of video pedagogy, in line with Richard Kilborn and John Izod's assertion that audiences generally view the documentary genre as a type of educational work or a citizenship duty.[23] The one exception was the case of the Mexican American workshop instructor, who avoided the pedagogic air of the video festival by encouraging students to "play" with the editing equipment rather than "learn" from it. On the whole, though, the creative work of storyboarding was more entertaining, because students could cross generic boundaries just as the programs they saw on television did. Like television, the "fiction effect" of storyboarding allowed them to imagine mobile and alternative worlds.[24] Just as viewers have found leisure in television's flowing segments and alternative realities, the video producers enjoyed their ability to adopt television's flow and mobility to the alternative realities in their storyboards.

The video festival and its materials raise the question of relevancy. In the video about altars, the youths made their documentary relevant to themselves by adding mass media elements from their favorite movies and television programs. The video not only extended the representational limits of the mass media that they consumed by making the video focus on their community in a positive way, it also put mass media tools in the service of progressive representations, bringing the signature trademarks of privately owned media into the public sphere.[25] This made the documentary pleasurable and a source of practical information about altars in the community: what they look like, who owns them, and what the altars mean to the owners. The mixing of fiction and nonfiction suggests that the hybrid mixture was the most relevant to the producers' lives because it made them visible in the most progressive way they could conceive of.

The aesthetics of the altars video itself exceeded the standard bounds of the student video documentary, as presented to them at the video festival. It incorporated mass media elements into its style, form, and content. The video opens to the refrain of the R&B song "Heaven" by Nu Flavor. While the song is about a man who prays to win a woman's affection, a montage of Virgin Mary statues and altars recontextualizes the words in the video. The rapid and rhythmically edited opening segments look more like a music video than a documentary, demonstrating the mass media's discursive influence from the beginning. Unsteady camera work and a rapid-fire zoom to an altar become visual complements to the trilling or crescendos in the song. Musical interludes with collages of altars not shown elsewhere, such as in the opening, are used throughout the video both to organize themes and break up the monotony of the interviews. After the initial two interviews, for example, an altar tumbles onto the screen with the bilingual pop song "Mystical Experience/ Experiencia Religiosa." The camera pans the altar vertically and horizontally before rolling out of the screen, leaving the viewer in the disjointed fragments of another interview with a middle-aged man. Another series of altars pulses according to the popular Tejano song "Le Pediré." Complete with an accordion and rhythm machine, it begins "Le pediré a una estrella / Que no me hagas sufrir más / Que te cuide adonde vayas / Que te vuelva a enamorar / Le pediré [I will ask a star / That you stop making me suffer / To take care of you wherever you go / That you fall in love again / I will ask]." The theme of the words is serious and romantic, but the rhythmic music and editing contribute to an upbeat feeling throughout the video.

Figure 7. Volunteers teaching each other video at San Anto Cultural Arts. *Photo taken by Carole Mayer.*

Yet the video was not exactly like the professionally polished ones they saw on television either. Both used roaming and unsteady camera action to replicate a "forced condensation of energy" in video footage, but in television, the rapid-fire intercuts between film and video, introductions and promotions, and animation and live action often overshadowed coherency.[26] The altars video instead used the camera movement and choppy editing together with interviews to heighten polysemy. Rather than provide a continuous narrative, which is central to classical Hollywood cinema, the onslaught of images displayed different altars, often without synchronous dialogue or titles, leaving the viewer to decipher the context. The repetition of interview questions provides continuity but also leaves unanswered questions. The quotes encompass a handful of themes, such as religious beliefs, Mexican American heritage, and divine miracles, but are left dangling without further development or a reasoned explanation. Together, the televisually inspired images and use of interviews left the video text open for viewers to interpret altars in any number of ways.

Humor further differentiated the altars video from mainstream documentary and fictional styles. In the video, the juxtapositions of serious and lighthearted messages created their own flow. First, a man describes the process of making the altar—building the form and laying the cement; the process is quite complicated. Yet when asked why he has an altar in the first place, he responds exasperatedly, "Well, 'cause we're Catholic, that's all." Then, a senior woman explains that her altar must protect her "porque a veces, yo camino solo y nunca me ha pasado nada [because sometimes I walk alone and nothing has ever happened to me]." Finally, the last woman says her altar has performed miracles; she just cannot remember them very well. The final interview ends with a crescendo of broadcast church music from San Fernando Cathedral, and the final "sí" of the oral interview. Then there is silence while four of the video production crew members, some of them previously unseen in front of the camera, put the altar back together for the woman they have interviewed. Seconds later, the video's credits include the mistakes made in shooting the video, just like in Sara's storyboard. A loud ska version of "Here Comes the Sun" blasts along to the errors and funny clips. Crew members shrug their shoulders, ignore the interviewee, prep for the camera, and flub their lines. The credits end with an extreme close-up of a card reading "San Anto" and a child reading, "How are altars different . . . [*a peal of laughter*]."

Humor served different functions in these examples. In one way, it subverted adult authority in the video, like a Bakhtinian carnivalesque.[27] The youths' subtle use of ironic adult quotations in the last two interviews reinforced their knowledge and ability as interviewers and camera operators. More overt humor, though, was also a mechanism for celebrating the everyday—just like in television or Jackie Chan movies, as Sara put it. In *Bloopers* programs, for instance, the display of production mistakes as television texts revealed how video production is part of daily life, whether it is the family making a home movie or the television actor missing a line. These mistakes have become so routine on television that they are format clichés.[28] Yet for the young producers, the humorous slapstick exemplified their ability to create an enjoyable documentary, one that would make everyone laugh as well as learn—an organic version of "edutainment" on the west side.

In reality, the SACA participants did not directly oppose the festival videos and the altars video in their conversations. Rather, the two forms exemplify how mass media aesthetics helped the youths define one video as "better" than another one. I often asked the participants to elaborate on why mass media aesthetics made the altars video more interesting to them. They often responded using binary terms, comparing the movie they wanted to accomplish and the documentary they wanted to avoid. For example: movies are fun. Documentaries are dull. Movies are on good television and at the theater. Documentaries are on the public station and at school. Movies are for seeing after work. Documentaries are things that teachers test you on. Movies are fast and exciting. Documentaries are slow and boring. In this way, the children associated mass media aesthetics not just with individual media texts

but also with their entire social environment. To rearticulate these comparisons, mass media aesthetics seemed comfortable to them. Mass media offered
a mobility beyond the repressive boundaries of school. Flexible media aesthetics
could promise creative choices beyond the imposed aesthetics of learning and
pedagogy.

The youths clearly felt that their video project represented them better
when they added mass media aesthetics. This in itself was not necessarily progressive.[29] The pastiche of images, music, and voices per se became progressive only because it helped the youths represent themselves with respect and
authority. As Coco Fusco and Pratibha Parmar both point out, mass media
aesthetics disassociated from their industrial conditions can actually stifle the
emergence of essentialistic images of people of color while undermining the
"colonialist fantasy" that Mexican American videos should look like Anglo-
produced documentaries.[30] The volunteers' favorite part of the altars video,
the mistakes at the end, was the section most closely modeled after a mass
media text they knew. In contrast, the relationship between altars, a Catholic tradition, and ethnic identity remained debatable to the teens. After all,
even though the ten crew members were Mexican Americans, they also included one Protestant who moved out of the neighborhood the previous year,
three monolingual English speakers who were unobservant Catholics, and six
observant Catholics who as first-generation immigrants considered themselves
Mexicans as easily as Americans. Thus despite their different relationships with
altars, the young producers unified in their search to use mass media aesthetics for self-representation. In the next section, the politics of recoding are further examined by comparing the degree to which the adolescents used mass
media to legitimate their video projects and, conversely, the degree to which
the video project could be used to improve upon the mass media. This ex-
amination is important, for it shows how the teens were both resistant and
complacent toward mass media consumption in their own video-making
process.

Recoding Genres and Contents

In my experiences working with SACA members, the Mexican American
youth participants celebrated and criticized mass media through their videos.
This is not surprising given the ambiguous relationships between Mexican
Americans and media. Historically, mass media industries have either ignored
Mexican American roles or used their aesthetics to create Mexican American stereotypes. In the 1990s, the vast majority of Latino representations were
of criminals, a modern adaptation of the "bandido" stereotype. In particular,

reality television programs "whose version of reality often consisted of white cops chasing . . . Hispanic robbers."[31] In such cases, television producers have used their techniques in the service of negative stereotypes that symbolically reinforced Mexican Americans' disempowerment from U.S. power structures.[32] Though the total number of Latino representations has risen through certain media genres (such as reality television programs, talk shows, and the growing proliferation of Spanish-language television programs), the lack of diversity over the entire spectrum of channels has relegated Mexican Americans to the edges of the medium's frame. Yet relevance is often in the eye of the beholder and studies of media audiences often have found that people with less social power in society interpret the most unrealistic programs as the most relevant to their lives.[33] Many scholars may have disregarded Latino representations in these commercial genres as purely negative, but viewers often adapt new narratives to the programs, making the images bear positive meanings.

"GO RICKI" RECODING

Talk shows, in particular, were positive forums for discussions of cultural identity. Talk shows in the 1990s marked the "popularization of identity politics on television."[34] The use of colloquial language legitimated urban modes of speech for people of color, while personal exclamations of private problems in the first or second person were visual representations of how the personal has become political. Finally, the talk show participants' multiple views of intimate issues subverted the notion that there was a singular, objective account of daily events. This was important in encouraging viewers to form their own opinions of the issues while revealing "performance behind the notion of truth."[35] Although talk shows often closed around certain preferred readings of cultural identity in the United States, the programs also destabilized stereotypes by empowering disfranchised citizens to speak publicly about themselves.[36]

It is this sense of empowerment that may have motivated my video crew's production of an interview with Ruth Behar, a Cuban American anthropologist who specializes in Latin American folk culture. Juan, Carlos, Elsa, Nora, Sara, and Ana arrived two hours early to prepare for the important interview. Juan and Carlos had already met Behar at a SACA interview for *El Placazo* and decided to make this interview better. In collaboration with the group, a "better" interview signified a talk show format. The teenagers put out a stage with two armchairs and hung a velvet cover over the wall to achieve a neat and professional background. Sara and Ana wrote questions on colorful index cards. Juan and Carlos practiced one-shots and two-shots on the camera, replicating standard camera shots in televised interviews. Elsa even brought a cup of water to the stage, noting that guests always have something to drink on talk shows. Thirty minutes before Behar's arrival, Ana practiced taking a sip of water before asking the question and looking sympathetically at both Behar's empty chair and the imaginary audience. At the last minute, the girls wrote "San Anto" on the back of each handheld question card "because that's the way it is on *Ricki Lake*," explained Sara. Before we began shooting, the "audience"—that is, four of the teens and myself—practiced applauding at the appropriate junctures. The end result was a "better" interview because it looked more like a televised talk show.

In this instance, the aesthetics of popular talk shows helped the youths set the stage for, in their minds, a professional interview. The mimicry of the talk show mise-en-scène, the audience rituals in terms of live interactivity, and the host's emotional performance were all standard features of televised talk shows the participants watched, including *Jerry Springer*, *Ricki Lake*, and *Cristina*. In particular, *Ricki Lake*, which Sara mentioned, was a "youth-oriented" talk show.[37] Through Lake's theatrical performances in support of or against her guest speakers, she involved young viewers and audience members in creating a public space for moral judgments about personal issues. At the same time, the program created a spectacle in which viewers were encouraged through the performances to label guests as absolutely righteous or deviant. In this sense, talk shows are ambiguous spaces, since they may actually reinforce "bad" guests' positions on the fringes of society.[38] However, for the crew members, their talk show did not ultimately invite these interactive elements.

While the crew copied some of the theatrical aspects of the talk show in their own interview, they could not bring themselves to reenact the excessively moralistic tone of the host and audience. The taping of the actual program deviated from the commercial talk show they had originally envisioned. After the detailed preparation of the set, Ana, the host, forgot most of her preplanned performance cues. Visibly shy in the presence of an adult authority, Ana began asking Behar short "yes" and "no" questions. Although Ana was curious about the personal side of being an anthropologist, with questions such as "Is it hard to be an anthropologist?" she did not pressure her guest. Ana abdicated her authority as the host and allowed her guest to take control of the interview—an anomaly in commercial talk show programming.[39] As a result, the interview did not disclose intimate details about their guest nor did it consolidate around a moral judgment of the guest. Afterward, Ana said she was so nervous she forgot to do all the things she "was supposed to" on the camera. This anxiety extended to the director, who said he had trouble moving the camera during the interview, and to the sound manager, who said she knew the sound quality was bad, but she did not want to stop the taping to tell the people on stage to speak up.

In this example, the participants' desire to do a talk show may have motivated them, but it did not sustain the actual production. This is important because even if they imagined talk shows as a forum for people like themselves, they did not have the confidence to feel they could enter that imaginary world. Yet the mimicry of certain elements held a value in themselves. The youths wanted to assert their own authority to Behar, the esteemed outsider. Throughout the process, they talked about setting up an interview that would impress the guest and show her how good they were at video. Although the final cut looked, ironically, much like the talking-head-style interviews common to community video programs in the 1970s, the teenagers felt good about trying to adapt the aesthetic prestige of a *Ricki Lake* or *Oprah*. In this sense, it made perfect sense that the video crew used only popular talk show aesthetics that would present a positive image of themselves and their guest. The talk show format was actually flexible enough to legitimate their own production without drawing on the potential negative exploitation that has accompanied many talk shows. The format, however, could only be stretched so far. In an environment where Mexican American children, particularly girls, are told to speak only when spoken to, the talk show taping had not overcome the authority structures in the west side itself. This suggests that all forms of media appropriation must be studied in the ways that they encourage creativity while reinforcing social hierarchies.

"HISPANIC CINDERELLA"

Even when the participants aimed directly to create a video that resisted a mass media text, they felt frustrated by the economic constraints of the project itself. This was most apparent in our brainstorming sessions, when youths conceptualized videos they felt they could not produce. In the case of a remake of *Cinderella* for a west side audience, video crew members wanted to remake the classic fairy tale to critique another version they saw on television. On 2 November 1997, four of the girls who worked on the Behar interview saw ABC's self-promoted "multicultural" *Cinderella*. The program targeted ethnic children specifically in the remake. An Internet advertisement promoted *Cinderella* in the following way: "Through revamping, TV fairy tales will remain classics because the inclusion of identifiable faces will allow children of all races to be a part of the dream. Alas! The magic has come alive for children of different ethnic backgrounds who enjoy the fairytales that we all have come to love and treasure over the years. . . . The essential theme of this fairytale 'that anything is possible in a world where dreams come true' really comes true for the myriad of young faces that for decades have been left out of America's fairytales."[40] Unfortunately, the girls did not feel included in ABC's promise of pluralism. They complained that the cast was almost completely African American, with Brandy and Whitney Houston playing the two leading female roles. Together with their friends, they decided to develop a video that would counter ABC's already-alternative *Cinderella*.

The title of the video varied between "Cenicienta," "The New Cinderella," or even "Hispanic Cinderella." Nora became particularly invested in brainstorming this project with Sara, Elsa, and Ana:

> N: We could use the castle at Brackenridge [Park] for the palace and Our Lady of Guadalupe for when they get married. We can use the house at San Anto.
> S: We need costumes and makeup. My aunt can play the queen.
> A: Yeah, she's named *Reina* [Queen].
> S: No, because she's really white.
> A: But there's too many scenes.
> VM: You don't have to do all of them.
> N: We don't have a carriage, but we could use a fancy white sports car with tinted windows. And instead of an orchestra, we can play *cumbia* in the ballroom.
> A: Yeah, and the sisters could be hoodrats.
> VM: Hoodrats?
> A: Sluts from the neighborhood that speak English and Mexican.

In Nora's vision of "Cenicienta," Cinderella was the local popular girl. She danced cumbia and rode in the white sports car with tinted windows, a high status vehicle on the west side of San Antonio. She gets married at a church, which all of the girls attend, and has a castle in a park that is their favorite for family outings. Coincidentally, we, as a group, had planned to have a picnic in the same park that month, illustrating the shared importance of Nora's video ideas. The group tended to like her plan and added their own ideas. Together, the video crew incorporated local geographic and cultural elements that represented themselves in contrast to an Anglo or African American Cinderella.

It is unclear in this case, however, to what degree the mass media appropriation was resistant. The girls may have resisted ABC's multicultural *Cinderella*, but their alternative ideas reinforced gendered and racialized hierarchies in the community at large. "Cenicienta" incorporated heterosexual models for masculine and feminine roles. In addition, the imagined good queen's whiteness and the evil stepsisters' Mexicanness (as "hoodrats") allude to the racial stereotypes that identify certain minorities as more virtuous on the basis of their lighter skin color. The allusion to racial stereotypes is even more complex because these representations might have been important fantasies for young people living in a world overdetermined by race. The racial and ethnic identity tags on the characters explore the contradictions of Mexican American identity in the real world. After all, the fair-skinned queen is a member of Sara's family; just as the "hoodrats" represent the tougher and more sexual girls who live in the neighborhood. The juxtaposition between a good family member and bad neighborhood girls in the video would allow the crew members to try out two very different roles for Mexican American girls in their community. Hence, the video's complicit use of racialized identities may have reinforced stereotypes, but it also may have broken them down.

The girls abandoned the "Cenicienta" video before ever shooting a scene, leaving these questions of racial identity unanswered. They became frustrated during our conversations about making their video look like "the real thing," which for them referred to the original Disney version of the movie. For example, Elsa was concerned that we needed scenes of the talking mice in the alcoves—a detail from the cartoon feature film. "How are we going to get the cartoon mice?" she asked earnestly. Nora responded, "Well, we could train some hamsters," causing the rest of the group to laugh. Soon after, the group began to question the feasibility of all of the scenes. Where would they get a pumpkin carriage or glass slippers? Their desire to reproduce the mass media text stifled their ability to decide on their own project. For all of the creativity among the group members, the desire to make a Disney cartoon was a constraint. The group soon turned to other fairy tales they wanted to adapt (*Beauty and the Beast* and *Sleeping Beauty*) and a reality program about a child abducted by aliens. Then summer came and the first-generation participants had to travel to Mexico to visit relatives, sapping the crew's energy to complete any of their ideas.

Within the constraints of SACA's technology, mass media appropriation played a highly ambivalent role in the youths' productions. Hal Foster distinguishes "appropriation" from "counter-appropriation" to define which mass media uses are more complacent or more resistant. In his argument, the counter-appropriation of mass media signifiers is a more resistant strategy because it recontextualizes the commercial meaning of signifiers in terms of minority producers' histories.[41] The local cultural icons and settings in "Cenicienta" would be examples of counter-appropriation. Foster also claims, though, that mere appropriation of mass media signifiers is not resistant because it does not counter the sign's original commercial intent, which tends to objectify minorities.[42] This distinction then does not explain why the girls saw their own reproduction of a talk show as more respectful when it directly copied *Ricki Lake*, or why they needed cartoon hamsters to enact "Cenicienta" the way they wanted. Further, Foster's definitions seem to suggest that technology-rich environments are more likely to appropriate mass media in a negative way simply because they can. Without equipment or staff, the SACA video crew had to counter-appropriate mass media if they wanted to "make do" with what they had. The fact that girls wanted to appropriate aesthetics to legitimate their own video productions must be read as part of a larger framework in which the industrial conditions of television production frustrated the youths from creating their own visions.

COMMERCIALIZING REALITY

The video crew's concern for making "real" television programs hence raised questions about the commercial structure behind the mass media aesthetics that the group willingly appropriated into its own programming. If television aims to sell audiences to advertisers, the video projects revealed other aims that nevertheless incorporated commercial concerns. Videos displayed consumption habits by representing what the youths were wearing and pointing to as fashionable. The use of popular music and intertextual references also displayed commodity consciousness, showing what the youths themselves were consuming or would like to consume. According to Daniel Sholle, the texts themselves, with their fragmented spectacles, pacifies audience members and positions them as consumers.[43] Yet, the video crew members seemed highly aware that consumption was a part of the television aesthetic, regardless of other programming features. As such, it was the dialectic between their desire to make a "real newscast" and the industrial features of the news that resulted in videos promoting consumption.

In the summer of 1998, SACA collaborated with volunteers at the neighboring social works organization to make a weekly newscast about the annual Inner City Development Summer Program. More than fifteen volunteers, mostly teen and preteen girls, trained on SACA's video camera. Over the course of six weeks, these volunteers worked in smaller crews. On Monday they developed story ideas; Tuesday through Thursday they shot the stories; Thursday and Friday they edited the stories together. The following Monday they showed the newscast to the entire group of summer program participants, over one hundred in all, and the process of making the next newscast continued. They completed four newscasts during that time, giving me a chance to watch the transformation of the video format over a short period.

From the beginning, the newscast functioned as the summer program's "bard" by relaying the participants' experiences back to them.[44] However, the participants' definition of news also demonstrated their sophisticated understanding of the discursive conventions of news production. In order to include as many summer program participants as possible and to describe the experiences of adults and children alike, the youths' newscasts used two modes of television news production: in studio and on location.[45] On-location stories tended to be either news events, such as the trip to the Children's Museum, or human interest stories, such as favorite lunch foods. After the first week, the reporters learned introductory and concluding comments for their story segments. They created scripts to introduce the participants to each other. All of these stories were prerecorded to be dropped into the studio broadcast, the second mode of the news production. Like the talk show, the physical set for the studio newscast replicated many standard broadcast news techniques. The anchor and co-anchors dressed in professional jackets to replicate their authority visually. They read from large cue cards and held papers to shuffle in their hands. They even engaged in small talk between stories and made comments like "Now we go to Bob" to signal the inserted news story. To the right of the news desk, an "on-site" reporter usually performed interviews with summer program staff or longtime members who could provide historical information about the summer program. Together, these elements made an inclusive form of news production that also replicated a professional newscast they might see on television.

Our first audience screening of the program was a success; adults and children alike laughed and clapped. Noting the segments that drew the most audible responses, the news crew adjusted their newscast so that, with each passing week, it more and more resembled a tabloid news program. Visual spectaculars, such as skating races and water slide feats, began to displace stories about the history of the camp and its members. In one sense, this was a positive move in the newscasts. Audacious visuals, vernacular language, and upbeat stories make tabloids more accessible and interesting to audiences. Unlike the distanced subjects and formats of news production, tabloids are "more anchored in the horizons of everyday life and its universe of experience."[46] By the third week of the summer, the youth newscasters were adept at picking stories with good visuals and action, such as the weekly roller-skating contests. In these stories, the youths chose the most comical shots—for instance, skaters falling down—to emphasize the most entertaining segments of footage.

In addition, the sensationalizing footage allowed the news crew to cut corners on our intense production schedule. One-liner jokes became a popular way to fill tape without having to actually develop a story. The pursuit of good visuals took less time than writing a script. Like tabloid television, the summer camp videos exploited the visual image to avoid "actual journalistic investigation" and save production time.[47] The repetition of successful story formulas saved time and effort because the crew did not have to think of completely original story ideas. For example, the youths preferred stories that asked participants about favorite things: music, movies, occupations, role models, and foods. Though the video newscast celebrated the local, the production logic of the program each week actually shared national tendencies toward thinning production values and time-saving devices.

The gradual politicization of the personal in human interest news stories accompanied other non-news stories about consumerism. This became most apparent in the final two weeks. Three of the most dedicated news crew members, Monica, Francis, and Nicki, decided that in order to be a "real newscast," the group needed to develop a series of advertisements to interrupt the news flow. Other crew members agreed. Together with two other girls—Monica's youngest sister and her best friend—they drew storyboards for two advertisements: one for the summer program snack shop and the other one for a fashion ad for jncos (a slang word for baggy jeans pronounced "jean-cos"). The commercials were simple in visuals and grammar. The snack shop consisted of a boyfriend and girlfriend holding hands and walking to the shop to order candy and crackers. It ended with a close-up on the two faces, joyfully eating and in love. Dialogue between the two teens deals with the snacks only. The jncos advertisement showed a girl wearing her pants during different summer program activities, such as swimming and playing tetherball, washing the pants, and then continuing to wear them. A jingle, "Jncos. Wear them. Wash them. Wear them again," accompanied the pictures. The students' need for commercial interruptions to make the newscast real powerfully illustrates John Corner's assertion that the advertisements "often work as a kind of *essential television*, using the generic system of broader television culture, with its grouped conventions of speech and image."[48] In other words, it was difficult for viewers in the late twentieth century to imagine television programs without commercials, since the two often used the same aesthetics and codes. For the girls working on the newscast, the commercials and the news reports were part of the same universe. Both used similar conventions to promote human interest issues at the summer program: the snack shop and a favorite fashion.

As with the "Cenicienta" video, the video crew never actualized the advertisements. In the first one, no boy would play the role of "boyfriend" for his peers. In the second advertisement, no one owned a pair of jncos to spotlight for the advertisement. Whereas the first advertisement showed the internal gender dynamics of the news program itself, the second showed the limits of the youths' class positions in the consumer market. Both cases demonstrated the fantasy involved in making commercials, whether it was having a boyfriend or possessing a pair of trendy pants. In the latter case, the Jncos ad would have concretized the youths' desires but not satisfied them, as they could not afford the central product of the advertisement. Nonetheless, they saw the newscast videos as increasingly better productions, even as the newscasts' commercialization threatened to alienate them.

Creativity and Constraint in Representing Mexican American Cultures

SACA youth participants used mass media texts to represent themselves through the videos they made and wanted to make. Mass media formats and aesthetics helped the participants sustain interest in a video project they could be proud of. They adopted formats and aesthetics that they saw as legitimate and relevant to their lives. These appropriations, however, were double-edged. Mass media both enabled and constrained their visions of themselves and their culture. On the one hand, they confounded boundaries between pleasure and knowledge in envisioning their citizenship. On the other hand, they imagined videos that would represent them as members of a mass-mediated community rather than in opposition to it. As such, they were easily co-opted into a nation-state that disciplined their membership through the available discourses of mass media texts.

The youths at SACA did not always have the will or persistence to finish every video project they imagined, but their ideas alone expressed their agency in defining themselves as young, ethnic, and gendered citizens. Mass media assisted them in that process. Open to interpretation and reinterpretation, the texts and their aesthetics provided participants with an arsenal of tools they could put to creative use. They erased binaries between fictional and nonfictional genres by hybridizing the two. In their productions, a commercial could provide knowledge and an interview could provide entertainment and emotional value. The participants were active in the video-making process, but not in ways that privileged institutionalized definitions of nonfiction as reality or documentary or as a dutiful repository for citizen knowledge.

The fact that their hybrid productions pleased them, however, should not be confused with some powerful sense of media resistance. The youths' working-class positions constrained their creativity, making some of their visions unattainable. When one of the video projects promoted consumption, the central feature of the advertisement was beyond SACA's and the volunteers' means. This was also true for other desired purchases during the video project: compact discs for background music, costumes for sets, a lavaliere microphone, etc. Rather than creating alternative means for communicating a message, participants felt they needed the mass media elements to make their work look more prestigious. These constraints support Justin Lewis and Sut Jhally's argument that video production does not necessarily equip students to criticize mass media and their commercial structures:

> It is sometimes assumed, for example, that a practical knowledge of video production will help demystify the world of television and promote a more analytical, critical perspective. . . . To the contrary, we have found that students are apt to be seduced by the form, to try to imitate commercial television, and, when their efforts fall short, regard the work of professionals purely in terms of their aesthetic or technical prowess. At best, teaching production as purely a set of technical skills leads to an analytical immersion rather than a critical distance.[49]

The problem lies in equating video production with strong forms of resistance, particularly when students seek to replicate themes in media texts that they already enjoy. In our case, the students' class constraints sometimes stalled the creative process when they became obsessed with their own technical limitations and inability to mimic certain mass media conventions or styles.

It is equally problematic, though, to rely on the traditional binaries when defining active and passive, information and pleasure, and progressive and conservative. These divisions date to the separations between video and television and carry on through academic scholarship and media literacy programs. By simply objectifying all student video productions as either resistant or co-opted, experts lose the ability to see how these Mexican American youths were *both* resistant and complacent toward mass media in their own productions. This is why the videos volunteers produced were just as important as the videos they felt they could not. The volunteers' mass-mediated ideas may have been rooted in their desires for status, respect, entertainment, mobility, and flexibility. Yet their actual productions reflected the limited resources they had, both in the San Anto video project and in their community. How else should one interpret the need for talking hamsters in "Cenicienta"? San Anto did not have computer access to create animation for their own video footage. Furthermore, there were almost no resources within the community to distribute and exhibit alternatives to mass mediated forms and contents. Yet given what they had, the youths represented themselves with respect and authority. It was this kind of limited resistance within the confines of the west side that could happen despite economic and political barriers. Albeit limited, their resistance to certain media messages pushed the representational boundaries of mass media, transforming them without eliminating them.

Conclusion

Cultural Affirmation and Consumer Alienation

Every year for the past century, San Antonio has hosted a festival in late April to, in the words of city organizers, celebrate the city's "rich and diverse cultures."[1] Called simply "Fiesta" much of the downtown becomes the stage for ten days of parades, performances, amusements, and all-night parties in the streets and plazas. Like many festivals, Fiesta represents the city as a multicultural metropolis, a place where African Americans, Asian Americans, and especially Mexican Americans can be identified as culturally "different" but equal in a pluralistically liberal society. The mariachi bands, the folkloric dancers, the taco vendors, and the souvenir sellers become aesthetic representations of the diversity that the city espouses about itself and then sells to visitors, both locally and to the outside world.[2] Fiesta sales have surpassed $200 million in recent years.[3]

Perhaps no better sign of the economic and cultural significance of Fiesta became epitomized in the organizers' choice of a grand marshal to lead the 1998 Flambeau Parade, which has been historically one of the largest events of the festival. The theme "Hollywood Nights" attracted approximately 415,000 people to gaze at elaborately decorated floats carrying imitators of their favorite television stars and movie icons.[4] At the head of the line, the grand marshal sat regally, performing the role of a representative of Fiesta, an attraction for the city and a sign of the cultural diversity of its peoples. For his part, Rinky, "the San Antonio Taco Bell Chihuahua," had little to say on the occasion.

Rinky, the cousin of the more publicized "Dinky the Chihuahua," earned his reputed spot for his participation in the nationwide television advertising campaign for Taco Bell throughout 1997 and 1998. His catchphrase, "Yo Quiero Taco Bell," made him both adored and despised by Mexican Americans who envisioned the dog as a metaphor for the representation of Mexican American culture in all mass media. Initially, Ornelas and Associates, a Mexican American owned agency from Dallas, tested the advertisements with Latinos who found the bilingual and bicultural dog cute.[5] However, the campaign also incited the ire of national Latino organizations, including the League of United Latin American Citizens (LULAC).[6] As former county commissioner, judge, and San Antonio media activist Albert Peña wrote in La Prensa: "Certainly there are many gorgeous Hispanic women and handsome Hispanic males who are available to cater to the growing Hispanic population. Save the Chihuahua for the dog shows. Yo no quiero Taco Bell."[7] Among the adolescents at San Anto, I heard far more of the former comment than the latter critique. One boy, who worked with a team drawing a picture of a "cool student" for an activity, explained why the group's sketch of the Taco Bell Chihuahua represented them: "Chihuahuas are cool. He's Mexican, like us. And we like Taco Bell, too." Identification with mass media, in this example, was both culturally cognizant and consumer motivated.

According to Benedict Anderson, every community has different ways of imagining itself.[8] For Mexican Americans in San Antonio, mass media representations have provided powerful yet contradictory ways to imagine themselves in relation to other Americans. The battle to enter mass media industries to produce media on their own terms has been part and parcel of Mexican Americans' struggle to be a part of a historical power bloc, one that is not oppositional to capitalism but instead accepts economic inequality while engaging in the politics of representation. Working with less financing and fewer resources than Anglo Americans, Mexican Americans have contributed to new hybrid forms of Mexican American culture as alternatives to mainstream media that still portray a largely white and middle-class nation. To do so, however, has demanded that Mexican Americans submit to market imperatives that continue to define Mexican Americans either as "authentic" or as undifferentiated members of a multicultural middle class. In either case, Mexican American culture becomes reduced to a collection of signs that can be made more specific for niche audiences or more generalized for mass or panethnic audiences. As people who have entrusted themselves with representing an imagined Mexican American community, media producers face a double-bind in trying to commodify a culture without alienating its consumers. The challenge for Mexican American media producers is worth pursuing, because, as Mike Featherstone points out, mass media are arguably necessary parts in the formation of the nation.[9] Mass media provide several lenses through which Mexican Americans can envision themselves as members of a liberal and pluralistic society. Children and teens, in particular, have used media texts and the practices surrounding their consumption to define themselves as young, ethnic, and gendered members in a world where they often have had limited agency over other aspects of their lives. Through media consumption, young Mexican Americans expose power relations that bind and distinguish them from their peers and elders in daily life. The texts themselves reinforce these bonds and distinctions, spurring a wealth of collective memories and personal aspirations. This means that media might crisscross the globe, but their texts are useful in very local ways.

Yet, as Rinky also illustrates, not all Mexican Americans feel the same ways about mass media representations. No one book could adequately describe all the different ways that Mexican Americans use, create, and think about mass media. This book focused mainly on two groups who historically have had deep interests in mass media as a means of personal and cultural expression. Mexican American media industry workers, from corporate executives to roadies, depended on cultural representations that have made some visions of Mexican Americans visible at the expense of others. Mexican American teens, on the other hand, transformed these representations to make themselves visible in their own personal ways. Undoubtedly, other Mexican Americans may cite very different relationships with mass media and their images. One group that is noticeably absent from the scope of this book has been the dedicated activists in Mexican American communities working to change media industries from outside. In San Antonio, a committed group of Mexican Americans continue to work as artists, intellectuals, and students dedicated to changing the structure of industrial media production through engaged resistance. Their work perhaps will form a new chapter for the future of Mexican Americans' relationship with media.

Interestingly, the biggest controversy in San Antonio the spring of the 1998 Fiesta was summed up in a letter to the editor of the *San Antonio Express-News*: "Rinky you fraud! So the people at the Fiesta Flambeau Parade Association put out the word that a Chihuahua will be featured in this year's Fiesta Flambeau. That can mean only one thing: Dinky, the fabulously famous talking Chihuahua from the Taco Bell commercials is coming to town. Yet, just as we were about to roll out the red carpet and put out the silver fire hydrant, we learn that it's a sham. It's not Dinky who will be in the parade, it's 'the San Antonio Taco Bell Chihuahua.'" Rinky, by this logic, could not be the esteemed grand marshal representing San Antonio and its cultures because he was not Dinky, the "real" Taco Bell Chihuahua. In this example, mass media industries and their representations can include and exclude its consumers simultaneously. The complaint pinpointed San Antonio's place after cities such as Los Angeles, New York, and Miami, which have little trouble attracting media stars and cultural icons. San Antonio, and by implication its people, might not have the economic status of other cities, but their culture deserves equal respect from the multinational companies that commodify it.

This leads to a final discussion of the city as the site where Mexican Americans' relationships with media have been fostered. Mexican Americans have long been involved in the production of mass media, but the struggles for recognition precipitated by the Chicano movements coincided with the city's search for a brand name in the new globalizing economy. By selling itself as *the* site for Mexican American cultural production and consumption, San Antonio—like Los Angeles, New York, and Miami—could outsource its own citizens in the service of higher revenues. While this has benefited some Mexican Americans in the city, it has effectively disfranchised many more who can only participate in civic life through continually reduced means of consumption.

The neoliberal state in the late twentieth century put cities into competition over corporate investment to offset shortages in federal spending and institutional support. City governments wooed businesses with tax breaks, loosened regulations, and modern educational, technological, and social infrastructures.[10] Media production was one site where San Antonio could struggle for competitive advantage by offering the right combination of cultural resources and economic incentives. Low wages and anti-union policies ensured a cheap labor pool for companies looking to outsource or move operations to a cheaper locale, while the expertise of Mexican American media producers helped mainstream companies reach a new demographic. The fact that over one thousand applicants appeared in a casting call for extras in *All the Pretty Horses* in 1999 demonstrated both the film company's mobility away from expensive sites in Hollywood and San Antonio laborers' eagerness for temporary six-dollar-an-hour jobs.[11] Few would be able to afford the price of a movie ticket on those wages alone, yet the city prided itself on the investment, offering sales and use tax exemptions through the Texas Film Commission to seal the deal.[12]

Mexican Americans who aligned with city officials created a symbiosis between cultural promotion and profitable marketing. Formulated as a cultural right, access to consumer markets became a rallying cry for Mexican

Americans at all levels of media industries, though few media workers actually had the political clout to propose deregulation as the primary solution to the perceived inequality. Those with the most power included Mexican Americans who merged their public and private identities in becoming cultural spokespeople for transnational capital. Lionel Sosa developed Hispanic advertising campaigns for Ronald Reagan in 1980 and nearly every Republican candidate running nationally and in Texas since. On the Democrats' side, four-time mayor and former Housing and Urban Development director Henry Cisneros was president and chief operating officer of Univision from 1997 to 2000. Upon accepting the position, Cisneros said he was "gratified to be joining the private sector with a company that affords me the opportunity to return to my Hispanic roots."[13] Understating his own role in supporting free enterprise in San Antonio while mayor, Cisneros also ignored the fact that his means of return to his roots was a national network that largely uses Mexican and Venezuelan programming to sell Hispanic audiences to a bevy of American advertisers. What stirred cultural pride for some Mexican Americans has made a profitable synergy for those in the highest positions of marketing that pride.

In the process, city officials and media executives shared an organizational culture that treated Mexican Americans more as clients than as political participants. Cultural tourism, such as the Fiesta and the Tejano Festival, became ways to both serve culture to a clientele public and to serve the public as commodities to a host of transnational industries, including hotel, restaurant, nightclub chains, and mailing list companies that then sold that information back to media industries. As director of the Tejano Music Association Robert Aurellano pointed out, the city and Tejano industry sought mutual economic benefits. "[Visitors] would come in just for the Fan Fair alone to hear all of the bands, and then they'll just stick around for the weekend to go to all of the nightclubs because all of the best Tejano bands in the state will be here," he explained. By treating their citizenry like demographic market segments, cities like San Antonio could score a win-win situation with corporations looking to target Mexican American communities.

Not everyone, however, has been a winner. Nonprofit media organizations, dependent on a combination of winnowing public funds and private donations, have had to reevaluate their missions in light of the city's pro-revenue stance. Unable to claim the numbers of clients that corporate-sponsored events can post, nonprofits developed new strategies to make do. Corporate partnerships promoted the good citizenship of private industries while ensuring that cultural organizations would not compete for a commercial market in the communities they served. City partnerships required the same organizations to reframe their constituents as "at-risk populations," a code phrase constructing Mexican Americans as both "different" and in need of "assimilation."[14] Even given the new reframing, not every nonprofit could defend their needs in the face of the city's market orientation. As much as the city promoted itself as a cultural Mecca for Mexican Americans, the sudden infliction of budget cuts on one nonprofit media organization after it hosted a gay film festival sent a clear message: only certain Mexican American media producers may be considered "risky" enough to merit the city's aid.[15] In this context, the tensions around Mexican Americans making their own media could be read as a struggle with the institutions that framed Mexican American community media funding as a business investment or a charitable gift for some of the city's most excluded citizens.

Just as serious has been the number of Mexican American citizens who are excluded from the city by virtue of their class. Turned toward market expansion, cities have contributed to the balkanization of their own citizens into a "cybergeoisie," who have socioeconomic security and high-tech access to global goods, and a class of "protosurps," who cannot make ends meet from their unstable occupations in the global economy.[16] The stratification of wealth ironically most affects the Mexican American children who represent both the cultural future and the plum market for media. Again, young Mexican Americans might have consumed more mass media, but the middle-class lifestyle portrayed in these texts was out of reach for the one out of three who was born into poverty.[17] Johanna Wyn and Rob White explain, "There is an increasing divergence in young people's experience between the products that are available for consumption by them, which on the surface appears to be 'inclusive,' and the reality of exclusion from expected standards of living. . . . The contradiction is also that although young people share cultural symbols and language derived from the media, they certainly do not share the means to buy the consumer goods which accompany these symbols."[18] Urged to consume while limited by parents' lack of class mobility, Mexican American young people were culturally included but economically excluded through their consumption. Their lack of consumer power, relative to middle-class teenagers, reinforced the limits of a cultural affirmation driven by media consumption.

Although the deteriorating conditions for Mexican American youths, as well as adults, is concerning, these citizens are not without hope. As the neoliberal state places the burden on cities to affirm cultural differences vis-à-vis opening access to consumer markets, the contradiction between citizenship and consumption become ever clearer to those who now see a dizzying array of cultural products—from Tejano concerts to Selena key chains—without the means to buy basic necessities.[19] The city will have to find new differences to justify why its members cannot buy into the fruits of globalization; and its members, who see the inequalities via media representations, will have to decide if the global economy represents their interests. One can only wait to see how cities, mass media industries, and the state participate in this struggle to represent and generate consumption, and how citizens disfranchised from consumption retaliate.

Notes

Introduction

1. A point well argued in Lauren Berlant, *The Queen of America Goes to Washington City* (Durham, N.C.: Duke, 1997).
2. For early resistance to stereotypes, see José E. Limón, "Stereotyping and Chicano Resistance: A Historical Dimension," in *Chicanos and Film: Representation and Resistance,* ed. Chon Noriega (Minneapolis: University of Minnesota Press, 1992). Chicano media activism is discussed in Chon Noriega, *Shot in America: Television, the State, and the Rise of Social Movement Cinema* (Minneapolis: University of Minnesota Press, 2000). The recent brownout is documented in Michael A. Fletcher, "Latinos Plan Boycott of Network TV; Goal of 'Brownout' Is Better Roles for Hispanics," *Washington Post,* 28 July 1999.
3. Ignacio M. García, *Chicanismo: The Forging of a Militant Ethos among Mexican Americans* (Tucson: University of Arizona Press, 1997).
4. Rosa Linda Fregoso, *The Bronze Screen: Chicana and Chicano Film Culture* (Minneapolis: University of Minnesota Press, 1993).
5. Philip Sonnichsen, "Los Madrugadores: Early Spanish Radio in California," *La Luz,* June 1977.
6. George Sánchez, *Becoming Mexican American: Ethnicity and Acculturation in Chicano Los Angeles, 1900–1943* (New York: Oxford University Press, 1993), 182.
7. Ibid., 171.
8. My reading of imagined communities builds on Benedict Anderson, *Imagined Communities* (London: Verso, 1983). Anderson argues that popular culture unifies disparate peoples. I would like to add that membership in those communities is not uniform or singular.
9. Noriega, *Shot in America.*
10. For a discussion of post-Fordism, see David Harvey, *The Condition of Postmodernity* (Oxford: Blackwell, 1989).
11. Rebecca Morales and Frank Bonilla, "Restructuring the New Inequality," in *Latinos in a Changing U.S. Economy: Comparative Perspectives on Growing Inequality,* ed. Rebecca Morales and Frank Bonilla (Newbury Park: Sage, 1993).
12. Brook Larmer, "Latino America," *Newsweek,* 12 July 1999.
13. Christie Haubegger, "The Legacy of Generation Ñ," *Newsweek,* 12 July 1999.
14. I borrowed this phrase from Marshall Berman, *All That's Solid Melts into Air* (New York: Simon & Schuster, 1982).
15. This work has been done by an ever-growing group of scholars, including David Buckingham, *Moving Images: Understanding Children's Emotional Responses to Television* (Manchester: Manchester University Press, 1996); David Morley, *Family*

Television: Cultural Power and Domestic Leisure (London: Comedia, 1986); Janice Radway, *Reading the Romance: Women, Patriarchy, and Popular Literature* (Chapel Hill: University of North Carolina Press, 1984); Ellen Seiter, Hans Borchers, Gabrielle Kreutzner, and Eva-Maria Warth, eds., *Remote Control: Television, Audiences, and Cultural Power* (London: Routledge, 1989); and John Tulloch and Henry Jenkins, *Science Fiction Audiences* (London: Routledge, 1995).

16. George Lipsitz, *Dangerous Crossroads: Popular Music, Postmodernism, and the Poetics of Place* (London: Verso, 1994), 88–90.

17. 1990 Census of Population and Housing Summary Tape File (HSTF), 3. Persons of Hispanic Origin in the United States, U.S. Department of Commerce, Bureau of the Census, Data User Services, 1994, Washington D.C.

18. Richard García, *Rise of the Mexican American Middle Class: San Antonio, 1929–1941* (College Station: Texas A & M University Press, 1991), 77–78.

19. Neil Foley, "Becoming Hispanic: Mexican Americans and the Faustian Pact with Whiteness," in *Reflexiones: New Directions in Mexican American Studies*, ed. Neil Foley (Austin: Center for Mexican American Studies, 1998).

20. García, *Rise of the Mexican American Middle Class*, 106.

21. Ibid.

22. Richard Flores, "Aesthetic Process and Cultural Citizenship: The Membering of a Social Body in San Antonio," in *Latino Cultural Citizenship: Claiming Identity, Space, and Rights*, ed. William Flores and Rina Benmayor (Boston: Beacon Press, 1997).

23. "Wealthiest Get Richer While Poor Get Poorer," *Austin American Statesman*, 18 December 1997, A3.

24. Bureau of Census, "1990 Census Lookup (1.4a)," Database C90STF3A, prepared by the Geography Division in Cooperation with the Housing Division, Bureau of the Census, Washington D.C., 1990.

25. *Hispanic Databook of U.S. Cities and Counties* (Milpitas, Calif.: Toucan Valley Publishers, 1994), 446–47.

26. Anne Hardgrove, *Community and Public Culture: The Marwari in Calcutta, c. 1989–1997*, World Wide Web, Columbia University E-book, 2002.

27. Betsy Guzmán, "The Hispanic Population: Census 2000 Brief," U.S. Census Bureau (Washington D.C., 2001), 2 (http://www.census.gov/prod/2001pubs/c2kbr01–3.pdf).

28. "Census Bureau Projects Doubling of Nation's Population by 2100," U.S. Census Bureau, Washington, D.C., 2000.

Chapter 1   **Mexican American Mass Media in San Antonio**

Parts of this chapter are reprinted, with permission, from Vicki Mayer, "From Segmented to Fragmented: Latino Media in San Antonio, Texas," *Journalism and Mass Communication Quarterly* 78, no. 2 (2001): 275–90.

1. Notable recent cultural histories of media include Susan Douglas, *Listening In: Radio and the American Imagination, from Amos 'n' Andy and Edward R. Murrow to Wolfman Jack and Howard Stern* (New York: Times Books, 1999); Susan Douglas, *Where the Girls Are: Growing Up Female with the Mass Media* (New York: Times Books, 1994); Michele Hilmes, *Hollywood and Broadcasting: From Radio to Cable, Illinois Studies in Communications* (Urbana: University of Illinois Press, 1990); Michele Hilmes, *Radio Voices: American Broadcasting, 1922–1952* (Minneapolis: University of Minnesota Press, 1997); Noriega, *Shot in America*; and Thomas Streeter, *Selling the Air: A Critique of the Policy of Commercial Broadcasting in the United States* (Chicago: University of Chicago Press, 1996).

2. Virginia Escalante, "In Pursuit of Ethnic Audiences: The Media and Latinos," *Renato Rosaldo Lecture Series Monograph*, 7th ser. (1991); Rosa Linda Fregoso, *The Bronze Screen: Chicana and Chicano Film Culture* (Minneapolis: University of Minnesota Press, 1993); Félix Gutiérrez and Jorge Schement, *Spanish Language Radio in the Southwestern United States* (Austin: Center for Mexican American Studies, 1979); Chon Noriega, "Introduction," in *The Ethnic Eye: Latino Media Arts*, ed. Chon Noriega and Ana López (Minneapolis: University of Minnesota Press, 1996); Noriega, *Shot in America*.

3. Carlos E. Cortéz, "Who Is Maria? What Is Juan? Dilemmas of Analyzing the Chicano Image in U.S. Feature Films," in *Chicanos and Film: Essays on Chicano Representation and Resistance*, ed. Chon Noriega (New York: Garland, 1992).

4. Mosco applied primarily quantitative data on race and gender to political-economic research in the United States to urge more political economists to study identity in the twenty-first century. Vincent Mosco, *The Political Economy of Communication: Rethinking and Renewal* (London: Sage, 1996).

5. América Rodríguez, "Made in the U.S.A.: The Constructions of Univision News" (Ph.D. diss., University of California, San Diego, 1993), 78.

6. "*La Prensa*, an Institution in Our Community," brochure, 1999.

7. Patricia Elena Constantakis, "Spanish-Language Television and the 1988 Presidential Elections: A Case Study of the 'Dual Identity' of Ethnic Minority Media" (Ph.D. diss., University of Texas, Austin, 1993). According to Constantakis, immigrant newspapers tend to be temporary publications, because they are oriented toward a population that either returns to the mother country or assimilates, making the publication irrelevant.

8. Victoria Lerner, "Los Exilados de la Revolución Mexicana y la Comunidad Chicana (1915–1930)," in *El México Olvidado I: La Historia Del Pueblo Chicano*, ed. David Maciel (Chihuahua, Mexico: Universidad Autónoma de Cuidad Juárez and University of Texas, El Paso, 1996).

9. David Montejano, *Anglos and Mexicans in the Making of Texas, 1836–1986* (Austin: University of Texas Press, 1987) 117–28.

10. Onofre de Stefano, "La Prensa of San Antonio and Its Literary Page, 1913 to 1915" (Ph.D. diss., University of California, Los Angeles, 1983).

11. Robert B. Horowitz, *The Irony of Regulatory Reform: The Deregulation of American Telecommunications* (New York: Oxford University Press, 1989).

12. This contradiction is well documented in Streeter, *Selling the Air: A Critique of the Policy of Commercial Broadcasting in the United States*.

13. Ibid., 102.

14. They write the broker's name was Lozano, but it is unclear if this was the same person as the owner of *La Prensa*. In Gutiérrez and Schement, *Spanish Language Radio*, 6.

15. Federico Subvervi-Vélez, "Media," in *The Hispanic-American Almanac: A Reference Work on Hispanics in the United States*, ed. Nicolás Kanellos (Detroit: Gale Research, 1993), 646.

16. Clemencia Rodríguez, *Fissures in the Mediascape: An International Study of Citizens' Media*, ed. Brenda Dervin, *Alternative Communication* (Cresskill, N.J.: Hampton Press, 2000), 142.

17. Rodríguez, "Made in the U.S.A.," 39.

18. Gutiérrez and Schement, *Spanish Language Radio*, 10.

19. Subvervi-Vélez, "Media," 647.

20. Gutiérrez and Schement, *Spanish Language Radio*, 10.

21. Subvervi-Vélez, "Media," 653.

22. Seth Fein, "Myths of Cultural Imperialism and Nationalism in Golden Age

Mexican Cinema," in *Fragments of a Golden Age: The Politics of Culture in Mexico, 1940–2000*, ed. Gilbert M. Joseph, Anne Rubenstein, and Eric Zolov (Durham: Duke University Press, 2001).

23. Rodríguez, *Fissures in the Mediascape*, 135.
24. Leo Grebler, Joan Moore, and Ralph Guzmán, 1970, in Gutiérrez and Schement, *Spanish Language Radio*, 11.
25. Gutiérrez and Schement, *Spanish Language Radio*, 58.
26. Subvervi-Vélez, "Media," 654.
27. George Sánchez, *Becoming Mexican American: Ethnicity and Acculturation in Chicano Los Angeles, 1900–1943* (New York: Oxford University Press, 1993), 182.
28. Rodríguez, "Made in the U.S.A.," 37.
29. Adding another intercultural layer to this story, most of these recordings are now held by Arhoolie Records, an Anglo-American owned company in California.
30. Guadalupe San Miguel Jr., "The Rise of Tejano Music in the Post–World War II, 1946–1964," *Journal of American Ethnic History* 19, no. 1 (1999).
31. Charles Rosson, "Flaco Jimenez," *Texas Monthly*, January 1998; accessed 19 September 1999 at http://www.texasmonthly.com/ranch/source/8848083651350/8848083661350.php.
32. Nicolas Valenzuela, "Organizational Evolution of a Spanish Language Television Network: An Environmental Approach" (Ph.D. diss., Stanford University, 1985).
33. Streeter, *Selling the Air*, 169–72.
34. Luis A. Noriega and Frances Leach, *Broadcasting in Mexico* (Boston: Routledge & Kegan Paul, 1979).
35. América Rodríguez, "Control Mechanisms of National News-Making: Britain, Canada, Mexico, and the United States," in *Questioning the Media: A Critical Introduction*, ed. John Downing, Ali Mohammadi, and Annabelle Sreberny-Mohammadi (Thousand Oaks, Calif.: Sage, 1995), 144.
36. John Sinclair, "Spanish-Language Television in the United States," *Studies in Latin American Popular Culture* 9 (1990): 39–63.
37. América Rodríguez, "Creating an Audience and Remapping a Nation: A Brief History of U.S. Spanish-Language Broadcasting 1930–1980," *Quarterly Review of Film and Video* 16, nos. 3–4 (1999).
38. Kenton Wilkinson, "Where Culture, Language, and Communication Converge: The Latin American Cultural-Linguistic Television Market" (Ph.D. diss., University of Texas, 1995).
39. Claudia Fernández and Andrew Paxman, *El Tigre: Emilio Azcárraga y su Imperio Televisa* (Mexico City: Grijalbo, 2000).
40. Subvervi-Vélez, "Media," 654.
41. Félix Gutiérrez and Jorge Schement, "Spanish International Network: The Flow of Television from Mexico to the United States," *Communication Research* 11, no. 2 (1984): 245.
42. Félix Gutiérrez and Jorge Schement, "Problems of Ownership and Control of Spanish-Language Media in the United States: National and International Concerns," in *Communication and Social Structure: Critical Studies in Mass Media Research*, ed. Emile McAnany, Jorge Schnitman, and Noreene Janus (New York: Praeger, 1981), 193.
43. Gutiérrez and Schement, "Spanish International Network," 246.
44. Gutiérrez and Schement, "Problems of Ownership and Control," 193.
45. América Rodríguez, "Commercial Ethnicity: Language, Class and Race in the Marketing of the Hispanic Audience," *Communication Review* 2, no. 3 (1997).
46. Lionel Sosa, *The Americano Dream: How Latinos Can Achieve Success in Business and in Life* (New York: Dutton, 1998).

47. Gutiérrez and Schement, "Spanish International Network," 246.
48. In 1996, Hispano Marketing billed $7.8 million (Megan Kamerick, "Hispano Marketing Hit with Recent Departures of Key Staff," *San Antonio Business Journal*, 21 April 1997; accessed 2 October 1999 at http://www.bizjournals.com/sanantonio/stories/1997/04/21/story7.html). Bromley, Aguilar & Associates billed $14.8 million in 1996 ("Advertising Age Ranks Bromley, Aguilar & Associates," *San Antonio Business Journal*, 21 April 1997; accessed 2 October 1999 at http://sanantonio.bizjournals.com/sanantonio/stories/1997/04/21/daily16.html) and $122 million in 1998 (Steve Krajewski, "Cartel Creativo's Defense Scores," *Adweek*, 21 December 1998). In 1997, KJS Spark billed $18 million ("Texaco Selects KJS as Advertising Agency for Hispanic Market," *San Antonio Business Journal*, 24 February 1997; accessed 2 October 1997 at http://sanantonio.bizjournals.com/sanantonio/stories/1997/02/24/daily13.html). In 1998, Cartel Creativo billed $27 million (Krajewski, "Cartel Creativo's Defense Scores").
49. Detailed histories of SIN/SICC can be found in John Sinclair, *Latin American Television: A Global View* (Oxford: Oxford University Press, 1999) and Wilkinson, "Where Culture, Language, and Communication Converge."
50. *Marketer's Guide to Media* (New York: BPI Communications, 1998).
51. *Broadcasting and Cable Yearbook 1999* (New Jersey: R. R. Bowker, 1999).
52. Gutiérrez and Schement, "Problems of Ownership and Control," 190.
53. Both Subvervi-Vélez, "Media" and Clint Wilson and Felix Gutiérrez, *Race, Multiculturalism, and the Media: From Mass to Class Communication* (Thousand Oaks, Calif.: Sage, 1995) hint at these positive effects.
54. Michael Curtin, "On Edge: Culture Industries in the Neo-Network Era," in *Making and Selling Culture*, ed. Richard Ohmann (Middletown: Wesleyan University Press, 1996), 190.
55. Joseph Turow, "Segmenting, Signalling, and Tailoring: Probing the Dark Side of Target Marketing," in *Critical Studies in Media Commercialism*, ed. Robin Andersen and Lance Strate (London: Oxford University Press, 2000), 244.
56. "*La Prensa*, an Institution in Our Community."
57. Ibid.
58. Melissa S. Monroe, "New Publication Seeks to Fill Void Left by Demise of KSJL," *San Antonio Business Journal*, 19 October 1998; accessed 2 October 1999 at http://sanantonio.bizjournals.com/sanantonio/stories/1998/10/19/story8.html.
59. Megan Kamerick, "Prime Time to Bring Many Operations under One Roof," *San Antonio Business Journal*, 20 April 1998; accessed 2 October 1999 at http://sanantonio.bizjournals.com/sanantonio/stories/1998/04/20/story3.html.
60. Melissa S. Monroe, "Bilingual Paper Hits the Streets in Alamo City," *San Antonio Business Journal*, 29 December 1997; accessed 2 October 1999 at http://sanantonio.bizjournals.com/sanantonio/stories/1997/12/29/story8.html.
61. Melissa S. Monroe, "Current Boosts Staff, Circulation," *San Antonio Business Journal*, 30 March 1998; 2 October 1999 at http://sanantonio.bizjournals.com/sanantonio/stories/1998/03/30/story8.html. This niche strategy was successful in assisting Alternative Media in selling all of its papers to another owner one year later, reaffirming that alternative presses are economically one of the strongest press markets in the United States (Eric Bates, "Chaining the Alternatives: What Started as a Movement Has Become an Industry," *Nation*, 29 June 1998). Soon after the buyout, *The Current* discontinued its editorial policy to target Hispanic readers, though the paper still strives for racial equity in editorial hires.
62. Among the web of partnerships, Televisa partnered with Venezuela's Venevisión for content and with PanAmSat, a U.S. company for satellite distribution throughout the Americas. In 1997, Sony bought Telemundo outright and partnered with TV Azteca in Mexico for content. Sinclair, *Latin American Television*, 109–14.

63. Néstor García Canclini, "North Americans or Latin Americans? The Redefinition of Mexican Identity and the Free Trade Agreements," in *Mass Media and Free Trade: NAFTA and the Cultural Industries*, ed. Emile McAnany and Kenton Wilkinson (Austin: University of Texas Press, 1996), 145–46.
64. Sinclair, *Latin American Television*, 115.
65. Subvervi-Vélez, "Media," 649.
66. Gutiérrez and Schement, *Spanish Language Radio*, 14.
67. Megan Kamerick, "Clear Channel Plans New Building," *San Antonio Business Journal*, 21 December 1998; accessed 2 October 1999 at http://sanantonio.bizjournals.com/sanantonio/stories/1998/12/21/story1.html; Debbie Nathan, "Spurs Merger Rampage," *San Antonio Current*, 14–20 October 1999.
68. Ratings gathered from Arbitron's online ratings service for summer and fall 1998 and spring 1999 (Radio y Musica Online, *Radio y Musica: San Antonio, Arbitron Personas 12+*, Radio Y Musica Inc., 9 April 1999; accessed 19 September 1999 at http://www.radiomusica.com/Arbitron/Sanantonio.html). Of Clear Channel's holdings, KXTN-FM, KROM-FM, KCOR-AM and KXTM-AM are Spanish-language formats (*Broadcasting and Cable Yearbook 1999* [New Jersey: R. R. Bowker, 1999]).
69. Mira Schwirtz, "Rates Soar in Quest to Woo Black Listeners," *Mediaweek*, 19 May 1998.
70. "Cox Buys Two Radio Stations in San Antonio," *San Antonio Business Journal*, 1 December 1997; accessed 2 October 1999 at http://sanantonio.bizjournals.com/sanantonio/stories/1997/12/01/daily17.html.
71. *Broadcasting and Cable Yearbook 1999* (New Jersey: R. R. Bowker, 1999).
72. Sí TV, "Bruce Barshop, Biography," San Antonio, 1999.
73. Elia Esparza, "Must Sí TV: Galavision and Producer Jeff Valdez Go Bilingual," *Hispanic*, May 1998, 24.
74. Based on a San Antonio-produced pilot entitled *Barbacoa*, The Brothers Garcia was reconfigured for a more generic panethnic consumer who predominantly speaks English. In 2000, the show aired Sundays at 5 P.M. eastern standard time.
75. From 1962 to 1966, KWEX and KMEX (in Los Angeles) together accumulated over $1 million in debt. Gutiérrez and Schement, "Spanish International Network," 252. Three decades later, both Univision and Telemundo nearly filed bankruptcy trying to finance their expansion. Wilkinson, "Where Culture, Language, and Communication Converge," 154.
76. Dan Schiller writes that the "two-tier marketing system" is characteristic of the new global economy. Dan Schiller, *Digital Capitalism: Networking the Global Market System* (Cambridge, Mass.: MIT Press, 1999), 140.
77. Ibid. Schiller predicts that market entry will become even more capital-intensive as cities transfer to digital broadcasting systems. San Antonio transferred to digital service in 2002.
78. Interview with Manuel Davila Jr., KEDA-AM General Sales Manager, 17 April 2001.
79. Turow, "Segmenting, Signalling, and Tailoring," 243.
80. Etienne Balibar describes "racial crisis" as a "threshold of intolerance," which, once crossed, leads to people acting out racialized postures that can be perceived as positive or negative by elites. Etienne Balibar, "Racism and Crisis," in *Race, Nation, Class: Ambiguous Identities*, ed. Etienne Balibar and Immanuel Wallerstein (London: Verso, 1991), 219.
81. Nicos Poulantzas, *Political Power and Social Classes*, ed. Timothy O'Hagan, trans. Timothy O'Hagan (London: Sheed and Ward, 1973), 301.

Chapter 2   Mexican Americans Making Media, Making Citizens

1. Descriptions of the ethnic and class inequalities between Mexican Americans and Anglo Americans in San Antonio in the pre–Civil Rights Era can be found in Rodolfo Acuña, *Occupied America: A History of Chicanos*, 3rd ed. (New York: Harper Collins, 1988); David Montejano, *Anglos and Mexicans in the Making of Texas, 1836–1986* (Austin: University of Texas Press, 1987); and Peter Skerry, *Mexican Americans: The Ambivalent Minority* (Cambridge: Harvard University Press, 1993).

2. Noriega, *Shot in America*, 25.

3. Ibid., 214 n. 37.

4. Ibid., 134. Noriega uses this phrase, popularized by Saul Alinsky, to describe mass media professionals in much the same terms that Alinsky described political and social organizers.

5. One of the most publicized schisms between media professionals and media activists in San Antonio occurred around the establishment of public access television in the mid–1970s. From interview with Pleas McNeel, 17 April 1998.

6. Simon Cottle, *Television and Ethnic Minorities: Producers' Perspectives* (Aldershot: Avebury, 1997), 11.

7. Peter Collins, "Negotiating Selves: Reflections on Unstructured Interviewing," *Sociological Research Online* 3, no. 3 (1998): para. 3.10.

8. M. M. Bakhtin, *The Dialogic Imagination: Four Essays*, ed. Michael Holquist, trans. Carol Emerson and Michael Holquist (Austin: University of Texas Press, 1981).

9. Stuart Hall, "Who Needs Identity?" in *Questions of Cultural Identity*, ed. Stuart Hall and Paul Du Gay (London: Sage, 1996).

10. Sosa, *The Americano Dream*.

11. Michael Omi and Henry Winant, *Racial Formation in the United States: From the 1960s to the 1990s* (London: Routledge, 1994).

12. David Novitz, "Art, Narrative, and Human Nature," *Philosophy and Literature* 13, no. 1 (1989); Robert Polkinghorne, "Human Existence and Narrative," in *Narrative Knowing and the Human Sciences* (Albany: State University of New York Press, 1988).

13. Michael Leiman, *The Political Economy of Racism: A History* (London: Pluto, 1993), 272. Although his argument focuses on African American communities and black capitalism, a parallel argument could apply to San Antonio's Mexican American community.

14. Sosa, *The Americano Dream*, 131.

15. Bill Ryan, *Making Capital from Culture: The Corporate Form of Capitalist Production* (Berlin: Walter de Gruyter, 1992).

16. Joseph Turow (*Media Industries: The Production of News and Entertainment* (New York: Longman, 1984), 136.

17. Omi and Winant, *Racial Formation in the United States*.

18. Frederic Jameson makes this distinction in discussing the difference between reading the political and the social into historical narratives. Whereas the political reading discusses the individual's resolutions of class tensions, the social reading more broadly addresses class conflict. Frederic Jameson, *The Political Unconscious: Narrative as a Socially Symbolic Act* (Ithaca, N.Y.: Cornell University Press, 1981), 81–84.

19. Noriega, *Shot in America*, 98.

20. Ibid., 133–38.

21. Noriega, "Introduction."

22. See also América Rodríguez, "Commercial Ethnicity: Language, Class and Race in the Marketing of the Hispanic Audience," *Communication Review* 2, no. 3 (1997).

23. The *Express-News*, owned by the Hearst Corporation, is atypical in its Hispanic hiring rates. In contrast, Rivard said only 3.46 percent of newsroom employees nationally are Hispanic compared with 11 percent of the population demographically. Rivard received *Editor & Publisher*'s "Editor of the Year Award" in April 2000, in part for his hiring efforts.

24. In *Television and Ethnic Minorities: Producers' Perspectives*, Simon Cottle found similar results in his interviews with BBC employees who worked in minority programming.

25. Although there are many women in media industries who occupy powerful positions, women are underrepresented in the areas of production, direction, writing, editing, and cinematography ("Women of the Year: They're Gaining Power in Hollywood and Using It to Make Films That Women Want to See," *Time*, 13 November 1995, and "Women in Film Underrepresented in Spite of Box Office Success," *Media Report to Women*, 1998).

26. This is also central to América Rodríguez's argument in *Making Latino News: Race, Language, Class* (Thousand Oaks: Sage, 1999).

27. Historians trace *música tejana* to the early 1900s, when the introduction of the accordion into small traveling bands of Mexicans harmonized with the bajo sexto and the guitar. Stylistic elements of Tejano can be found in several predecessors from the past century, including conjunto, orquestra, and Chicano music. For example, see Manuel H. Peña, *Música Tejana: The Cultural Economy of Artistic Transformation* (College Station: Texas A & M University Press, 1999); Manuel H. Peña, *The Texas-Mexican Conjunto: History of a Working-Class Music* (Austin: University of Texas Press, 1985); Jose Reyna, "Notes on Tejano Music," *Perspectives on Mexican American Studies* 1 (1988). Producers tended to trace Tejano back to more personal referents, such as when a family member started playing or when they became fans. Those who focused on the industrial development of the market also mentioned the Guadalupe Conjunto Festival and the Tejano Music Awards as important events in Tejano history in 1980–81.

28. Ironically, the group played "Talk to Me," a crossover rock 'n' roll song.

29. For a similar argument about Latinos in marketing and advertising agencies, see Arlene Dávila, *Latinos Inc.: The Marketing and Making of a People* (Berkeley: University of California Press, 2001), 47.

30. One radio announcer explained it this way: "If there was, you know, some Jewish name I couldn't pronounce, I wouldn't want to mispronounce it and the person would say, you know, that's a little disrespectful. . . . By the same token, you know, Hispanic names should remain Hispanic names. You know there's times that I've done functions here in San Antonio and . . . when I see names that, that I'm not familiar with, I make it a point to ask because I think it's a sign of respect when you at least make a concerted effort to get it right."

31. This argument conforms in many ways with the argument for Latino cultural citizenship expounded by authors in William Flores and Rina Benmayor, eds., *Latino Cultural Citizenship: Claiming Identity, Space, and Rights* (Boston: Beacon Press, 1997). According to them, public recognition of Mexican American culture, particularly through language, is a cultural right of all citizens.

32. Carlos Guerra, "City Gets Free Ride Off Tejano's Millions," *San Antonio Express-News*, 23 March 1996.

33. Several interviews with people involved in all parts of the industry reconfirmed this figure when asked about their earnings.

34. Paul Frank, "Star Shines on Us All," *International Musician*, April 2000.
35. Rodolfo Rosales, *The Illusion of Inclusion: The Untold Political Story of San Antonio*, Center for Mexican American Studies History, Culture and Society Series (Austin: University of Texas Press, 2000), 138.
36. Interview with Arthur Emerson, 12 February 1999.
37. Bureau of Census, "Census Bureau, Los Angeles–Based Hispanic Organization Form Census 2000 Outreach and Promotion Partnership, " 24 March 1999; accessed 21 February 2002 at http://www.census.gov/Press-Release/www/1999/cb99-cn12s.html.
38. Sut Jhally, "Advertising at the Edge of the Apocalypse," in *Critical Studies in Media Commercialism*, ed. Robin Andersen and Lance Strate (Oxford: Oxford University Press, 2000).
39. For an analysis of Puerto Rican identification as a basis for sponsorship, see Arlene Dávila, "Mapping Latinidad: Language and Culture in the Spanish TV Battlefront," *Television and New Media* 1, no. 1 (2000).
40. Noriega calls this the "schizo-cultural limbo" of Chicano media professionals in *Shot in America*, 33–35.
41. Notions of symbolic capital and cultural fields are appropriate in explaining how Mexican Americans may have cultural capital (or power) in one segment of musical production, but that, on the whole, that segment is subordinated in the general industry. Pierre Bourdieu, *Distinction: A Social Critique of the Judgement of Taste*, trans. Richard Nice (Cambridge: Harvard University Press, 1984).
42. John Hartley, *The Uses of Television* (London: Routledge, 1999), 159.
43. Tying democracy to consumer choice has a long history that extends to the beginnings of consumer societies, as Dávila points out in *Latinos Inc.* (p. 47). See also Stuart Ewen and Elizabeth Ewen, *Channels of Desire: Mass Images and the Shaping of American Consciousness* (Minneapolis: University of Minnesota Press, 1992).

Chapter 3   Tensions in the Tejano Industry

1. Peña, *Música Tejana*.
2. Ibid., 51, 92. Corporate recording labels, such as Columbia and RCA-Victor, first noticed Mexican American musical production in the 1930s but retreated during the war years, when the same labels refocused their capital toward Latin American musical production and distribution. At that time, San Antonio was the center of Mexican American musical investment until Mexico City outpaced the U.S. city for corporate investment in Latino musical production. Then CBS-Discos emerged in 1979, followed by RCA. Two other companies subsumed these companies, respectively Sony Discos and BMG (John Lannert, "Two Decades of Sony Discos," *Billboard*, 20 November 1999). When Sony Discos purchased distribution rights for San Antonio's Cara Records in 1989, they dominated the field until senior executive José Behar left to join EMI-Latin (Ramiro Burr, *The Billboard Guide to Tejano and Mexican Regional Music* [New York: Billboard Books, 1999]). Behar then bought out Cara's contracts with their artists and created new stars; one of the first was Selena, who signed a distribution agreement with EMI in 1989.
3. Arista/Nashville also had a short investment in Tejano from 1993 to 1998. Abel Salas, "Record Label Abandons Tejano Experiment," *Hispanic*, September 1998.
4. According to one of the family members and station programmer, Güero Polcas, KEDA later adopted the subtitle "Radio Jalapeño" to prevent confusion for listeners.
5. Smythe alluded to the commodity audience when he said that "audiences themselves are themselves 'intermediate' products—i.e. their production is a marketing

cost, not an end in itself." Dallas Smythe, "The Role of Mass Media and Popular Culture in Defining Development," in *Counterclockwise: Perspectives on Communication, Dallas Smythe*, ed. Thomas Guback (Boulder, Colo.: Westview, 1994), 251. For her astute application of Smythe to the history of American radio, see Kathleen Newman, "Critical Mass: Advertising, Audiences, and Consumer Activism" (Ph.D. diss., Yale University, 1997).

6. Ramiro Burr, "The Year of Tejano? Artists Score Firsts, Revenues Jump in 1992," *Houston Chronicle*, 20 December 1992.

7. This included 104.9-FM and 106.5-FM in Houston, 99.1-FM and 107.9-FM in Dallas, and 99.9-FM in Corpus Christi.

8. Bill Hobbs, "Industry Singing Praises of Tejano Music," *Amusement Business*, 28 March–3 April 1994.

9. Burr, "The Year of Tejano?"; Hobbs, "Industry Singing Praises of Tejano Music."

10. Ramiro Burr, "Tejano Getting Its Due but Must Seize Its Future," *San Antonio Express-News*, 12 February 1995.

11. Carlos Guerra, "City Gets Free Ride Off Tejano's Millions," *San Antonio Express-News*, 23 March 1996.

12. Ramiro Burr, "The State of Tejano: The Industry Appears to Be Limping Along as It Searches to Revive the Glory Years It Enjoyed a Decade Ago," *San Antonio Express News*, 4 April 2001.

13. Several articles confirmed this feeling, including Joe Nick Patoski, "Tuned Out," *Texas Monthly*, May 2000; Ramiro Burr, "Fresh Talent, Variety Key to Strong—but Changing—Regional and Tejano Markets," *Billboard*, 28 August 1999; Burr, "The State of Tejano"; Ramiro Burr, "Young Blood; Labels Scramble for New Talent to Save Tejano," *Houston Chronicle*, 30 July 2000.

14. The latter position can be found in Peña, *Música Tejana*.

15. My approach thus differs from that presented in Lucien Goldmann, *Cultural Creation in Modern Society*, trans. Bart Grahl (Saint Louis: Telos, 1976). Goldmann asserted that art reflects the social class of the people who produced it. While Tejano undoubtedly had a large working-class following, it was not reflective of any unified experiences of its producers. Rather, this chapter is heavily influenced by the work of Pierre Bourdieu in *Distinction* and *The Field of Cultural Production: Essays on Art and Literature*, ed. Randal Johnson (New York: Columbia University Press, 1993). In Bourdieu's work, producers born into and schooled in particular habits bring a set of dispositions, knowledge areas, and competencies to a field of cultural production. This approach allows for individuals from different backgrounds and with different skills and attitudes to contribute to Tejano music, regardless of what the music ultimately signifies for its consumers.

16. For a discussion of the politics of crossover, especially African Americans' exclusion from rock 'n' roll genres despite their strong participation in the music, see Reebee Garofalo, *Rockin' Out: Popular Music in the U.S.A.* (Needham Heights, Mass.: Allyn and Bacon, 1997).

17. Maria Elena Cepeda, "Mucho Loco for Ricky Martin; or the Politics of Chronology, Crossover, and Language within the Latin(o) Music 'Boom,'" *Popular Music and Society* 24, no. 3 (2000).

18. Russell Sanjek, *Pennies from Heaven: The American Popular Music Business in the Twentieth Century* (New York: De Capo, 1996), 666. Sanjek also writes about this trend, though in different terms, across music industries in the 1980s and 1990s.

19. Jeff Leeds, "Company Town: Univision to Expand into Music Business," *Los Angeles Times*, 18 April 2001.

20. Peña, *Música Tejana*, 180.

21. This clause has served Q well in the case of Selena, Quintanilla's daughter. After

her death, Q produced and distributed both compilation songs and "greatest hits" compact discs to eager fans.

22. Raoul Hernandez, "Parallel Universe," *Austin Chronicle*, 9 February 1998.

23. Bourdieu, *The Field of Cultural Production*.

24. Ibid., 43. This resonates with Bourdieu's observation that writing is one of the least "professionalized" jobs, leaving wide boundaries to debate who is a member of the field.

25. David Harvey, *The Condition of Postmodernity* (Oxford: Blackwell, 1989); Krishan Kumar, *From Post-Industrial to Post-Modern Society: New Theories of the Contemporary World* (Oxford: Blackwell, 1995).

26. Raúl Coronado Jr., "Selena's Good Buy: Texas Mexicans, History, and Selena Meet Transnational Capitalism," *Aztlán* 26, no. 1 (2001): 77. Coronado calls Selena's mainstreaming effect on Tejano the "Selena package."

27. Developed out of a Frankfurt school model, many authors seem to take this position, arguing that commercialism degraded local musical forms. See, for example, Peña, *Música Tejana*; and Richard A. Patterson, *Creating Country Music: Fabricating Authenticity* (Chicago: University of Chicago Press, 1997).

28. Joli Jenson, *Nashville Sound: Authenticity, Commercialization, and Country Music* (Nashville: Vanderbilt University Press, 1998).

29. This trend started early in the 1990s when prominent companies sought artists in order to attract Latino consumers. See Ramiro Burr, "Skyrocketing Tejano Takes Center Stage," *Houston Chronicle*, 4 March 1992.

30. On authenticity codes in hip-hop, see Kembrew McLeod, "Authenticity within Hip-Hop and Other Cultures Threatened with Assimilation," *Journal of Communication Inquiry* 49, no. 2 (1999).

31. A two-and-three agreement is a contract that guarantees two albums with Sony's option to record three more albums. "New Faces: Regional Mexican Talent to Watch in 2000," *Billboard*, 26 August 2000.

32. The translations here are fuzzy. "El Gordito" means, literally, "the chubby guy," but it is really a term of endearment. The words of the final verse were "Que bien te queda el dicho que se dicen / Con dinero baila el perro y tu de pasada" until the final line changed to "No aprecias algo hasta que la pierdes."

33. Super 16mm film is identifiable by the black borders on the top and bottom of the picture. It is this kind of production that marks high-status programs in televisual discourse. John Caldwell, *Televisuality: Style, Crisis, and Authority in American Television* (New Jersey: Rutgers University Press, 1995).

34. Ramiro Burr, "Grupo Vida Joins Dixie Chicks on Road Trip," *Houston Chronicle*, 26 November 2000.

35. Susan Bordo, *Unbearable Weight: Feminism, Western Culture and the Body* (Berkeley: University of California Press, 1993).

36. Bourdieu, *The Field of Cultural Production*, 111.

37. Jenson, *Nashville Sound*, 49.

38. Direct advertising would include selling packages to clubs hosting bands that weekend. Nontraditional revenue would range from marketing products from the event site to selling demographic information about "free-ticket" winners who called the radio station. I could not confirm how much of these revenues were raised for this actual event.

39. Bourdieu, *The Field of Cultural Production*.

40. Presumably, as the concentration of newspapers and publishers continues to shrink nationally, Burr will remain the authoritative voice of Tejano music in critical circles.

41. On cultural matrixes in music, see Keith Negus, *Music Genres and Corporate Cultures* (London: Routledge, 1999), 16.

42. Simon Frith, "Music and Identity," in *Questions of Cultural Identity*, ed. Stuart Hall and Paul Du Gay (London: Sage, 1996).

Chapter 4   *Representations of Kids and* La Familia

1. "The Other America," sponsored by the Esperanza Peace and Justice Center, also has featured Latino films each fall.
2. CineFestival curator Ray Santisteban said Portillo refused to screen the film until she made some last-minute changes to the piece.
3. Noriega, *Shot in America*; Clara Rodríguez, ed., *Latin Looks: Images of Latinas and Latinos in the U.S. Media* (Boulder, Colo.: Westview, 1998).
4. Arlene Dávila, *Latinos Inc.: The Marketing and Making of a People*. (Berkeley: University of California Press, 2001).
5. The location of the event was arguably an international site, but it reflected the choice of the film's local sponsors and their personal ties to the Hard Rock's management.
6. Gary Keller, *Hispanics and United States Film: An Overview and Handbook* (Tempe, Ariz.: Bilingual Press, 1994); Arthur G. Pettit, *Images of Mexican Americans in Fiction and Film* (College Station: Texas A & M University Press, 1980); Charles Ramírez Berg, "Stereotyping in Films in General and of the Hispanic in Particular," in Rodríguez, *Latin Looks*.
7. The problems of identifying Mexican Americans for quantitative studies is addressed in Cortéz, "Who Is Maria? What Is Juan?"
8. National Council of La Raza, "Out of the Picture: Hispanics in the Media," Washington, D.C., 1994.
9. Clara Rodríguez, "Keeping It Reel? Films of the 1980s and 1990s," in Rodríguez, *Latin Looks*, 180. See also Robert Lichter and Daniel Amundson, "Distorted Reality: Hispanic Characters in TV Entertainment," in Rodríguez, *Latin Looks*.
10. Liz Kotz, "Unofficial Stories: Documentaries by Latinas and Latin American Women," in Rodríguez, *Latin Looks*, 203.
11. For a review of Chicana feminist literature, see Aida Hurtado, "'Sitios y Lenguas': Chicanas Theorize Feminism," *Hypatia* 13, no. 2 (1998).
12. Lynn Spigel, *Welcome to the Dreamhouse: Popular Media and Postwar Suburbs* (Durham: Duke University Press, 2001).
13. Santiago Nieves and Frank Algarin, "Two Film Reviews: My Family/Mi Familia and the Perez Family," in Rodríguez, *Latin Looks*, 221.
14. Victoria Getis, "Experts and Juvenile Deliquency, 1900–1935," in *Generations of Youth: Youth Cultures and History in Twentieth-Century America*, ed. Joe Austin and Michael Evans (New York: New York University Press, 1998).
15. Mario Gamio, *Mexican Immigration to the United States: A Study of Human Migration* (New York: Dover, 1971); Celia S. Heller, *Mexican American Youth: Forgotten Youth at the Crossroads* (New York: Random House, 1966); William Madsen, *The Mexican-Americans of South Texas*, 2nd ed. (New York: Holt, Rinehart and Winston, 1973); Arthur. J. Rubel, "The Family," in *Mexican-Americans in the United States: A Reader*, ed. John Burma (Cambridge, Mass.: Schenkman Publishing, 1970).
16. Scholars equally applied these characteristics to their assessment of the "traditional Mexican family" without regard for the differences in location or social conditions. From Carmen Carrillo-Beron, "Traditional Family Ideology in Relation to Locus of Control: A Comparision of Chicano and Anglo Women" (San Francisco: R & E Research Associates, 1974).
17. Alfredo Mirandé, *The Chicano Experience: An Alternative Perspective* (Notre Dame: University of Notre Dame Press, 1985), 149. For a review of this literature, see

also Beatriz Pesquera, "Work and Family: A Comparative Analysis of Professional, Clerical and Blue-Collar Chicana Workers" (Ph.D. diss., University of California, 1985), and Josephine Méndez-Negrete, "'Dime Con Quien Andas': Notions of Chicano and Mexican American Families," *Families in Society: The Journal of Contemporary Human Services* 81, no. 1 (2000).

18. Henry Jenkins, "Her Royal Majesty: On the Sentimental Value of Reading *Lassie*," in *Kids Media Culture*, ed. Marsha Kinder (Durham: Duke University Press, 1999).

19. Richard Griswold del Castillo, *La Familia: Chicano Families in the Urban Southwest, 1848 to the Present* (Notre Dame: University of Notre Dame Press, 1984).

20. Ibid., 46.

21. Ibid., 51.

22. Ibid., 71.

23. Alan Riding, *Distant Neighbors: A Portrait of the Mexicans* (New York: Vintage, 1989).

24. Leo Grebler, Joan W. Moore, and Ralph Guzmán, *The Mexican-American People: The Nation's Second Largest Minority* (New York: Free Press, 1970).

25. Marta Tienda, "Familism and Structural Assimilation of Mexican Immigrants in the United States," *International Migration Review* 14, no. 3 (1980).

26. Alfredo Mirandé and Evangelina Enriquez, *La Chicana: The Mexican American Woman* (Chicago: University of Chicago Press, 1979), 116.

27. Pesquera, "Work and Family: A Comparative Analysis of Professional, Clerical and Blue-Collar Chicana Workers"; Denise Segura, "Chicanas and Mexican Immigrant Women in the Labor Market" (Ph.D. diss., University of California, 1986).

28. Jennifer Willis-Rivera and Alberto González, "Reconceptualizing Gender through Intercultural Dialogue: The Case of the Tex-Mex Madonna," *Women and Language* 20, no. 1 (1999): 9.

29. June Loy, "Corpus: A Home Movie for Selena," *Fabula* 3, no. 3 (1999); accessed 12 February 1999 at http://www.fabulamagazine.com/Volume3Issue3.html.

30. Dávila, *Latinos Inc.*, 94.

31. Lionel Sosa, *The Americano Dream*, 111.

32. Betty G. Farrell, *Family: The Making of an Idea, an Institution, and a Controversy in American Culture* (Boulder, Colo.: Westview, 1999).

33. Vincent Brook, "From the Cozy to the Carceral: Trans-Formations of Ethnic Space in the Goldbergs and Seinfeld," *Velvet Light Trap* 44 (1999); George Lipsitz, *Time Passages: Collective Memory and American Popular Culture* (Minneapolis: University of Minnesota Press, 1990); Barbara Wilinsky, "Before the Networks Reinvented the Family: Chicago Television's Portrait of America," *Quarterly Review of Film and Video* 16, nos. 3–4 (1999).

34. Rodríguez, "Creating an Audience and Remapping a Nation," 364.

35. I. Schneiderman, "Growth among Hispanic, Asian Markets, Teen Boys and Young Drivers Will All Be Factors," *DNR* 29, no. 114 (1999): 42.

36. Dávila, *Latinos Inc.*, 95.

37. Coronado, "Selena's Good Buy," 66.

38. John Hartley, *The Uses of Television* (London: Routledge, 1999).

39. U.S. Census Bureau, *Statistical Abstract of the United States: 2001*, 121st ed. (Washington, D.C.: GPO, 2001), 51–52.

40. 1990 Census of Population and Housing Summary Tape File (HSTF), 3. Persons of Hispanic Origin in the United States, U.S. Department of Commerce, Bureau of the Census, Data User Services, Washington D.C., 1994.

41. "Changes in Family Finances from 1989 to 1992: Evidence from the Survey of Consumer Finances," *Federal Reserves Bulletin* 80, no. 10 (1994).

42. Richard Butsch, "Class and Gender in Four Decades of Television Situation Comedy: Plus Ça Change," *Critical Studies in Mass Communication* 9, no. 4 (1992).
43. Pierrette Hondagneu-Sotelo and Ernestine Avila, "'I'm Here, but I'm There': The Meanings of Latina Transnational Motherhood," *Gender and Society* 11, no. 5 (1997).
44. Mary Romero, "Life as the Maid's Daughter: An Exploration of the Everyday Boundaries of Race, Class, and Gender," in *Feminisms in the Academy*, eds. Abigail Stewart and Domna Stanton (Ann Arbor: University of Michigan Press, 1995).
45. Two other shows about Mexican Americans focus on familial relations, *Resurrection Boulevard* on Showtime and *The George Lopez Show* on ABC, though both have clear antecedents in other types of programming, such as *The Sopranos* and *Roseanne*.
46. Ella Shohat and Robert Stam, *Unthinking Eurocentrism: Multiculturalism and the Media* (London: Routledge, 1994), 183.

Chapter 5   Mexican American Alternative Media

Parts of this chapter are reprinted, with permission, from Vicki Mayer, "Capturing Cultural Identity/Creating Community: A Grassroots Video Project in San Antonio, Texas," *International Journal of Cultural Studies* 3, no. 1 (2000): 57–78.

1. The history of the fight for public access in San Antonio was pieced from interviews with some of the activists at the time, including Mario Salas, Pleas McNeel, and Don Friedkin.
2. Richard Griswold del Castillo and Arnoldo de León, *North to Aztlán: A History of Mexican Americans in the United States* (New York: Twayne, 1996), 47.
3. Ibid., 94–97. See also Peter Skerry, *Mexican Americans: The Ambivalent Minority* (Cambridge, Mass.: Harvard, 1993).
4. Raymond Williams, "Base and Superstructure in Marxist Cultural Theory," in *Problems in Materialism and Culture: Selected Essays* (London: Verso, 1980).
5. García, *Chicanismo*.
6. Charles R. Morris, *American Catholic: The Saints and Sinners Who Built America's Most Powerful Church* (New York: Vintage, 1997).
7. Skerry, *Mexican Americans*.
8. *Hispanic Databook of U.S. Cities and Counties* (Milpitas, Calif.: Toucan Valley Publishers, 1994); 1990 Census of Population and Housing Summary Tape File (HSTF), 3. Persons of Hispanic Origin in the United States, U.S. Department of Commerce, Bureau of the Census, Data User Services, Washington, D.C., 1994.
9. Bill Minutaglio, "A Way out of Welfare: San Antonio Project Emphasizes Career Skills Trainees Need to Land, Keep Higher-Paying Jobs," *Dallas Morning News*, 24 February 1997; "San Antonio Council Praised for Linking Tax Breaks, Wages," *Dallas Morning News*, 4 July 1998.
10. School data collected from the Texas Education Administration's Web site for the period 1997–99. It can be found at http://www.tea.state.tx.us.
11. Richard García, *Rise of the Mexican American Middle Class: San Antonio, 1929–1941* (College Station: Texas A & M University Press, 1991).
12. The group's organizers specifically prohibited anyone who was not Mexican American, female, and working class to join the group. The group organizers only permitted me to come in to perform interviews and occasionally help the program with recruitment and lectures. After six months trying to observe the group, I finally gave up.
13. In *Shot in America*, Chon Noriega observes that Chicano nationalism has wavered

between various political and ideological poles but has always insisted on an ethnic essence that defines the group.

14. José A. Burciaga, *Drink Cultura: Chicanismo* (Santa Barbara: Joshua O Dell, 1993). It should also be noted that graffiti and plagiarism violate authorship by defacing or stealing the artist's original intent.

15. Freire's liberationary pedagogy certainly draws on a Catholic discourse while going beyond it in his desire to use the pedagogy to stimulate revolution. In San Antonio, Catholic priests have adopted certain aspects of liberational theology while operating within existing democratic governance structures. Edmundo Rodríguez, "The Hispanic Community and Church Movements: Schools of Leadership," in *Hispanic Catholic Church Culture in the U.S.: Issues and Concerns*, ed. J. Dolan and A. F. Deck (Notre Dame: University of Notre Dame Press).

16. Paulo Freire, *Pedagogy of the Oppressed*, trans. M. Ramos Bergman (New York: Seabury, 1974).

17. Although SACA began providing some stipend money to lead mural artists in 1999, the countless hours that muralists spent was hardly compensated by the two-hundred-dollar stipend.

18. Barbara Epstein, *Political Protest and Cultural Revolution: Nonviolent Direct Action in the 1970s and 1980s* (Berkeley: University of California Press, 1991), 126, 59.

19. García's *Chicanismo* addresses essentialism in Chicano arts movements in the 1960s and 1970s.

20. Michael Sandel, "The Procedural Republic and the Unencumbered Self," *Political Theory* 12 (1984).

21. Kenneth Grasso, "Introduction: Catholic Social Thought and the Quest for an American Public Philosophy," in *Catholicism, Liberalism, and Communitarianism: The Catholic Intellectual Tradition and the Foundations of Democracy*, ed. Kenneth Grasso, Gerard Bradley, and Robert Hunt (London: Rowman and Littlefield, 1995), 4.

22. Robert Bellah, Richard Madsen, William Sullivan, Ann Swidler, and Steven Tipton, *The Good Society* (New York: Knopf, 1991), 281.

23. Mario Barrera, *Beyond Aztlán: Ethnic Autonomy in Comparative Perspective* (New York: Praeger, 1988).

24. "The emphasis was on contributions and participation, not insurgency," writes David Abalos, *Latinos in the United States: The Sacred and the Political* (Indiana: Notre Dame University Press, 1986), 141.

25. Virgilio Elizondo, "Foreword," in *El Cuerpo De Cristo: The Hispanic Presence in the U.S. Catholic Church*, ed. Peter Casarella and Raúl Gómez (New York: Crossroad, 1998).

26. José E. Limón, *Mexican Ballads, Chicano Poems: History and Influence in Mexican-American Social Poetry* (Berkeley: University of California Press, 1992), 81–3.

27. García, *Chicanismo*, 87.

28. Juan Gómez Quiñones, *Chicano Politics: Reality and Promise* (Albuquerque: University of New Mexico Press, 1990), 140.

29. Virgilio Elizondo, *Galilean Journey: The Mexican American Promise* (New York: Orbis, 1983), 18, 30.

30. Each of the readers contributed information that I have integrated into this final copy, including clarification of quotations, jargon, factual information, additional context for events, and different interpretations of SACA's multicultural identity.

31. With the exception of Manny, all other names are pseudonyms to protect the anonymity of the human subjects.

32. In particular, the video project needed editing equipment to achieve independence from other organizations and to give more community members access to the

technology. In the past, SACA had to borrow editing equipment from other arts organizations or the local cable television provider. This was ineffective for many reasons, including the organizations' reluctance to let adolescents operate the expensive equipment, the inability to schedule times and transportation after school or on weekends, and the incompatibility of different editing systems (linear and digital).

33. Over the next month, this project evolved into a narrative about a girl who explores various dance styles in San Antonio before deciding to be a break-dancer.

34. Aida Hurtado, *The Color of Privilege* (Ann Arbor: University of Michigan Press, 1997).

35. Tomás Ybarra-Frausto, "Rasquachismo: A Chicano Sensibility," in *Chicano Art: Resistance and Affirmation, 1965–1985,* ed. Griswold Del Castillo, Teresa McKenna, and Yvonne Yarbro Bejarano (Los Angeles: University of California Press, 1991), 104–5. According to Ybarra-Frausto, Chicano cultural arts, both their texts and production, explicitly critiqued the liberal pluralist and mass capitalist ideology that reinforced an Anglocentric, middle-class culture in the United States. He explains that Chicano poets not only sought "new forms and a new vocabulary" based on Mexican American *corrido* ballads, but also attempted to establish an underground production, distribution, and exhibition circuit separate from commodity-driven culture markets.

36. For a discussion of the divisions within self-identified Chicano arts movements in the 1960s, see García, *Chicanismo,* 82. Despite the heterogeneity of the cross-class arts group, each one stressed the preservation of Mexican American working-class cultural practices as authentic and often romanticized signs of cultural identity.

37. Avoidance of confrontational subjects or personal criticism in civic organizations is typical in the United States, as found by Nina Eliasoph in *Avoiding Politics: How Americans Produce Apathy in Everyday Life* (Cambridge: Cambridge University Press, 1998).

38. This ethic is similar to what Fatima Rony calls a "third-eye sensibility," in *The Third Eye: Race, Cinema, and Ethnographic Spectacle* (Durham: Duke, 1996), 207.

39. My findings in this case were similar to those in Olga Vasquez, "La Clase Mágica: Imagining Optimal Possibilities in a Bilingual Community of Learners" (unpublished manuscript).

40. This seems similar to what Ybarra-Frausto, in "Rasquachismo: A Chicano Sensibility," calls a "rasquache" aesthetic in which the poor image quality actually communicates a "Chicano sensibility." At the same time, I do not want to ignore the video crew's actual desire to use more professional-looking footage over Ybarra-Frausto's description of a conscious decision *not* to use professional-looking footage.

41. Barbara Epstein, *Political Protest and Cultural Revolution,* 207.

42. Although the festival accepts Spanish-language submissions, the organizers preferred translated works that could reach all of San Antonio's English-speaking population, too.

43. Cindy Hing-Yuk Wong, "Understanding Grassroots Audiences: Imagination, Reception and Use in Community Videography," *Velvet Light Trap* 42 (1998).

44. Sean Cubitt, *Timeshift: On Video Culture* (London: Routledge, 1991), 19.

45. Clemencia Rodríguez, "A Process of Identity Deconstruction: Latin American Women Producing Video Stories," in *Women in Grassroots Communication: Furthering Social Change,* ed. Pilar Riaño (Thousand Oaks, Calif.: Sage, 1994).

46. Jennifer Bing-Canar and Mary Zerkel, "Reading the Media and Myself: Experiences in Critical Media Literacy with Young Arab American Women," *Signs* 23, no. 3 (1998): 735.

47. Dee Dee Halleck, *Hand-Held Visions: The Impossible Possibilities of Community Media* (New York: Fordham University Press, 2002), 385.

Chapter 6   Searching for Media Consumption and Cultural Identities

Earlier versions of selections from this chapter can be found in Vicki Mayer, "Pop Goes the World," *Emergences: Journal of Media and Composite Cultures* 11, no. 2 (2001): 307–22, and Vicki Mayer, "Living Telenovelas / Telenovelizing Life: Mexican-American Girls' Identities and Transnational Telenovelas," *Journal of Communication* 53, no. 3 (2003): pages to be announced. They have been reprinted with permission of the publishers, Carfax (www.tand.co.uk) and Oxford University Press.

1. Berman, *All That's Solid Melts into Air*.
2. Jean Jackson, "I Am a Fieldnote: Fieldnotes as a Symbol of Professional Identity," in *Fieldnotes: The Makings of Anthropology*, ed. Roger Sanjek (Ithaca, N.Y.: Cornell University Press, 1990), 14.
3. Roger Hart, Collette Daiute, and Selim Iltus, "Developmental Theory and Children's Participation in Community Organizations," *Social Justice* 24, no. 3 (1998): 38.
4. Ellen Seiter, *Television and New Media Audiences* (Oxford: Clarendon, 1999).
5. Lynn Spigel, *Make Room for TV: Television and the Family Ideal in Postwar America* (Chicago: University of Chicago Press, 1992).
6. John Caldwell, *Televisuality: Style, Crisis, and Authority in American Television* (New Brunswick: Rutgers University Press, 1995), 160.
7. As project facilitator, it was my job to balance my part-time role as educator and youth caretaker in deciding when to police "media talk" and when to allow it. In this regard, my role structured to some degree when media were acceptable conversation topics and when they were not. Although I was not always conscious of my regulating power, I enforced my class and age power by trying to control when "media talk" was an acceptable part of the education and care-taking process. In "Making Distinctions in Audience Research: Case Study of a Troubling Interview," *Cultural Studies* 4, no. 1 (1990), Ellen Seiter explains that this power differential is unavoidable, given the class and social status that researchers' media discourses have in relation to their subjects.
8. Barbara Renaud González, "Latinos Won't Find Success in Football," *San Antonio Express News*, 26 October 1997.
9. Seiter, *Television and New Media Audiences*, 87.
10. These television programs were the highest Nielsen-rated programs in the San Antonio DMA for teen viewers, as noted in the Nielsen ratings for 1998 ("Nielsen Station Index: Viewers in Profile" [San Antonio, Texas, 1998]). Although telenovelas may be underrated by Nielsen, the girls' tastes overlap with the larger demographic group. Similarly, Arbitron ratings showed KTFM as one of the two highest-rated radio stations in San Antonio in 1999. Radio y Musica Online, *Radio y Musica: San Antonio, Arbitron Personas 12+* (Radio y Musica Inc., 9 April 1999; accessed 19 September 1999 at http://www.radiomusica.com/Arbitron/Sanantonio.html.
11. Raymond Williams, *Television: Technology and Cultural Form* (Hanover, Conn.: Wesleyan University Press, 1992).
12. Mary Ellen Brown, "Soap Opera and Women's Talk: The Pleasures of Resistance," in *Communication and Human Values*, ed. Robert White and Michael Traber (London: Sage, 1994).
13. The girls preferred the new station; KTFM leaned toward more rap and hip hop in 2000.

14. Robert C. Allen, *Speaking of Soap Operas* (Chapel Hill: University of North Carolina Press, 1985), 3.

15. Ien Ang, *Living Room Wars: Rethinking Media Audiences for a Postmodern World* (London: Routledge, 1996), 92–93.

16. Marita Soto, "Memoria y Olvido de Mujer: El Amor en las Telenovelas," in *Telenovela: Los relatos de una historia de amor* (Buenos Aires: Atuel, 1996).

17. This type of modern telenovela contrasts with other Latin American sub-genres, such as the Brazilian social-realist novela and the Argentine neo-baroque novela. Gustavo Aprea and Rolando Mendoza Martínez, "Hacía una Definición del Género Telenovela," in *Telenovela: Los Relatos de una Historia de Amor* (Buenos Aires: Atuel, 1996). The modern telenovela is also distinctly different from American and British soap operas, as discussed by Allen, *Speaking of Soap Operas,* and Tamar Liebes and Sonia Livingstone, "The Structure of the Family and Romantic Ties in the Soap Opera: The Ethnographic Approach," *Communication Research* 21, no. 6 (1994).

18. Luis Terán, *Lágrimas de Exportación* (Mexico City: Clío, 2000).

19. Fernández and Paxman, *El Tigre,* 254.

20. Shohat and Stam, *Unthinking Eurocentrism.*

21. First, Ricardo's Aunt Rosaura, a rich widow, does not accept the indigenous bride and works to undermine the relationship. Second, Ricardo's high-school sweetheart and sister return from Europe to tempt Ricardo away from his wife. Finally, María Isabel's former domestic colleague, Amargura, jealously schemes to break up the two when she cannot reconcile with her abusive husband.

22. This argument has been made in Jesús Martín-Barbero, *De los Medios a los Mediaciones: Comunicación, Cultura y Hegemonía* (Barcelona: Editorial Gustavo Gili, 1987).

23. Bordo, *Unbearable Weight.*

24. Lesley Holdom, "Backstreet Boys: Pop Goes the Boy Bands," *Launch.com,* 2 September 2000; accessed 19 June 2001 at http://launch.yahoo.com/artist/news.asp?artistID=1001612.

25. Cepeda, "Mucho Loco for Ricky Martin."

26. Douglas, *Listening In,* 33.

27. Gayle Wald, "Just a Girl? Rock Music, Feminism, and the Construction of Female Youth," *Signs* 23, no. 3 (1998).

28. On rap and hip hop's "politics of fulfillment," see Paul Gilroy, *The Black Atlantic: Modernity and Double Consciousness* (Cambridge: Harvard, 1993), 37.

29. The girls got much of their information about each band member through Web sites at the local public library. They recommended *NSYNC's official Web site and specialized fan sites with information on each member, such as Justin Timberlake's bio from http://www.geneofun.on.ca/nsync/bios/justin.html.

30. Even a SACA staff member noted to me in July 1999 how the *NSYNC phenomenon had built a bond between the sisters that superceded their usual bickering and teasing.

31. Mary Harron, "McRock: Pop as a Commodity," in *Facing the Music,* ed. Simon Frith (New York: Pantheon, 1988), 176–77.

32. Valerie Walkerdine, *Schoolgirl Fictions* (London: Verso, 1990).

33. Elizabeth Fox, "The Rise (and Fall?) of the Telenovela Abroad," *InterMedia: The Journal of the International Institute of Communications* 25, no. 1 (1997).

34. Jesús Martín-Barbero, "Matrices Culturales de las Telenovelas," *Estudios sobre las Culturas Contemporâneas* 2, nos. 4–5 (1988).

35. Jonathon Epstein, "Introduction: Misplaced Childhood: An Introduction to the

Sociology of Youth and Their Music," in *Adolescents and Their Music: If It's Too Loud, You're Too Old*, ed. Jonathon Epstein (New York: Garland Publishing, 1994).

36. Phillip Brian Harper, "Passing for What? Racial Masquerade and the Demands of University Pressward Mobility," *Callaloo* 21, no. 2 (1998).

Chapter 7 **Videotaping the Future?**

1. Also mentioned in David Gauntlett, *Video Critical: Children, the Environment and Media Power* (Luton, England: University of Luton, 1996), 85.
2. Shaun Moores, *Interpreting Audiences: The Ethnography of Media Consumption* (London: Sage, 1993), 117.
3. Deidre Boyle, *Subject to Change: Guerrilla Television Revisited* (New York: Oxford University Press, 1997), 12.
4. Ibid., 33–34.
5. Alexandra Juhasz, *AIDS-TV: Identity, Community, and Alternative Video* (Durham, N.C.: Duke University Press, 1995), 8–9.
6. Janine Marchessault, "Amateur Video and the Challenge for Change," in *Mirror Machine: Video and Identity*, ed. Janine Marchessault (Toronto: XYZ Books, 1995), 17–18.
7. Martin Walsh, *The Brechtian Aspect of Radical Cinema*, ed. Keith M. Griffiths (London: BFI, 1981).
8. Marchessault, "Amateur Video," 19.
9. For the distinction between Lukacsian and Brechtian approaches to artistic production, see Terry Lovell, *Pictures of Reality: Aesthetics, Politics, Pleasure* (London: BFI, 1980), 74.
10. Kevin Dowler, "Interstitial Aesthetics and the Politics of Video at the Canada Council," in *Mirror Machine: Video and Identity*, ed. Janine Marchessault (Toronto: XYZ Books, 1995).
11. John Caldwell, *Televisuality*, 264–65.
12. Ibid., 264–70.
13. Ibid., 283.
14. Aired on Univision, these programs are Spanish-language versions of *Candid Camera* and *COPS* respectively.
15. Sean Cubitt, *Timeshift: On Video Culture* (London: Routledge, 1991), 19.
16. John Caldwell, "Racial Off-Worlds: Interactivity, Digital Theory, and Hybrid Borderlands," *Emergences: The Journal of Contemporary Media and Composite Cultures* 9, no. 2 (1999).
17. Hal Foster, *Recodings: Art, Spectacle, Cultural Politics* (Port Townsend: Bay Press, 1985).
18. John Corner, *Popular Television in Britain: Studies in Cultural History* (London: BFI, 1991), 264.
19. Bill Nichols, *Representing Reality: Issues and Concepts in Documentary* (Bloomington: Indiana University Press, 1991), 180.
20. Charlotte Brunsdon, "Problems with Quality," *Screen* 31, no. 1 (1990).
21. Caldwell, *Televisuality*, 21.
22. Mike Wayne, *Theorizing Video Practice* (London: Lawrence & Wishart, 1997), 66.
23. Richard Kilborn and John Izod, *An Introduction to Television Documentary: Confronting Reality* (Manchester: Manchester University Press, 1997).
24. Margaret Morse, "An Ontology of Everyday Distraction: The Freeway, the Mall, and Television," in *Logics of Television: Essays in Cultural Criticism*, ed. Patricia Mellencamp (Bloomington: Indiana University Press, 1990).

25. Wayne, *Theorizing Video Practice*, 74.
26. Mitchell Stephens, *The Rise of the Image, the Fall of the Word* (New York: Oxford, 1998), 132.
27. Chuck Kleinhans, "Cultural Appropriation and Subcultural Expression: The Dialectics of Co-optation and Resistance," Northwestern University Center for the Humanities Lecture, 14 November 1994.
28. Tim O' Sullivan, "Nostalgia, Revelation and Intimacy: Tendencies in the Flow of Modern Television," in *The Television Studies Book*, ed. Christine Geraghty and David Lusted (London: Arnold, 1998), 203.
29. Foster, *Recodings*.
30. Coco Fusco, *English Is Broken Here: Notes on Cultural Fusion in the Americas* (New York: New Press, 1995), 142. See also Prathiba Parmar, "That Moment of Emergence," in *Postmodern After-Images: A Reader in Film, Television and Video*, ed. Peter Brooker and Will Brooker (London: Arnold, 1997).
31. Lichter and Amundson, "Distorted Reality," 71.
32. Berg, "Stereotyping in Films."
33. See, for example, Ann Gray, *Video Playtime: The Gendering of a Leisure Technology* (London: Routledge, 1992), and Sut Jhally and Justin Lewis, *Enlightened Racism: The Cosby Show, Audiences, and the Myth of the American Dream* (Boulder Colo.: Westview, 1992).
34. Jane Shattuc, "'Go Ricki': Politics, Perversion, and Pleasure in the 1990s," in *The Television Studies Book*, ed. Christine Geraghty and David Lusted (London: Arnold, 1998), 213.
35. Ibid., 219.
36. Jane Shattuc, *The Talking Cure: TV, Talk Shows and Women* (New York: Routledge, 1997), 195.
37. Shattuc, "'Go Ricki,'" 214.
38. Joshua Gamson, *Freaks Talk Back: Tabloid Talk Shows and Sexual Non-Conformity* (Chicago: University of Chicago Press, 1998).
39. Sonia Livingstone and Peter Lunt, *Talk on Television: Audience Participation and Public Debate* (London: Routledge, 1994).
40. Quoted from the Web site http:// www.worldafricanet.com /html/cinderella.html.
41. Foster, *Recodings*, 169.
42. Ibid., 168.
43. Daniel Sholle, "Buy Our News: Tabloid Television and Commodification," *Journal of Communication Inquiry* 17, no. 1 (1993): 70–71.
44. John Fiske and John Hartley, *Reading Television* (London: Methuen, 1978).
45. John Corner, *Television Form and Public Address* (London: Edward Arnold, 1995), 56.
46. Peter Dahlgren, *Television and the Public Sphere: Citizenship, Democracy, and the Media* (London: Sage, 1995), 61.
47. Caldwell, *Televisuality*, 224.
48. Corner, *Television Form and Public Address*, 106.
49. Justin Lewis and Sut Jhally, "The Struggle over Media Literacy," *Journal of Communication* 48, no. 1 (1998): 115.

Conclusion   Cultural Affirmation and Consumer Alienation

1. "About Fiesta San Antonio," *San Antonio Fiesta Commission*, April 1998; accessed 7 October 2002 at http://www.fiestasa.org/about.html.

2. Lisa Lowe, *Immigrant Acts: On Asian American Cultural Politics* (Durham, N.C.: Duke University Press, 1996), 86.

3. "About Fiesta San Antonio."

4. John Gutierrez-Mier, Daniel Vargas, and Cynthia Klekar, "'Stars' Shine at Parade: Hollywood Theme Is a Hit with Fiesta Crowd," *San Antonio Express News*, 26 April 1998.

5. "Protestan contra Adviso de Taco Bell: Grupo Latino Affirma que Uso de Perro Chihuahua ofende a esta comunidad," *La Opinion*, 18 August 1998.

6. Armando Botello, "Boicot contra Taco Bell y Jack in the Box: Dicen que los Comerciales con Perritos Chihuahuas Son Denigrantes y un Insulto a Todos los Mexicanos," *La Opinion*, 14 July 1998.

7. Albert Peña, "Chihuahua!" *La Prensa de San Antonio*, 26 July 1998.

8. Benedict Anderson, *Imagined Communities* (London: Verso, 1983).

9. Mike Featherstone, *Undoing Culture: Globalization, Postmodernism and Identity, Theory, Culture & Society* (London: Sage, 1995), 109.

10. Stephen Graham and Simon Marvin, *Telecommunications and the City: Electronic Spaces, Urban Places* (London: Routledge, 1996).

11. Jennifer Walsh, "For Some, Casting Call Is a Family Affair," *San Antonio Express News*, 13 February 1999.

12. "Sales and Use Tax Exemptions Available to Film/Video Producers," *Texas Film Commission*, May 2002; accessed 13 October 2002 at http://www.governor.state.tx.us/film/salestax.htm.

13. "Cisneros Lands Quickly," *CNN* 23 January 1997; accessed 7 October at 2002 http://www.cnn.com/ALLPOLITICS/1997/01/23/briefs/.

14. Janine Marchessault, "Amateur Video and the Challenge for Change," in *Mirror Machine: Video and Identity*, ed. Janine Marchessault (Toronto: XYZ Books, 1995), 20.

15. Judith H. Dobrzynski, "San Antonio Reduces Aid to the Arts by 15 Percent," *New York Times*, 13 September 1997.

16. Michael Dear and Steven Flusty, "The Postmodern Urban Condition," in *Spaces of Culture: City—Nation—World*, ed. Mike Featherstone and Scott Lash (London: Sage, 1999), 76.

17. U.S. Bureau of Census, "Census Bureau Updates Profile of Nation's Hispanic Groups," 8 March 2000; accessed 12 October 2002 at http://www.census.gov/Press-Release/www/2000/cb00–38.html.

18. Johanna Wyn and Rob White, *Rethinking Youth* (London: Sage, 1997), 124.

19. Néstor García Canclini, *Consumidores y Ciudadanos: Conflictos Multiculturales de la Globalización* (Miguel Hidalgo, Mexico: Grijalbo, 1995), 36.

Bibliography

Abalos, David. *Latinos in the United States: The Sacred and the Political*. Notre Dame: Notre Dame University Press, 1986.

Acuña, Rodolfo. *Occupied America: A History of Chicanos*. 3rd ed. New York: Harper Collins, 1988.

"Advertising Age Ranks Bromley, Aguilar & Associates." *San Antonio Business Journal*, 21 April 1997.

Allen, Robert C. *Speaking of Soap Operas*. Chapel Hill: University of North Carolina, 1985.

Anderson, Benedict. *Imagined Communities*. London: Verso, 1983.

Ang, Ien. *Living Room Wars: Rethinking Media Audiences for a Postmodern World*. London: Routledge, 1996.

Aprea, Gustavo, and Rolando Mendoza Martínez. "Hacía una Definición del Género Telenovela." In *Telenovela: Los Relatos de una Historia de Amor*, 17–30. Buenos Aires: Atuel, 1996.

Bakhtin, M. M. *The Dialogic Imagination: Four Essays*. Translated by Carol Emerson and Michael Holquist. Edited by Michael Holquist. Austin: University of Texas Press, 1981.

Balibar, Etienne. "Racism and Crisis." In *Race, Nation, Class: Ambiguous Identities*, edited by Etienne Balibar and Immanuel Wallerstein, 217–27. London: Verso, 1991.

Barrera, Mario. *Beyond Aztlán: Ethnic Autonomy in Comparative Perspective*. New York: Praeger, 1988.

Bates, Eric. "Chaining the Alternatives: What Started as a Movement Has Become an Industry." *Nation*, 29 June1998, 11–17.

Bellah, Robert, Richard Madsen, William Sullivan, Anne Swidler, and Stephen Tipton. *The Good Society*. New York: Knopf, 1991.

Berlant, Lauren. *The Queen of America Goes to Washington City*. Durham, N.C.: Duke University Press, 1997.

Berman, Marshall. *All That's Solid Melts into Air*. New York: Simon & Schuster, 1982.

Bing-Canar, Jennifer, and Mary Zerkel. "Reading the Media and Myself: Experiences in Critical Media Literacy with Young Arab American Women." *Signs* 23, no. 3 (1998): 735–43.

Bordo, Susan. *Unbearable Weight: Feminism, Western Culture and the Body*. Berkeley: University of California Press, 1993.

Botello, Armando. "Boicot contra Taco Bell y Jack in the Box: Dicen que los Comerciales con Perritos Chihuahuas Son Denigrantes y un Insulto a Todos los Mexicanos." *La Opinion*, 14 July 1998, 4A.

Bourdieu, Pierre. *Distinction: A Social Critique of the Judgement of Taste*. Translated by Richard Nice. Cambridge: Harvard University Press, 1984.
———. *The Field of Cultural Production: Essays on Art and Literature*. Edited by Randal Johnson. New York: Columbia University Press, 1993.
Boyle, Deidre. *Subject to Change: Guerrilla Television Revisited*. New York: Oxford University Press, 1997.
Broadcasting and Cable Yearbook 1999. New Jersey: R. R. Bowker, 1999.
Brook, Vincent. "From the Cozy to the Carceral: Trans-Formations of Ethnic Space in the Goldbergs and Seinfeld." *Velvet Light Trap* 44 (1999): 54–67.
Brown, Mary Ellen. "Soap Opera and Women's Talk: The Pleasures of Resistance." In *Communication and Human Values*, edited by Robert White and Michael Traber. London: Sage, 1994.
Brunsdon, Charlotte. "Problems with Quality." *Screen* 31, no. 1 (1990): 67–90.
Buckingham, David. *Moving Images: Understanding Children's Emotional Responses to Television*. Manchester: Manchester University Press, 1996.
Burciaga, José A. *Drink Cultura: Chicanismo*. Santa Barbara: Joshua O Dell, 1993.
Burr, Ramiro. *The Billboard Guide to Tejano and Mexican Regional Music*. New York: Billboard Books, 1999.
———. "Fresh Talent, Variety Key to Strong—but Changing—Regional and Tejano Markets." *Billboard*, 28 August 1999, LM–1.
———. "Grupo Vida Joins Dixie Chicks on Road Trip." *Houston Chronicle*, 26 November 2000, 7.
———. "Skyrocketing Tejano Takes Center Stage." *Houston Chronicle*, 4 March 1992, 1.
———. "The State of Tejano: The Industry Appears to Be Limping Along as It Searches to Revive the Glory Years It Enjoyed a Decade Ago." *San Antonio Express-News*, 4 April 2001, 1G.
———. "Tejano Getting Its Due but Must Seize Its Future." *San Antonio Express-News*, 12 February 1995, 21.
———. "The Year of Tejano? Artists Score Firsts, Revenues Jump in 1992." *Houston Chronicle*, 20 December 1992, 19.
———. "Young Blood: Labels Scramble for New Talent to Save Tejano." *Houston Chronicle*, 30 July 2000, 13.
Butsch, Richard. "Class and Gender in Four Decades of Television Situation Comedy: Plus Ça Change." *Critical Studies in Mass Communication* 9, no. 4 (1992): 387–99.
Caldwell, John. "Racial Off-Worlds: Interactivity, Digital Theory, and Hybrid Borderlands." *Emergences: The Journal of Contemporary Media and Composite Cultures* 9, no. 2 (1999): 373–87.
———. *Televisuality: Style, Crisis, and Authority in American Television*. New Brunswick: Rutgers University Press, 1995.
Carrillo-Beron, Carmen. "Traditional Family Ideology in Relation to Locus of Control: A Comparision of Chicano and Anglo Women." Research Report 73. San Francisco: R & E Research Associates, 1974.
"Census Bureau Projects Doubling of Nation's Population by 2100." *Census Brief*. Washington, D.C.: U.S. Department of Commerce, 2000.
Cepeda, Maria Elena. "Mucho Loco for Ricky Martin; or the Politics of Chronology, Crossover, and Language within the Latin(o) Music 'Boom.'" *Popular Music and Society* 24, no. 3 (2000): 55–72.
Cisneros Lands Quickly (Web site). CNN, 1997 (cited 7 Oct. 2002). Available from http://www.cnn.com/ALLPOLITICS/1997/01/23/briefs/.

Collins, Peter. "Negotiating Selves: Reflections on Unstructured Interviewing." *Sociological Research Online* 3, no. 3 (1998): 55 pars.

Constantakis, Patricia Elena. "Spanish-Language Television and the 1988 Presidential Elections: A Case Study of the 'Dual Identity' of Ethnic Minority Media." Ph.D. diss., University of Texas, Austin, 1993.

Corner, John. *Popular Television in Britain: Studies in Cultural History*. London: BFI, 1991.

———. *Television Form and Public Address*. London: Edward Arnold, 1995.

Coronado, Raúl, Jr. "Selena's Good Buy: Texas Mexicans, History, and Selena Meet Transnational Capitalism." *Aztlán* 26, no. 1 (2001): 59–100.

Cortéz, Carlos E. "Who Is Maria? What Is Juan? Dilemmas of Analyzing the Chicano Image in U.S. Feature Films." In *Chicanos and Film: Essays on Chicano Representation and Resistance*, edited by Chon Noriega, 74–93. New York: Garland, 1992.

Cottle, Simon. *Television and Ethnic Minorities: Producers' Perspectives*. Aldershot: Avebury, 1997.

"Cox Buys Two Radio Stations in San Antonio." *San Antonio Business Journal*, 1 Dec. 1997.

Cubitt, Sean. *Timeshift: On Video Culture*. London: Routledge, 1991.

Curtin, Michael. "On Edge: Culture Industries in the Neo-Network Era." In *Making and Selling Culture*, edited by Richard Ohmann, 181–202. Middletown: Wesleyan University Press, 1996.

Dahlgren, Peter. *Television and the Public Sphere: Citizenship, Democracy, and the Media*. London: Sage, 1995.

Dávila, Arlene. *Latinos Inc.: The Marketing and Making of a People*. Berkeley: University of California Press, 2001.

———. "Mapping Latinidad: Language and Culture in the Spanish TV Battlefront." *Television and New Media* 1, no. 1 (2000): 75–94.

Dear, Michael, and Steven Flusty. "The Postmodern Urban Condition." In *Spaces of Culture: City—Nation—World*, edited by Mike Featherstone and Scott Lash, 64–85. London: Sage, 1999.

Dobrzynski, Judith H. "San Antonio Reduces Aid to the Arts by 15 Percent." *New York Times*, 13 Sept. 1997, 17L, 18N.

Douglas, Susan. *Listening In: Radio and the American Imagination, from Amos 'n' Andy and Edward R. Murrow to Wolfman Jack and Howard Stern*. New York: Times Books, 1999.

———. *Where the Girls Are: Growing up Female with the Mass Media*. New York: Times Books, 1994.

Dowler, Kevin. "Interstitial Aesthetics and the Politics of Video at the Canada Council." In *Mirror Machine: Video and Identity*, edited by Janine Marchessault, 35–50. Toronto: XYZ Books, 1995.

Eliasoph, Nina. *Avoiding Politics: How Americans Produce Apathy in Everyday Life*. Cambridge: Cambridge University Press, 1998.

Elizondo, Virgilio. "Foreword." In *El Cuerpo de Cristo: The Hispanic Presence in the U.S. Catholic Church*, edited by Peter Casarella and Raúl Gómez, 9–20. New York: Crossroad, 1998.

———. *Galilean Journey: The Mexican American Promise*. New York: Orbis, 1983.

Epstein, Barbara. *Political Protest and Cultural Revolution: Nonviolent Direct Action in the 1970s and 1980s*. Berkeley: University of California Press, 1991.

Epstein, Jonathon. "Introduction: Misplaced Childhood: An Introduction to the Sociology of Youth and Their Music." In *Adolescents and Their Music: If It's Too Loud, You're Too Old*, edited by Jonathon Epstein, xiii–xxxiiiv. New York: Garland, 1994.

Escalante, Virginia. "In Pursuit of Ethnic Audiences: The Media and Latinos." *Renato Rosaldo Lecture Series Monograph*, 7th ser. (1991): 29–54.

Esparza, Elia. "Must Sí TV: Galavisión and Producer Jeff Valdez Go Bilingual." *Hispanic*, May 1998, 20–30.

Ewen, Stuart, and Elizabeth Ewen. *Channels of Desire: Mass Images and the Shaping of American Consciousness*. Minneapolis: University of Minnesota Press, 1992.

Farrell, Betty G. *Family: The Making of an Idea, an Institution, and a Controversy in American Culture*. Boulder, Colo.: Westview, 1999.

Featherstone, Mike. *Undoing Culture: Globalization, Postmodernism and Identity, Theory, Culture and Society*. London: Sage, 1995.

Fein, Seth. "Myths of Cultural Imperialism and Nationalism in Golden Age Mexican Cinema." In *Fragments of a Golden Age: The Politics of Culture in Mexico, 1940–2000*, edited by Gilbert M. Joseph, Anne Rubenstein, Eric Zolov, and Elena Poniatowska, 159–98. Durham: Duke University Press, 2001.

Fernández, Claudia, and Andrew Paxman. *El Tigre: Emilio Azcárraga y su Imperio Televisa*. Mexico City: Grijalbo, 2000.

Fiske, John, and John Hartley. *Reading Television*. London: Methuen, 1978.

Fletcher, Michael A. "Latinos Plan Boycott of Network TV; Goal of 'Brownout' Is Better Roles for Hispanics." *Washington Post*, 28 July 1999, 1.

Flores, Richard. "Aesthetic Process and Cultural Citizenship: The Membering of a Social Body in San Antonio." In *Latino Cultural Citizenship: Claiming Identity, Space, and Rights*, edited by William Flores and Rina Benmayor, 124–51. Boston: Beacon Press, 1997.

Flores, William, and Rina Benmayor, eds. *Latino Cultural Citizenship: Claiming Identity, Space, and Rights*. Boston: Beacon Press, 1997.

Foley, Neil. "Becoming Hispanic: Mexican Americans and the Faustian Pact with Whiteness." In *Reflexiones: New Directions in Mexican American Studies*, edited by Neil Foley, 53–70. Austin: Center for Mexican American Studies, 1998.

Foster, Hal. *Recodings: Art, Spectacle, Cultural Politics*. Port Townsend: Bay Press, 1985.

Fox, Elizabeth. "The Rise (and Fall?) of the Telenovela Abroad." *Intermedia* 25, no. 1 (1997): 37–39.

Frank, Paul. "Star Shines on Us All." *International Musician*, April 2000, 12–13.

Fregoso, Rosa Linda. *The Bronze Screen: Chicana and Chicano Film Culture*. Minneapolis: University of Minnesota Press, 1993.

Freire, Paulo. *Pedagogy of the Oppressed*. Translated by M. Ramos Bergman. New York: Seabury, 1974.

Frith, Simon. "Music and Identity." In *Questions of Cultural Identity*, edited by Stuart Hall and Paul Du Gay, 108–27. London: Sage, 1996.

Fusco, Coco. *English Is Broken Here: Notes on Cultural Fusion in the Americas*. New York: New Press, 1995.

Gamio, Mario. *Mexican Immigration to the United States: A Study of Human Migration*. New York: Dover, 1971.

Gamson, Joshua. *Freaks Talk Back: Tabloid Talk Shows and Sexual Non-Conformity*. Chicago: University of Chicago Press, 1998.

García, Ignacio M. *Chicanismo: The Forging of a Militant Ethos among Mexican Americans*. Tucson: University of Arizona Press, 1997.

García, Richard. *Rise of the Mexican American Middle Class: San Antonio, 1929–1941*. College Station: Texas A&M University Press, 1991.

García Canclini, Néstor. *Consumidores y Ciudadanos: Conflictos Multiculturales de la Globalización*. Miguel Hidalgo, Mexico: Grijalbo, 1995.

———. "North Americans or Latin Americans? The Redefinition of Mexican Identity and the Free Trade Agreements." In *Mass Media and Free Trade: NAFTA and the Cultural Industries*, edited by Emile McAnany and Kenton Wilkinson, 142–56. Austin: University of Texas Press, 1996.

Garofalo, Reebee. *Rockin' Out: Popular Music in the U.S.A.* Needham Heights, Mass: Allyn and Bacon, 1997.

Gauntlett, David. *Video Critical: Children, the Environment and Media Power.* Luton, England: University of Luton, 1996.

Getis, Victoria. "Experts and Juvenile Deliquency, 1900–1935." In *Generations of Youth: Youth Cultures and History in Twentieth-Century America*, edited by Joe Austin and Michael Evans, 21–35. New York: New York University, 1998.

Gilroy, Paul. *The Black Atlantic: Modernity and Double Consciousness.* Cambridge, Mass.: Harvard, 1993.

Goldmann, Lucien. *Cultural Creation in Modern Society.* Translated by Bart Grahl. Saint Louis: Telos, 1976.

Graham, Stephen, and Simon Marvin. *Telecommunications and the City: Electronic Spaces, Urban Places.* London: Routledge, 1996.

Grasso, Keith. "Introduction: Catholic Social Thought and the Quest for an American Public Philosophy." In *Catholicism, Liberalism, and Communitarianism: The Catholic Intellectual Tradition and the Foundations of Democracy*, edited by Kenneth Grasso, Gerald Bradley, and Robert Hunt, 1–14. London: Rowman and Littlefield, 1995.

Gray, Ann. *Video Playtime: The Gendering of a Leisure Technology.* London: Routledge, 1992.

Grebler, Leo, Joan W. Moore, and Ralph Guzmán. *The Mexican-American People: The Nation's Second Largest Minority.* New York: Free Press, 1970.

Griswold del Castillo, Richard. *La Familia: Chicano Families in the Urban Southwest, 1848 to the Present.* Notre Dame: University of Notre Dame Press, 1984.

Griswold del Castillo, Richard, and Arnoldo de León. *North to Aztlán: A History of Mexican Americans in the United States.* New York: Twayne, 1996.

Guerra, Carlos. "City Gets Free Ride Off Tejano's Millions." *San Antonio Express-News*, 23 March 1996, 1.

Gutiérrez, Félix, and Jorge Schement. "Problems of Ownership and Control of Spanish-Language Media in the United States: National and International Concerns." In *Communication and Social Structure: Critical Studies in Mass Media Research*, edited by Emile McAnany, Jorge Schnitman, and Noreene Janus, 181–203. New York: Praeger, 1981.

———. "Spanish International Network: The Flow of Television from Mexico to the United States." *Communication Research* 11, no. 2 (1984): 241–58.

———. *Spanish Language Radio in the Southwestern United States.* Austin: Center for Mexican American Studies, 1979.

Gutierrez-Mier, John, Daniel Vargas, and Cynthia Klekar. "'Stars' Shine at Parade: Hollywood Theme Is a Hit with Fiesta Crowd." *San Antonio Express-News*, 26 April 1998.

Guzmán, Betsy. "The Hispanic Population: Census 2000 Brief." *Census Brief*, 8. Washington D.C.: U.S. Census Bureau, 2001.

Hall, Stuart. "Who Needs Identity?" In *Questions of Cultural Identity*, edited by Stuart Hall and Paul Du Gay, 1–17. London: Sage, 1996.

Halleck, Dee Dee. *Hand-Held Visions: The Impossible Possibilities of Community Media.* New York: Fordham University Press, 2002.

Hardgrove, Anne. *Community and Public Culture: The Marwari in Calcutta c. 1989–1997.* World Wide Web, Columbia University E-book, 2002.

Harper, Phillip Brian. "Passing for What? Racial Masquerade and the Demands of Upward Mobility." *Callaloo* 21, no. 2 (1998): 381–97.

Harron, Mary. "McRock: Pop as a Commodity." In *Facing the Music*, edited by Simon Frith, 173–220. New York: Pantheon, 1988.

Hart, Roger, Collette Daiute, and Selim Iltus. "Developmental Theory and Children's Participation in Community Organizations." *Social Justice* 24, no. 3 (1998): 33–63.

Hartley, John. *The Uses of Television*. London: Routledge, 1999.

Harvey, David. *The Condition of Postmodernity*. Oxford: Blackwell, 1989.

Haubegger, Christie. "The Legacy of Generation Ñ." *Newsweek*, 12 July 1999, 61.

Heller, Celia S. *Mexican American Youth: Forgotten Youth at the Crossroads*. New York: Random House, 1966.

Hernandez, Raoul. "Parallel Universe." *Austin Chronicle*, 9 Feb. 1998.

Hilmes, Michele. *Hollywood and Broadcasting: From Radio to Cable, Illinois Studies in Communications*. Urbana: University of Illinois Press, 1990.

———. *Radio Voices: American Broadcasting, 1922–1952*. Minneapolis: University of Minnesota Press, 1997.

Hing-Yuk Wong, Cindy. "Understanding Grassroots Audiences: Imagination, Reception and Use in Community Videography." *Velvet Light Trap* 42 (1998): 91–102.

Hispanic Databook of U.S. Cities and Counties. Milpitas, Calif.: Toucan Valley Publishers, 1994.

Hobbs, Bill. "Industry Singing Praises of Tejano Music." *Amusement Business*, 28 March–3 April 1994, 15–17.

Hondagneu-Sotelo, Pierrette, and Ernestine Avila. "'I'm Here, but I'm There': The Meanings of Latina Transnational Motherhood." *Gender and Society* 11, no. 5 (1997): 548–70.

Horowitz, Robert B. *The Irony of Regulatory Reform: The Deregulation of American Telecommunications*. New York: Oxford University Press, 1989.

Hurtado, Aida. *The Color of Privilege*. Ann Arbor: University of Michigan Press, 1997.

———. "'Sitios y Lenguas': Chicanas Theorize Feminism." *Hypatia* 13, no. 2 (1998): 134–52.

Jackson, Jean. "I Am a Fieldnote: Fieldnotes as a Symbol of Professional Identity." In *Fieldnotes: The Makings of Anthropology*, edited by Roger Sanjek, 3–34. Ithaca: Cornell University Press, 1990.

Jameson, Frederic. *The Political Unconscious: Narrative as a Socially Symbolic Act*. Ithaca: Cornell University Press, 1981.

Jenkins, Henry. "Her Royal Majesty: On the Sentimental Value of Reading *Lassie*." In *Kids Media Culture*, edited by Marsha Kinder. Durham: Duke University Press, 1999.

Jenson, Joli. *Nashville Sound: Authenticity, Commercialization, and Country Music*. Nashville: Vanderbilt University Press, 1998.

Jhally, Sut. "Advertising at the Edge of the Apocalypse." In *Critical Studies in Media Commercialism*, edited by Robin Andersen and Lance Strate, 27–39. Oxford: Oxford University Press, 2000.

Jhally, Sut, and Justin Lewis. *Enlightened Racism: The Cosby Show, Audiences, and the Myth of the American Dream*. Boulder, Colo.: Westview, 1992.

Juhasz, Alexandra. *AIDS-TV: Identity, Community, and Alternative Video*. Durham: Duke University Press, 1995.

Kamerick, Megan. "Clear Channel Plans to Buy New Building." *San Antonio Business Journal*, 21 December 1998.

———. "Hispano Marketing Hit with Recent Departures of Key Staff." *San Antonio Business Journal*, 21 April 1997.

————. "Prime Time to Bring Many Operations under One Roof." *San Antonio Business Journal*, 20 Apr. 1998.

Keller, Gary. *Hispanics and United States Film: An Overview and Handbook*. Tempe, Ariz.: Bilingual Press, 1994.

Kilborn, Richard, and John Izod. *An Introduction to Television Documentary: Confronting Reality*. Manchester: Manchester University Press, 1997.

Kotz, Liz. "Unofficial Stories: Documentaries by Latinas and Latin American Women." In *Latin Looks: Images of Latinas and Latinos in the U.S. Media*, edited by Clara Rodríguez, 200–213. Boulder, Colo.: Westview Press, 1998.

Krajewski, Steve. "Cartel Creativo's Defense Scores." *Adweek*, 21 December 1998, 3.

Kumar, Krishan. *From Post-Industrial to Post-Modern Society: New Theories of the Contemporary World*. Oxford: Blackwell, 1995.

Lannert, John. "Two Decades of Sony Discos." *Billboard*, 20 November 1999, 52.

Larmer, Brook. "Latino America." *Newsweek*, 12 July 1999, 48–51.

Leeds, Jeff. "Company Town: Univision to Expand into Music Business." *Los Angeles Times*, 18 April 2001, 6.

Leiman, Michael. *The Political Economy of Racism: A History*. London: Pluto, 1993.

Lerner, Victoria. "Los exilados de la Revolución Mexicana y la comunidad Chicana (1915–1930)." In *El México Olvidado I: La Historia del Pueblo Chicano*, edited by David Maciel, 45–60. Chihuahua: Universidad Autónoma de Ciudad Juárez and University of Texas, El Paso, 1996.

Lewis, Justin, and Sut Jhally. "The Struggle over Media Literacy." *Journal of Communication* 48, no. 1 (1998): 109–20.

Lichter, Robert, and Daniel Amundson. "Distorted Reality: Hispanic Characters in TV Entertainment." In *Latin Looks: Images of Latinas and Latinos in the U.S. Media*, edited by Clara Rodríguez, 57–72. Boulder, Colo.: Westview, 1998.

Liebes, Tamar, and Sonia Livingstone. "The Structure of the Family and Romantic Ties in the Soap Opera: The Ethnographic Approach." *Communication Research* 21, no. 6 (1994): 717–41.

Limón, José E. *Mexican Ballads, Chicano Poems: History and Influence in Mexican-American Social Poetry*. Berkeley: University of California, 1992.

————. "Stereotyping and Chicano Resistance: A Historical Dimension." In *Chicanos and Film: Representation and Resistance*, edited by Chon Noriega, 3–17. Minneapolis: University of Minnesota Press, 1992.

Lipsitz, George. *Dangerous Crossroads: Popular Music, Postmodernism, and the Poetics of Place*. London: Verso, 1994.

————. *Time Passages: Collective Memory and American Popular Culture*. Minneapolis: University of Minnesota Press, 1990.

Livingstone, Sonia, and Peter Lunt. *Talk on Television: Audience Participation and Public Debate*. London: Routledge, 1994.

Lovell, Terry. *Pictures of Reality: Aesthetics, Politics, Pleasure*. London: BFI, 1980.

Lowe, Lisa. *Immigrant Acts: On Asian American Cultural Politics*. Durham: Duke University Press, 1996.

Madsen, William. *The Mexican-Americans of South Texas*. 2nd ed. New York: Holt, Rinehart and Winston, 1973.

Marchessault, Janine. "Amateur Video and the Challenge for Change." In *Mirror Machine: Video and Identity*, edited by Janine Marchessault, 13–25. Toronto: XYZ Books, 1995.

Marketer's Guide to Media. New York: BPI Communications, 1998.

Martín-Barbero, Jesús. *De los Medios a los Mediaciones: Comunicación, Cultura y Hegemonía*. Barcelona: Editorial Gustavo Gili, 1987.

————. "Matrices Culturales de las Telenovelas." *Estudios sobre las Culturas Contemporáneas* 2, no. 4–5 (1988): 137–63.

McLeod, Kembrew. "Authenticity within Hip-Hop and Other Cultures Threatened with Assimilation." *Journal of Communication Inquiry* 49, no. 2 (1999): 132–50.

Méndez-Negrete, Josephine. "'Dime Con Quien Andas': Notions of Chicano and Mexican American Families." *Families in Society: The Journal of Contemporary Human Services* 81, no. 1 (2000): 42–48.

Miguel, Guadalupe San, Jr. "The Rise of Tejano Music in the Post–World War II, 1946–1964." *Journal of American Ethnic History* 19, no. 1 (1999): 26–49.

Minutaglio, Bill. "A Way out of Welfare: San Antonio Project Emphasizes Career Skills Trainees Need to Land, Keep Higher-Paying Jobs." *Dallas Morning News*, 24 February 1997, 1.

Mirandé, Alfredo. *The Chicano Experience: An Alternative Perspective*. Notre Dame: University of Notre Dame Press, 1985.

Mirandé, Alfredo, and Evangelina Enriquez. *La Chicana: The Mexican American Woman*. Chicago: University of Chicago Press, 1979.

Monroe, Melissa S. "Bilingual Paper Hits the Streets in Alamo City." *San Antonio Business Journal*, 29 December 1997.

————. "Current Boosts Staff, Circulation." *San Antonio Business Journal*, 30 March 1998.

————. "New Publication Seeks to Fill Void Left by Demise of KSJL." *San Antonio Business Journal*, 19 October 1998.

Montejano, David. *Anglos and Mexicans in the Making of Texas, 1836–1986*. Austin: University of Texas Press, 1987.

Moores, Shaun. *Interpreting Audiences: The Ethnography of Media Consumption*. London: Sage, 1993.

Morales, Rebecca, and Frank Bonilla. "Restructuring the New Inequality." In *Latinos in a Changing U.S. Economy: Comparative Perspectives on Growing Inequality*, edited by Rebecca Morales and Frank Bonilla, 1–27. Newbury Park: Sage, 1993.

Morley, David. *Family Television: Cultural Power and Domestic Leisure*. London: Comedia, 1986.

Morris, Charles R. *American Catholic: The Saints and Sinners Who Built America's Most Powerful Church*. New York: Vintage, 1997.

Morse, Margaret. "An Ontology of Everyday Distraction: The Freeway, the Mall, and Television." In *Logics of Television: Essays in Cultural Criticism*, edited by Patricia Mellencamp, 193–221. Bloomington: Indiana University Press, 1990.

Mosco, Vincent. *The Political Economy of Communication: Rethinking and Renewal*. London: Sage, 1996.

Nathan, Debbie. "Spurs Merger Rampage." *San Antonio Current*, 14–20 October 1999, 7.

Negus, Keith. *Music Genres and Corporate Cultures*. London: Routledge, 1999.

"New Faces: Regional Mexican Talent to Watch in 2000." *Billboard*, 26 August 2000, LM1-LM3.

Newman, Kathleen. "Critical Mass: Advertising, Audiences, and Consumer Activism." Ph.D. diss., Yale University, 1997.

Nichols, Bill. *Representing Reality: Issues and Concepts in Documentary*. Bloomington: Indiana University Press, 1991.

Nieves, Santiago, and Frank Algarin. "Two Film Reviews: *My Family/Mi Familia* and *The Perez Family*." In *Latin Looks: Images of Latinas and Latinos in the U.S. Media*, edited by Clara Rodríguez, 221–24. Boulder, Colo.: Westview, 1998.

Noriega, Chon. "Introduction." In *Chicanos and Film: Essays on Chicano Representation and Resistance*, edited by Chon Noriega, xi–xxvi. New York: Garland, 1992.

————. "Introduction." In *The Ethnic Eye: Latino Media Arts*, edited by Chon Noriega and Ana López, ix–xxii. Minneapolis: University of Minnesota Press, 1996.

————. *Shot in America: Television, the State, and the Rise of Social Movement Cinema*. Minneapolis: University of Minnesota Press, 2000.

Noriega, Luis A., and Frances Leach. *Broadcasting in Mexico*. Boston: Routledge & Kegan Paul, 1979.

Novitz, David. "Art, Narrative, and Human Nature." *Philosophy and Literature* 13, no. 1 (1989): 57–74.

Omi, Michael, and Henry Winant. *Racial Formation in the United States: From the 1960s to the 1990s*. London: Routledge, 1994.

O'Sullivan, Tim. "Nostalgia, Revelation and Intimacy: Tendencies in the Flow of Modern Television." In *The Television Studies Book*, edited by Christine Geraghty and David Lusted, 198–211. London: Arnold, 1998.

"Out of the Picture: Hispanics in the Media." Research Report. Washington, D.C.: National Council of La Raza, 1994.

Parmar, Pratibha. "That Moment of Emergence." In *Postmodern After-Images: A Reader in Film, Television and Video*, edited by Peter Brooker and Will Brooker, 279–86. London: Arnold, 1997.

Patoski, Joe Nick. "Tuned Out." *Texas Monthly*, May 2000, 21–24.

Patterson, Richard A. *Creating Country Music: Fabricating Authenticity*. Chicago: University of Chicago Press, 1997.

Peña, Albert. "Chihuahua!" *La Prensa de San Antonio*, 26 July 1998, 2A.

Peña, Manuel H. *Música Tejana: The Cultural Economy of Artistic Transformation*. College Station: Texas A&M University Press, 1999.

————. *The Texas-Mexican Conjunto: History of a Working-Class Music*. Austin: University of Texas, 1985.

Pesquera, Beatriz. "Work and Family: A Comparative Analysis of Professional, Clerical and Blue-Collar Chicana Workers." Ph.D. diss., University of California, 1985.

Pettit, Arthur G. *Images of Mexican Americans in Fiction and Film*. College Station: Texas A&M University Press, 1980.

Polkinghorne, Robert. "Human Existence and Narrative." In *Narrative Knowing and the Human Sciences*, 125–55. Albany: State University of New York Press, 1988.

Poulantzas, Nicos. *Political Power and Social Classes*. Translated by Timothy O'Hagan. Edited by Timothy O'Hagan. London: Sheed and Ward, 1973.

"Protestan contra Adviso de Taco Bell: Grupo Latino Affirma que Uso de Perro Chihuahua Ofende a Esta Comunidad." *La Opinión*, 18 August 1998, 3A.

Quiñoñes, Juan Gómez. *Chicano Politics: Reality and Promise*. Albuquerque: University of New Mexico Press, 1990.

Radway, Janice. *Reading the Romance: Women, Patriarchy, and Popular Literature*. Chapel Hill: University of North Carolina Press, 1984.

Ramírez Berg, Charles. "Stereotyping in Films in General and of the Hispanic in Particular." In *Latin Looks: Images of Latinas and Latinos in the U.S. Media*, edited by Clara Rodríguez, 104–20. Boulder, Colo.: Westview, 1998.

Renaud González, Barbara. "Latinos Won't Find Success in Football." *San Antonio Express-News*, 26 October 1997, 1G.

Reyna, Jose. "Notes on Tejano Music." *Perspectives on Mexican American Studies* 1 (1988): 33–45.

Rodríguez, América. "Commercial Ethnicity: Language, Class and Race in the Marketing of the Hispanic Audience." *Communication Review* 2, no. 3 (1997): 283–309.

————. "Control Mechanisms of National News-Making: Britain, Canada, Mexico, and the United States." In *Questioning the Media: A Critical Introduction*, edited

by John Downing, Ali Mohammadi and Annabelle Sreberny-Mohammadi, 128–
46. Thousand Oaks, Calif.: Sage, 1995.

——. "Creating an Audience and Remapping a Nation: A Brief History of U.S.
Spanish-Language Broadcasting, 1930–1980." *Quarterly Review of Film and Video*
16, nos. 3–4 (1999): 357–74.

——. "Made in the U.S.A.: The Constructions of Univision News." Ph.D. diss.,
University of California, San Diego, 1993.

——. *Making Latino News: Race, Language, Class.* Thousand Oaks, Calif.: Sage, 1999.

Rodríguez, Clara. "Keeping It Reel? Films of the 1980s and 1990s." In *Latin Looks:
Images of Latinas and Latinos in the U.S. Media,* edited by Clara Rodríguez, 180–
84. Boulder, Colo.: Westview, 1998.

——, ed. *Latin Looks: Images of Latinas and Latinos in the U.S. Media.* Boulder, Colo.:
Westview, 1998.

Rodríguez, Clemencia. "Fissures in the Mediascape: An International Study of Citizens' Media." *Alternative Communication.* Cresskill, N.J.: Hampton Press, 2000.

——. "A Process of Identity Deconstruction: Latin American Women Producing
Video Stories." In *Women in Grassroots Communication: Furthering Social Change,*
edited by Pilar Riaño, 149–60. Thousand Oaks, Calif.: Sage, 1994.

Rodríguez, Edmundo. "The Hispanic Community and Church Movements: Schools
of Leadership." In *Hispanic Catholic Church Culture in the U.S.: Issues and Concerns,* edited by J. Dolan and A. F. Deck, 206–39. Notre Dame: University of Notre
Dame Press.

Romero, Mary. "Life as the Maid's Daughter: An Exploration of the Everyday Boundaries of Race, Class, and Gender." In *Feminisms in the Academy,* edited by Abigail
Stewart and Domna Stanton. Ann Arbor: University of Michigan Press, 1995.

Rony, Fatima Toby. *The Third Eye: Race, Cinema, and Ethnographic Spectacle.* Durham:
Duke University Press, 1996.

Rosales, Rodolfo. *The Illusion of Inclusion: The Untold Political Story of San Antonio,*
Center for Mexican American Studies History, Culture and Society Series. Austin:
University of Texas Press, 2000.

Rosson, Charles. "Flaco Jimenez." *Texas Monthly,* January 1998.

Rubel, Arthur J. "The Family." In *Mexican-Americans in the United States: A Reader,*
edited by John Burma, 211–24. Cambridge, Mass.: Schenkman Publishing, 1970.

Salas, Abel. "Record Label Abandons Tejano Experiment." *Hispanic,* September 1998,
14.

"San Antonio Council Praised for Linking Tax Breaks, Wages." *Dallas Morning News,*
4 July 1998, 40.

Sánchez, George. *Becoming Mexican American: Ethnicity and Acculturation in Chicano
Los Angeles, 1900–1943.* New York: Oxford University Press, 1993.

Sandel, Michael. "The Procedural Republic and the Unencumbered Self." *Political
Theory* 12 (1984): 81–96.

Sanjek, Russell. *Pennies from Heaven: The American Popular Music Business in the Twentieth Century.* New York: De Capo, 1996.

Schiller, Dan. *Digital Capitalism: Networking the Global Market System.* Cambridge,
Mass.: MIT Press, 1999.

Schneiderman, I. "Growth among Hispanic, Asian Markets, Teen Boys and Young Drivers Will All Be Factors." *DNR* 29, no. 114 (1999): 42.

Schwirtz, Mira "Rates Soar in Quest to Woo Black Listeners." *Mediaweek,* 19 May 1998,
20–24.

Segura, Denise. "Chicanas and Mexican Immigrant Women in the Labor Market."
Ph.D. diss., University of California, 1986.

Seiter, Ellen. "Making Distinctions in Audience Research: Case Study of a Troubling Interview." *Cultural Studies* 4, no. 1 (1990): 61–84.

———. *Television and New Media Audiences*. Oxford: Clarendon, 1999.

Seiter, Ellen, Gabrielle Kreutzner, Eva Marie Warth, and Hans Borchers, eds. *Remote Control: Television, Audiences, and Cultural Power*. London: Routledge, 1989.

Shattuc, Jane. "'Go Ricki': Politics, Perversion, and Pleasure in the 1990s." In *The Television Studies Book*, edited by Christine Geraghty and David Lusted, 212–27. London: Arnold, 1998.

———. *The Talking Cure: TV, Talk Shows and Women*. New York: Routledge, 1997.

Shohat, Ella, and Robert Stam. *Unthinking Eurocentrism: Multiculturalism and the Media*. London: Routledge, 1994.

Sholle, Daniel. "Buy Our News: Tabloid Television and Commodification." *Journal of Communication Inquiry* 17, no. 1 (1993): 56–73.

Sinclair, John. *Latin American Television: A Global View*. Oxford: Oxford University Press, 1999.

———. "Spanish-Language Television in the United States." *Studies in Latin American Popular Culture* 9 (1990): 39–63.

Skerry, Peter. *Mexican Americans: The Ambivalent Minority*. Cambridge: Harvard University Press, 1993.

Smythe, Dallas. "The Role of Mass Media and Popular Culture in Defining Development." In *Counterclockwise: Perspectives on Communication, Dallas Smythe*, edited by Thomas Guback, 247–62. Boulder, Colo.: Westview, 1994.

Sonnichsen, Philip. "Los Madrugadores: Early Spanish Radio in California." *La Luz*, June 1977, 15–18.

Sosa, Lionel. *The Americano Dream: How Latinos Can Achieve Success in Business and in Life*. New York: Dutton, 1998.

Soto, Marita. "Memoria y Olvido de Mujer: El Amor en las Telenovelas." In *Telenovela: Los Relatos de una Historia de Amor*, 91–96. Buenos Aires: Atuel, 1996.

Spigel, Lynn. *Make Room for TV: Television and the Family Ideal in Postwar America*. Chicago: University of Chicago Press, 1992.

Stefano, Onofre de. "La Prensa of San Antonio and Its Literary Page, 1913 to 1915." Ph.D. diss., University of California, Los Angeles, 1983.

Stephens, Mitchell. *The Rise of the Image, the Fall of the Word*. New York: Oxford, 1998.

Streeter, Thomas. *Selling the Air: A Critique of the Policy of Commercial Broadcasting in the United States*. Chicago: University of Chicago Press, 1996.

Subvervi-Vélez, Federico. "Media." In *The Hispanic-American Almanac: A Reference Work on Hispanics in the United States*, edited by Nicolás Kanellos, 621–74. Detroit: Gale Research, 1993.

Terán, Luis. *Lágrimas de Exportación*. Mexico City: Clío, 2000.

"Texaco Selects LKS as Advertising Agency for Hispanic Market." *San Antonio Business Journal*, 24 February 1997.

Tienda, Marta. "Familism and Structural Assimilation of Mexican Immigrants in the United States." *International Migration Review* 14, no. 3 (1980): 383–408.

Tulloch, John, and Henry Jenkins. *Science Fiction Audiences*. London: Routledge, 1995.

Turow, Joseph. *Media Industries: The Production of News and Entertainment*. New York: Longman, 1984.

———. "Segmenting, Signalling, and Tailoring: Probing the Dark Side of Target Marketing." In *Critical Studies in Media Commercialism*, edited by Robin Andersen and Lance Strate, 239–49. London: Oxford University Press, 2000.

U.S. Census Bureau. *Statistical Abstract of the United States: 2001*. 121st ed. Washington, D.C.: GPO, 2001.

Valenzuela, Nicolas. "Organizational Evolution of a Spanish Language Television Network: An Environmental Approach." Ph.D. diss., Stanford University, 1985.

Vasquez, Olga. "La Clase Mágica: Imagining Optimal Possibilities in a Bilingual Community of Learners." Unpublished manuscript.

Wald, Gayle. "Just a Girl? Rock Music, Feminism, and the Construction of Female Youth." *Signs* 23, no. 3 (1998): 585–609.

Walkerdine, Valerie. *Schoolgirl Fictions*. London: Verso, 1990.

Walsh, Jennifer. "For Some, Casting Call Is a Family Affair." *San Antonio Express-News*, 13 February 1999.

Walsh, Martin. *The Brechtian Aspect of Radical Cinema*. Edited by Keith M. Griffiths. London: BFI, 1981.

Wayne, Mike. *Theorizing Video Practice*. London: Lawrence & Wishart, 1997.

Wilinsky, Barbara. "Before the Networks Reinvented the Family: Chicago Television's Portrait of America." *Quarterly Review of Film and Video* 16, nos. 3–4 (1999): 271–88.

Wilkinson, Kenton. "Where Culture, Language, and Communication Converge: The Latin American Cultural-Linguistic Television Market." Ph.D. diss., University of Texas, 1995.

Williams, Raymond. "Base and Superstructure in Marxist Cultural Theory." In *Problems in Materialism and Culture: Selected Essays*, 31–49. London: Verso, 1980.

———. *Television: Technology and Cultural Form*. Hanover: Wesleyan University Press, 1992

Willis-Rivera, Jennifer, and Alberto González. "Reconceptualizing Gender through Intercultural Dialogue: The Case of the Tex-Mex Madonna." *Women and Language* 20, no. 1 (1999): 9–12.

Wilson, Clint, and Felix Gutiérrez. *Race, Multiculturalism, and the Media: From Mass to Class Communication*. Thousand Oaks, Calif.: Sage, 1995.

"Women in Film Underrepresented in Spite of Box Office Success." *Media Report to Women* 26, no. 3 (1998): 1–3.

"Women of the Year: They're Gaining Power in Hollywood and Using It to Make Films That Women Want to See." *Time*, 13 November 1995, 96–100.

Wyn, Johanna, and Rob White. *Rethinking Youth*. London: Sage, 1997.

Ybarra-Frausto, Tomás. "Rasquachismo: A Chicano Sensibility." In *Chicano Art: Resistance and Affirmation, 1965–1985*, edited by Griswold Del Castillo, Teresa McKenna and Yvonne Yarbro Bejarano, 152–62. Los Angeles: University of California Press, 1991.

Index

activism. *See* media activism and Chicano movements

advertising, executives, 18, 23–25, 27, 34–35, 42, 57, 60, 85; family depictions in, 84–87; industry, 18, 24, 37–38; low rates for, 35; talent, 28–29, 30; targeted, 14

Advertising Age, 18

affirmative action, 11

Aguilar, Adolfo, 18, 23–25, 27, 34–35, 42, 85

Aguilera, Christina, 48, 55

"Altars on the West Side" (documentary), 105, 107–118, 154–55, 157–160

alternative media, Mexican-American production of, 93–118; Spanish-language, xiv; as training ground, 93; use of for self-representation, 93

American Bandstand, 39

American Dream, 27, 73, 80, 86, 87, 88, 141

American Family, 91–92

American Federation of Musicians, 40

American identity, xii. *See also* assimilation

American Society of Composers, Authors, and Publishers (ASCAP), 40

Anderson, Benedict, 172, 179n8. *See also* imagined communities

Anglo Americans, dominance in media industry, 24; media representations of,

89; in San Antonio, 4, 5; and wealth, 16, 89

arts investment, 41

arts organizations, xiii. *See also* San Anto Cultural Arts

assimilation, of family, 80, 84, 86; of individuals, 101, 136, 176; of media workers, 24, 30, 43; in Tejano music, 71

Association of Hispanic advertising Agencies (AHAA), 18, 41, 42

Astol, Lalo, 5

audiences, xv, 2–17, 44, 47–48, 91, 130, 152–153, 187n5

authenticity, and co-optation, 66; and marketing, 55, 174; in media, 138; in music, 189n30; in Tejano industry, 46, 55–58, 61–63, 65–70; in video production, 151–52, 156

Ayala, Tony, 70–71

Azcárraga Vidaurreta, Don Emilio, 7–8, 9

Azcárraga Milmo, Emilio, 10

Barbacoa, 77, and class, 89–90; family in, 75–77, 78–84, 85–87, 89–90; gender roles in, 73, 77, 81, 90; legacy of, 91, 184n74; and positive representations of Mexican Americans in, 72–73, 75–76; youth in, 88

Behar, Ruth, 161–162

Berman, Marshall, 179n14, 195n1

biculturalism, 25–27, 31; of MA youth, 76–77

213

About the Author

Vicki Mayer is a media scholar, producer, and fan. After being a journalist, community media advocate, and mass media consumer much of her life, she earned a doctorate in communication from the University of California, San Diego. She is currently an assistant professor of communication at Tulane University.